The Bible Speaks Today

Series Editors: J. A. Motyer (OT)
John R. W. Stott (NT)

The Message of Mark

The mystery of faith

Titles in this series

The Message of Genesis 1-11
The Dawn of Creation
David Atkinson

The Message of Genesis 12—50
From Abraham to Joseph
Joyce G. Baldwin

The Message of Ruth
The Wings of Refuge
David Atkinson

The Message of Chronicles
One Church, One Faith, One Lord
Michael Wilcock

The Message of Job
Suffering and Grace
David Atkinson

The Message of Ecclesiastes
*A Time to Mourn,
and a Time to Dance*
Derek Kidner

The Message of Jeremiah
Against Wind and Tide
Derek Kidner

The Message of Daniel
The Lord Is King
Ronald S. Wallace

The Message of Hosea
Love to the Loveless
Derek Kidner

The Message of Amos
The Day of the Lion
J. A. Motyer

**The Message of the
Sermon on the Mount
(Matthew 5—7)**
Christian Counter-Culture
John R. W. Stott

The Message of Mark
The Mystery of Faith
Donald English

The Message of Luke
The Saviour of the World
Michael Wilcock

The Message of 1 Corinthians
Life in the Local Church
David Prior

The Message of 2 Corinthians
Power in Weakness
Paul Barnett

The Message of Galatians
Only One Way
John R. W. Stott

The Message of Ephesians
God's New Society
John R. W. Stott

The Message of Philippians
Jesus Our Joy
J. A. Motyer

**The Message of Colossians
and Philemon**
Fullness and Freedom
R. C. Lucas

The Message of 2 Timothy
Guard the Gospel
John R. W. Stott

The Message of Hebrews
Christ Above All
Raymond Brown

The Message of James
The Tests of Faith
J. A. Motyer

The Message of 1 Peter
The Way of the Cross
Edmund P. Clowney

The Message of John's Letters
Living in the Love of God
David Jackman

The Message of Revelation
I Saw Heaven Opened
Michael Wilcock

The Message of Mark

The mystery of faith

Donald English

Inter-Varsity Press
Leicester, England
Downers Grove, Illinois, U.S.A.

InterVarsity Press
P.O. Box 1400, Downers Grove, IL 60515, USA
38 De Montfort Street, Leicester LE1 7GP, England

InterVarsity Press®, U.S.A., is the book-publishing division of InterVarsity Christian Fellowship®, a student movement active on campus at hundreds of universities, colleges and schools of nursing in the United States of America, and a member movement of the International Fellowship of Evangelical Students. For information about local and regional activities, write Public Relations Dept., InterVarsity Christian Fellowship, 6400 Schroeder Rd., P.O. Box 7895, Madison, WI 53707-7895.

Inter-Varsity Press, England, is the book-publishing division of the Universities and Colleges Christian Fellowship (formerly the Inter-Varsity Fellowship), a student movement linking Christian Unions in universities and colleges throughout the United Kingdom and the Republic of Ireland, and a member movement of the International Fellowship of Evangelical Students. For information about local and national activities write to UCCF, 38 De Montfort Street, Leicester LE1 7GP.

Study guide: Jo Bramwell

USA ISBN 0-8308-1231-8
UK ISBN 0-85110-968-3

Printed in the United States of America

Library of Congress Cataloging-in-Publication Data

English, Donald.
    The message of Mark: the mystery of faith/Donald English.
      p.   cm.—(The Bible speaks today)
    Includes bibliographical references.
    ISBN 0-8308-1231-8
    1. Bible. N.T. Mark—Commentaries. I. Bible. N.T. Mark.
  English. New International. 1992. II. Title. III. Series.
    BS2585.3.E54   1992
    226.3'07—dc20   92-6112
                                       CIP

British Library Cataloguing in Publication Data

A catalogue record for this book is available from the British Library.

17	16	15	14	13	12	11	10	9	8	7	6	5	4	3	2	1
05	04	03	02	01	00	99	98	97	96	95	94	93	92			

General preface

The Bible Speaks Today describes a series of both Old Testament
and New Testament expositions, which are characterized by a
threefold ideal: to expound the biblical text with accuracy, to relate
it to contemporary life, and to be readable.

These books are, therefore, not 'commentaries', for the commentary seeks rather to elucidate the text than to apply it, and tends
to be a work rather of reference than of literature. Nor, on the
other hand, do they contain the kind of 'sermons' which attempt
to be contemporary and readable without taking Scripture seriously
enough.

The contributors to this series are all united in their convictions
that God still speaks through what he has spoken, and that nothing
is more necessary for the life, health and growth of Christians than
that they should hear what the Spirit is saying to them through his
ancient – yet ever modern – Word.

J. A. MOTYER
J. R. W. STOTT
Series Editors

For Carol and Maxine

Contents

General preface   5
Author's preface   9
Abbreviations   11
Bibliography   12
Introduction   14

1. The beginning (1:1–13)   25
2. The ministry opens up (1:14 – 3:6)   48
3. Words and deeds in Galilee (3:7 – 6:13)   81
4. Missionary outreach beyond Galilee in spite of the
    disciples' limitations (6:14 – 8:26)   127
5. Going to Jerusalem (8:27 – 10:52)   158
6. Jesus enters Jerusalem (11:17 – 13:37)   184
7. Passion and resurrection (14:1 – 16:20)   211

Study guide   244

Author's preface

I am particularly grateful for the privilege of writing an exposition of Mark's gospel for *The Bible Speaks Today series*. The gap between many scholarly commentaries and much devotional literature is a serious one which does damage to our understanding of the Bible. I warm to the threefold ideal set out in the General Preface. It requires rigorous study of the biblical text, a study which faces the difficulties involved and is open to questions that have to be asked. Yet it also recognizes that Scripture was not given by God as a subject only for academic study. It is the story of God's grace and righteousness revealed uniquely in Jesus Christ. As such it calls for more than serious study – it invites a response of faith and a life lived that is appropriate to that faith. Scholarship and devotion ought not to be alternatives. Each needs the other.

Mark's gospel fits very aptly into such an approach. At first sight it is a simple account of the ministry of Jesus, with lots of stories, plenty of action, a large amount of human interest, and some very straight and searching statements, mostly from Jesus himself. Yet a serious reading of this gospel raises all kinds of questions. If Jesus is what the Christian church says he is, why doesn't he make more of it in the gospel, do more to press people into believing it, go out of his way to make it easy for the crowds to believe? And why, on the other hand, with so much evidence in front of them, did people find it so hard to see who he was, and to commit themselves to God through him? Why is the steady progress of good deeds by Jesus matched by a growing resistance to all he stood for? Why do his disciples find it so difficult to believe and understand, when it all seems so clear to us?

There are also technical questions about the origin of Mark's gospel, about the aims of Mark in writing it, about the construction, and about the contents and why they are arranged as they are.

Bible study has nothing to fear from questions like this. If it is

9

about truth then the questions must be asked. But the attitude with which the questions are asked is important too. The books of the Bible are written 'from faith to faith'. They are not meant to be an almanac of all available knowledge. Neither are they written simply to stimulate academic interest. Nor do they reveal their treasures to the cynic. An openness to the truth is required if the truth is to be perceived and received. This theme is central to Mark's gospel.

I first came to this gospel as a young Christian, and was struck by its forthrightness, and by the picture of Jesus it contained. Later as a preacher, and as a Travelling Secretary with the UCCF (in the days when it was the Inter-Varsity Fellowship) I found it was the gospel to which, again and again, I referred those interested in faith, or newly into faith. Later still, as a theological college lecturer, I found myself expounding Mark and facing some of the deeper questions this gospel raises. I wrote, at the invitation of the World Methodist Council, six short studies, for use around the world.

This exposition is the next step in a journey of exploration, a journey which never fails to reveal more than I had discovered before, and to promise even more if I am willing to look beyond what is obvious and to allow it to speak to my own life and setting. It will be evident that I still have a long way to go, but I am grateful for the personal enrichment that has come from producing this book.

The Faculty, led by Dean Jim Waits, and students of Candler School of Theology, Emory University, Atlanta, Georgia, provided an excellent context of devotion and study which enabled the major part of the writing of the book to be completed. I express warmest thanks to them.

I am deeply grateful to Mrs Eva Scrivener and Miss Jan Dale for their patient typing and re-typing of the manuscript; to Frank Entwistle and Colin Duriez with their colleagues on the IVP staff; and to the New Testament Editor John Stott, whose eye for detail misses very little, and yet who never loses sight of the larger scene.

Lastly I am in debt to all those who over the years have helped me understand the Bible more sensitively and to perceive depths and heights which I might have missed without their fellowship. My prayer is that others will be inspired in the same way by this exposition.

DONALD ENGLISH

Abbreviations

GNB The Good News Bible (NT 1966, 4th edition 1976; OT 1976).

NIV The New International Version of the Bible (1973, 1978, 1984).

RSV The Revised Standard Version of the Bible (NT 1946; 2nd edition 1971; OT 1952).

Bibliography

Anderson, Hugh, *The Gospel of Mark* (New Century Bible Commentary; Oliphants, 1976; Marshall, Morgan & Scott/Eerdmans, 1981).

Best, Ernest, *Mark: The Gospel as Story* (T. & T. Clark, 1983).

Blanch, Stuart, *Encounters with Jesus* (Hodder & Stoughton, 1988).

Cole, R. A., *The Gospel According to St Mark* (Tyndale New Testament Commentaries; Tyndale Press, 1961; 2nd edition Inter-Varsity Press, 1990).

Cranfield, C. E. B., *The Gospel According to St Mark* (Cambridge University Press, 1959).

Davies, John D. and Vincent, John, *Mark at Work* (Bible Reading Fellowship, 1986).

Denney, James, *The Death of Christ* (1902; revised and abridged by R. V. G. Tasker; Tyndale Press, 1951).

Dunham, Maxie, *The Gospel of Mark* (Cokesbury, 1988).

English, Donald, *Discipleship the Hard Way – Studies in Mark's Gospel* (Methodist Church, Home Mission Division, 1977).

English, Donald, *The Meaning of the Warmed Heart* (Methodist Church, Home Mission Division, 1987).

Gould, Ezra, P., *The Gospel according to St Mark* (International Critical Commentary, T. & T. Clark, 1896, reprinted 1983).

Guy, H. A., *The Gospel of Mark* (Macmillan/St Martin's Press, 1968).

Hargreaves, John, *A Guide to St Mark's Gospel* (TEF Study Guide 2, 3rd edition SPCK, 1979).

Hooker, Morna D., *The Message of Mark* (Epworth, 1983).

Martin, Ralph P., *Where the Action is* (Regal Books Division, Gospel Light Publications, USA, 1977).

Martin, Ralph P., *Mark: Evangelist and Theologian* (Paternoster Press, 1972).

12

Marxen, Willi, *Mark the Evangelist*, translated by R. A. Harrisville (Abingdon Press, 1969).

McGinley, Hugh (ed.), *The Year of Mark* (Deskbooks and the Joint Board of Christian Education of Australia and New Zealand, 1984).

Moule, C. F. D., *The Gospel According to Mark* (Cambridge Bible Commentary; Cambridge University Press, 1965).

Nineham, D. E., *The Gospel of St Mark* (Pelican Gospel Commentaries; Penguin, 1963).

Robinson, J. M., *The Problem of History in Mark* (SCM Press, 1957; reissued in *The Problem of History in Mark and other Marcan Studies*, Fortress Press, 1982).

Stott, John R. W., *Men With a Message* (IVP, 1954), published in the USA as *Basic Introduction to the New Testament* (Eerdmans/IVP, 1964).

Swete, H. B., *The Gospel According to St Mark* (1898).

Taylor, Vincent, *The Gospel According to St Mark* (Macmillan, 1952).

Weaver, Walter P., *Mark* (Basic Bible Commentary; Cokesbury, 1988).

Williamson, Lamar, Jr., *Mark* (Interpretation – A Bible Commentary for Teaching and Preaching; John Knox Press, 1983).

Introduction

Our first question must be: 'Why should we read Mark's gospel at all?' There is the obvious answer that it is there, and that we don't want to miss anything. There is further the now widely accepted fact that Mark's was the first of the New Testament gospels to be written, and was used by Matthew and Luke. But the other New Testament gospels are longer, and each has a more apparent distinctiveness – Matthew with the strongly Jewish background, Luke with his commitment to outcast groups, and John with the great I AM themes. What has Mark to offer by comparison with these?

It used to be thought that Mark was, by contrast, a simple, straightforward account of the story of Jesus, set out chronologically. That approach shouldn't be wholly abandoned, since in broad terms it remains true. It also safeguards some important insights into Mark's intention, not least the way in which he shows the shadow of the cross hanging over the ministry of Jesus from the very beginning.

Yet it is equally clear that Mark shows little interest in close or detailed historical linkage between one story and the next. Nor does he include material vital to a pure historian concerning Jesus' ancestry, birth or childhood. It is not a biography of Jesus. What happened after the resurrection is largely omitted too, if, as will be suggested later, the original version of Mark's gospel ended at Mark 16:8. He is equally free of pressure to provide exact geographical locations. Stories move from scene to scene without explanation. It is clear that something else concerns him much more. This 'something else' is the most important element in the introduction to the reading of the gospel itself. It uncovers the purpose of the writer and the prospect for the reader.

The best way to discover the intention of Mark is to read *his own expression of purpose*, wherever he has tried to make it plain.

We can go on to examine *focal points of the teaching contained* in the gospel. What Mark emphasizes should help us to grasp his purpose more clearly. Then there is the task of *reading the stories* Mark tells, trying sympathetically to get into them, and to discern the reason for their presence in the gospel from within the account itself. Questions of *the materials on which Mark drew* are not unimportant, but they must not distract our attention from the texture of the gospel itself. We need to try also to *understand the people* who figure in the stories. They are important for a discovery of what the gospel is about. Other people are important, too. There are *those for whom the gospel was first written*. What we can know or surmise about their attitudes, experiences and needs will help us better to see how Mark's gospel related to them. And *we must not forget ourselves* as we, under the inspiration of the same Spirit who led the writer, seek to be addressed by him through the Scripture as we take it up now.

The task is not a simple one. It has some of the characteristics of solving a mystery! But it is deeply challenging and spiritually rewarding for all who are willing to commit themselves to it. The element of commitment will be constantly present.

Mark's purpose

There is no ambiguity here! The opening thirteen verses set it out with breathtaking clarity.[1]

There is, first, the idea of 'The beginning of the gospel' (1:1). Something new is being launched. Much has been made of Mark's use, for the first time, of gospel as a way of tabulating the good news (which is what 'gospel' means) in a written form. There is something more significant even than that, however. The word 'gospel' had a meaning prior to that of either 'message' or 'written document'. It was originally used to describe 'an epoch-making event'. For example, the birth of the future Emperor Augustus was described as 'gospel', meaning a happening which would change world history. Mark certainly offers gospel as good news. Equally clearly he is presenting it for the first time as a whole account in written form. Perhaps most important of all however he is announcing an event after which the history of the world will never again be the same.

At the centre of this event is Jesus Christ. Mark makes it clear that the person at the heart of his story establishes continuity with God's previous activity in the world, hence the quotations from

[1] See pp. 25ff.

the Old Testament (1:2–3). There is also a testimony from John the Baptist, seen as the prophet promised in the Old Testament who would precede the coming of the Messiah – God's anointed who delivers Israel (1:4–8). After John, if he is properly regarded in Old Testament terms, the next will be the Messiah.

This is precisely what the voice from heaven, during John's baptism of Jesus, makes clear. The 'You are my Son' of 1:11 provides the closing bracket of the parenthesis which began with 'the Son of God' in 1:1. Mark could hardly be clearer about his view of who Jesus is.

We seem to be on the same track when Mark describes the beginning of Jesus' ministry. He announces nothing less than 'the kingdom of God'. Because it has drawn, or is drawing, near, people must repent and believe the gospel (1:14–15).

This picture of the Messiah sent from God is made even more compelling by the demonstration, beyond words of preaching, in the miracles Jesus performed. For the first eight chapters of this gospel there is a quite breathless presentation of one work of power after another. Mark needs to keep using the word 'immediately' because he is hurrying his readers along from one example of the release of divine energy to the next.

If this gospel was written as some kind of training material for new Christians, or for early Christian evangelists, as some have suggested, then the evidence so far is clear and convincing. The powerful Son of God overcomes all problems brought to him. The kingdom of God is focused on him. Those who come to him in need are taught, healed and delivered. 'We have never seen anything like this!' (2:12), becomes the appropriate response.

It is much too simple a conclusion, however, to assume that Mark's sole intention is to portray Jesus as the powerful Son of God. It is probably not even his main purpose. The high Christology of the first thirteen verses, and the excitement of the miracles in the first eight chapters, are increasingly seen in Mark's gospel as the necessary preliminary to something else.

The first hint about that 'something else' comes at the outset of Jesus' preaching ministry as Mark records it. People are called not just to hear that the kingdom of God is imminent, but to do something about it. They should 'repent and believe the good news'. We are justified in picking up that theme also as the gospel unfolds. Mark is pointing us to a double thrust in his message. It is about *who Jesus is*. It is also about *how people should respond* to Jesus. *These two themes run right through the Gospel of Mark.* They form the basic materials for the telling of the story of Jesus.

Neither of those themes stays the same as the gospel unfolds.

What is more, the development of each points us towards a more accurate definition of Mark's purpose.

Who Jesus is

There has been a long tradition of noting the significant change in the tone and direction of Jesus' ministry in Mark's gospel after the accounts of Peter's confession at Caesarea Philippi 'You are the Christ' (8:27–30) and of the transfiguration of Jesus (9:2–13), where the emphasis is again on the identity of Jesus. 'This is my Son, whom I love. Listen to him!' Before this time the concentration is on addressing the crowds, with attention to who Jesus might be. After it there is more concentration on training the disciples, and the focal point about Jesus is not who he is but what he has come to accomplish. This is particularly encapsulated in three repetitive passages (8:31; 9:31; 10:32–34). There is great value in that perception of the way Jesus lovingly helped his disciples towards the truth about himself and his vocation.

What has also to be recognized, however, and what is perhaps even more germane to Mark's purpose in gathering the material together in this way, is that these two stories (at Caesarea Philippi and on the transfiguration mountain) also make a significant change in the presentation of the two key themes so far: namely, who Jesus is, and how we should respond to him.

What is noticeable about the *identity of Jesus* is the striking alteration of strategy in his ministry, without any loss in its authority. From Mark 8 onwards Jesus goes steadily on to the confrontation with the religious authorities, speaking as he goes about the inevitability of suffering, rejection and death for himself. The all-powerful healer and miracle-worker suddenly becomes the one who submits to the fate of crucifixion (8:31, *etc.*), despite protests from Peter about such a course (8:32). He knows the pain that will be involved (14:32–42). He does not even defend himself against false evidence at his trial (14:61).

Yet at no point does Mark give any impression of Jesus being anything other than in total control of the situation. The contrast is not between a time of self-assured success, followed by a period of uncontrollable decline. Jesus walks from one phase to the other with determination and confidence. He predicts what will happen. We are given to feel that even at his trial he knows better than anyone else what is happening. The demonstration of power in the first half of the gospel, and the lowly path to the cross in the second are part of the one process of doing the will of his Father, part of the one way of being who he is and of doing what he came to do.

17

They belong inextricably together. That will be a vital clue as we try to discern Mark's message about Jesus and the kingdom of God.

The same point is made in a different way if we consider the *titles used of Jesus* in Mark's gospel. The two most significant are 'Son of God' and 'Son of Man'.

The background of *Son of God* is in Old Testament passages like 2 Samuel 7:14; Psalms 2:7 and 89:26–27. It is used sometimes of Israel's kings and sometimes of the messianic king who will come to deliver God's people. When the title is used in Mark the reader has to decide in the context which use is the more likely. The accounts of the baptism of Jesus, the transfiguration, and the trial before the Sanhedrin require a messianic interpretation. The comment on the text will argue that the same is true when the demon-possessed cry out and call Jesus 'Son of God'. There may be something more subtle about the use of this title towards the end of the gospel. At the crucifixion of Jesus, the centurion in charge of the soldiers remarks, 'Surely this man was (the/a) Son of God'. Whichever translation we prefer, it may still be that the centurion had a much more earthy view of Jesus when he used such language. But Mark could be making a point which will come out even more clearly below, namely, that those who have eyes to see will perceive that the soldier's words were more meaningful than he knew. If so, then we are very near to the heart of Mark's gospel. But that is to jump ahead.

Alongside the use of Son of God is the more frequent use of *Son of Man*. The background in the Old Testament is again varied. In Psalm 8:4 it refers to humankind. In Daniel 7:1 it refers to a heavenly figure honoured by God. In Ezekiel it is the prophet's way of being addressed by God.

Mark makes clear that this is Jesus' favoured way of describing himself. It occurs in the gospel at a number of points which bring together the two titles or variations of them. In 8:29 Peter affirms Jesus as 'the Christ' (meaning 'the Anointed One', the Messiah). He is praised for the insight. It is a true perception. At once, however, when Jesus speaks of his future, he uses, not Messiah, but Son of Man, and he speaks of the necessary suffering which lies ahead. The title Son of Man, with its much more lowly connotations than Christ, Messiah, Son of God, is being used to interpret the others. When, at his trial, Jesus admits to being 'the Christ, the Son of the Blessed One', he goes on immediately to interpret that confession in terms of the future of 'the Son of Man'. When seeking to make abundantly clear to his disciples where the way forward lay in the work of salvation he had come to achieve, Jesus uses Son of Man language to communicate it (10:45). At the centre of the gospel are the three prophetic statements about his death, each cast in terms of 'Son of Man'.

To jump ahead once more, it is noteworthy that words about Jesus' future are accompanied by sayings about the nature of discipleship in the kingdom. Again we are moving nearer to the central purpose of this gospel, 'like master, like servant'.

We come across the same emphasis by yet another route when considering the use of *kingdom of God* in Mark. Jesus begins by announcing that the kingdom is drawing, or has already drawn, near. The strong implication is that it has drawn near in him. As the story unfolds it becomes even clearer that he is the focal point of that kingdom. His power over disease, nature and demons celebrates the kingdom. He even assures people of divine forgiveness, to the chagrin of the religious leaders (2:1–12). People who show interest in coming to terms with the kingdom of God receive instruction in how to follow Jesus. Perhaps one can put it most accurately by saying that if he is not the king of the kingdom, since God is, he is at least the model of kingship. People can see in him God's way of being king.

If the disciples in any way perceived that, and Peter's affirmation at Caesarea Philippi suggests that they might have done so, then we can understand their horror, expressed in Peter's words straight after his testimony to Jesus, at the thought of Jesus going to death in Jerusalem at the hands of others. His picture of the future did not coincide with theirs, even though he affirmed their view of him as the Christ, the Son of God. It was not that the titles were wrong. He was warning them against the accretions of centuries, whereby the Messiah was seen in terms of the model of kingship developed by earthly kings.

Jesus allowed the use of the traditional titles, but recast their meaning through his own way of being king – certainly being in control and seeing to the heart of things, but also showing lowly submission to his Father, and eventually suffering so that the kingdom might be truly established in the lives of men and women.

We are right, therefore, to see the person and work of Jesus as a focal point of Mark's account. But we should also notice that as the gospel progresses the picture of Jesus changes from the all-powerful conquering centre of divine energy, to the lowly, unresistant, suffering one. What his followers, and the crowds, and his opponents found difficult to see, to which Mark wishes to draw his readers' attention, is that this also was a release of divine energy, far more significant than the power strategy which had preceded it, necessary though it was. We may have to confess that we, too,

19

have difficulty with that, a point of great importance if discipleship means following our Master.

We have now looked at one of the main strands of Mark's account namely, who Jesus is. We have seen that this theme changes across the length of the gospel in two ways. 'Who Jesus is' moves from an emphasis on a miracle worker to lowly dying servant, though without loss of authority. And 'who Jesus is' becomes, in the second half, the basis for concentrating on 'what Jesus came to do'.

The response to Jesus

Each of these variations of the theme is vital for the other main emphasis to which we now turn. We have already identified it as *how people should respond to Jesus*.

Mark indicates Jesus' stress on this element by recording his earliest exhortation. Because the kingdom of God is at hand, his hearers should 'repent and believe the good news' (1:15). Followed as it is by the series of miracles which Jesus performed, one would expect a welcome response to such an appeal, coming as it does from the person at the centre of the transformations taking place in people's lives. Here too, however, as with the portrayal of the person of Jesus, so with the response people make, there is a development of theme into something different from the initial portrayal.

To the question, 'How do people in Mark's gospel show faith in Jesus?', the answer, to put it bluntly, is that mostly they don't! His family misunderstand and try to deflect him from his course. His own townspeople are almost jealous of him and certainly refuse to accept his claims. The religious leaders are at first cool and later directly antagonistic to the point of seeking his death. The crowd follows, enjoying the teaching and being amazed by it, but in the end they do nothing to save him. Even his disciples, and not least Peter, struggle to understand without ever properly doing so, and get things badly wrong. Some of the women are at least faithful as far as the crucifixion, but even their faith fails them at the very end.

Only two groups seem to give anywhere near the expected response – the desperate and the demoniacs. The latter at least show signs of knowing who Jesus is; but they get no further because recognition leads to resistance, not faith, till they are delivered. The desperate alone are seen to be faithful. They have nowhere else to go, and no future to hope for without a cure. In the main they cast themselves on Jesus and find all that they need, and more.

One explanation of this phenomenon of unbelief is *the sinfulness of the human heart*. Mark makes this plain by drawing particular attention to what it means to follow Jesus. It is likely, as some commentators suggest, that the pattern of concentrating half the gospel on miracles and the other half on the passion is deliberate. The pattern is presented to underline the fact that discipleship is not an unending experience of supernatural power revealed in miracles and powerful teaching. Discipleship is also about lowly, costly obedience to the will of God, in facing the sinfulness and evil of human nature in the world. The disciples particularly illustrate how difficult it is for human beings to accept that side of the life of faith. They seem to enjoy all the wonderful works, but they recoil at the talk of the cost. They argue about who will have the seats of honour, both his and theirs. Peter, whose testimony may well lie behind much of what Mark writes, is a particular example both of the good intentions and of the dismal failures of those who were encountered by Jesus.

So one part of the mystery of unbelief is the power of sin in people's lives. That is not the only, nor even the most important, reason for lack of true discipleship in this gospel, however. There is a second development of the discipleship theme in Mark. Put simply, it is that the people in the story are not able to come to proper discipleship *because they do not yet know the full story*. They are faced by Jesus before his death and resurrection. If true discipleship is, as Jesus keeps on making clear, to carry our cross after him, and to discover God's care for us as we do, then they are bound to be unable to perceive its total meaning before he dies and rises, though those who are desperate enough seem to make the breakthrough.

Evidence that this is part of the intention of the gospel is seen in the way that, from the very beginning, the shadow of the cross hangs over the story. Mark is not alone in describing the baptism of Jesus by John, with all its implications for our understanding of the death of Jesus for our sins. It signifies his association with our sins, since he had none of his own. But in Mark there is also the early saying about not fasting while the bridegroom is with you, but only when the bridegroom 'is taken away'. Then there is the dramatic change in the middle of the gospel, marked by the repeated prophecy of death, with the resurrection also promised. And half the gospel is given to the passion, including the resurrection. When one adds the way that Jesus speaks of discipleship as taking up one's cross and following him, the importance of the death and resurrection of Jesus as the model for discipleship becomes powerfully clear.

21

It is at this point that we can perceive part of the reason for seeing Mark's gospel as owing something to the theology of Paul. The reality and power of sin in the world is a pillar of Paul's teaching. So is the centrality of the death of Jesus as its solution. Above all, Paul sees the Christian life as a daily experience of dying and rising with Christ, which is symbolized in baptism. Mark benefitted from Paul as well as from Peter, another reason why this gospel is so basic to the faith of Christians.

From the various roads towards an understanding of the purpose of the Gospel of Mark we have now looked at Mark's own declared intention. We have followed the presentation of the material and the way it develops. Attention has been given especially to major themes of the gospel: the identity and ministry of Jesus and the nature and demands of discipleship. The two have come together in the focus on the death and resurrection of Jesus as properly the climax of all that he came to do and as the secret of true discipleship. As we have covered this ground we have noticed the people in the story and the nature of their varied participation.

Mark's readership . . . and us

We may now ask about *those for whom the Gospel of Mark was written.* Here we are unavoidably faced with trying to discern from the text itself who they were and why they were the recipients.

Some outside evidence may be inferred from the content. Of the four suggested destinations (Egypt, Antioch, Galilee and Rome) the last would seem still to be the most likely. The people addressed include a majority of Gentiles, since Mark needs to explain Jewish customs. Yet he is not apparently writing to a church torn by Jewish-Gentile power struggles within its life. The spread of the Gospel of Mark, and its use by other gospel writers, suggests that a reliable and strong church stood behind it. The obvious relevance to the 'suffering' element in discipleship hints at a place and time of recent or current persecution. Rome under Nero certainly provides just such a scenario, and is supported by the likelihood that the gospel was written after the death of the apostle Peter, and probably of Paul too. Some time after AD 64 is indicated, and before the destruction of Jerusalem in AD 70 which is still in the future in the gospel, taking the prophetic element of the gospel seriously.

If Rome is the place then the readership is a varied group. The need for some exposition of suffering in the Christian life would be important. Was there also a tendency in such circumstances to want a particularly powerful form of Christianity in order to counter, at a supernatural level, the persecution being experienced at the natural level? Or was there a view of Jesus which so emphasized his divine nature and power that awareness of his humanity and understanding of human need was deficient? Were so many Christians wondering why, with a Saviour who was Son of God, they should be suffering at all? The answers cannot reach any degree of certainty, but somewhere in that set of suggestions there is probably a fair account of some of the questions being asked.

In response Mark assures them of a strong and lowly Jesus, whose very suffering became an avenue of salvation (a point powerfully made by Peter on the Day of Pentecost, Acts 2:36–39).

The view of authorship taken here is that the writer was John Mark, to whom reference is found in Acts 12:12, 25; 15:37–39; Colossians 4:10; 2 Timothy 4:11 and Philemon 24. He was evidently close to Peter and, after an initial failure, travelled with Paul. His pedigree is therefore strong!

It is clear that Mark did not try to present a chronological biography of Jesus, as a modern historian might. He had at his disposal material from spoken and written sources, and personal testimony from the apostle Peter. All this he sifted and presented in a way which enabled him to communicate those things he felt called to make plain. Such a view of the origin of this gospel in no sense diminishes the work of the Holy Spirit in inspiring this part of Holy Scripture. It adds to the sense of purpose behind the gospel, and it acknowledges the vital part of the author. It lifts us healthily clear of views of inspiration which require nothing of the author but the capacity to write words received from heaven. At the other end of the spectrum, it delivers us from views of Mark stringing together isolated segments of tradition with very little purpose other than to include as many as possible. Above all, it concentrates our attention on the text itself, as speaking for itself. There is a mystery about the divine inspiration of human effort, and we do well to acknowledge it and receive Holy Scripture as it is, from the hand of God through the minds of human beings committed to be channels of his will.

How are we to receive and read Mark's gospel? Much in the cultural detail of the first century is strange to us. We need to work hard at understanding it and its significance for those described in the gospel, and for those to whom it first came. We must be conscious, too, of the traditions and thought forms and experiences which shape our perceptions as we read the Bible. These also need to come under the judgment of God the Spirit as we read. But at depth, as the Spirit who inspires the writer inspires the reader, we may perceive fundamental themes which challenge us as directly as they did the earliest readers. Such topics as the nature of the king-

23

dom of God and our part in it; the identity and authority of Jesus our Lord; the centrality of his death and resurrection; their implications for our discipleship; and our own vision of and commitment to mission – all these stand out as part of Mark's contribution to our spirituality and service. His direct and deep engagement with them, and with us, can enrich us immensely.

Mark 1:1–13
1. The beginning

1. The meaning of the words and phrases (1:1)

The beginning of the gospel about Jesus Christ, the Son of God.

a. The beginning . . .

The Good News version 'This is' ('This is the Good News . . .') misses an obvious link with the Genesis story 'In the beginning'. Mark is establishing the fact that God is making a new start – new in the sense that it is a great step forward, but not new in leaving everything else behind, as will soon be evident. The first impression created by this gospel, however, is that something has happened which deserves careful attention.

b. . . . of the gospel

Now we begin to see why we should watch closely. The word 'gospel' has various meanings for us. It suggests a message proclaimed (as in 'Did he preach the gospel?'), or a book of the Bible (we are studying the Gospel according to Mark). Originally, however, it meant neither. It represented 'good news' in the sense of announcing some significant event which made a change in world history, like the birth of the Roman Emperor Augustus.[1] There is an essential historicity to the Christian message.

When the Old Testament roots of 'the gospel' are explored we begin to see why it is so important. In the form of a verb in Hebrew ('to announce good news') it means 'the in-breaking of God's kingly rule, the advent of his salvation, vengeance, vindication'.[2]

[1] Martin, *Action*, p. 10.
[2] Cranfield, p. 35. See, for example, Is.40:9; 41:27; 52:7; 60:6; 61:1; Na. 1:15; Pss. 50:9; 96:2).

The focus is on God's chosen people, but the implications range far wider, especially when, as at the coming of Jesus, they are under foreign rule. God's in-breaking has world significance. Those who witness it must tell it.

c. . . . about Jesus Christ

Mark begins to do just that for his readers. The reason the gospel is an event of world-changing implications is that it is 'the gospel about Jesus Christ'.

We now have a technical problem. Does 'the gospel about Jesus Christ' mean the gospel he preached, or the gospel of which he is the content? A glance at 1:14 clearly indicates the former, but Mark's gospel as a whole requires the latter. For once we can accept both meanings. The gospel is the good news Jesus preached; and he is at the heart of the good news. The messenger is also the message. This is unlike that other messenger we shall read about in a moment, John the Baptist (1:2–8), who made a clear distinction between himself and the one of whom he spoke, and who saw himself decreasing as the person at the heart of the good news increased (Jn. 3:30).

We understand this identification of message and messenger better as we look at the names of this person who is the centre of the message.

d. Jesus

This was a common name among Jews until the second century AD, after which Jews ceased using it to avoid connection with Jesus Christ, and Christians did not use it commonly, out of respect for their Lord. The name means 'Yahweh is salvation', and Matthew draws particular attention to that (Mt. 1:21): '*You are to give him the name Jesus because he will save his people from their sins.*'

e. Christ

Though we use this as a name it is primarily a title, and means 'the anointed one', or the Messiah. This was the one for whom the Jewish nation had waited for many years, longing for him particularly in days of oppression by others, as was their case now under the Romans. They had much to learn about what God intended by sending his anointed one, but for the moment Mark signals the link between the Saviour and the Messiah in the one who is the heart of the good news.

26

f. Son of God

There is some difficulty over the earliest texts here, some including 'Son of God' and others excluding it. One simply has to sum up the evidence on each side and make up one's own mind. Certainly it is usually assumed that such high Christology is more likely to have been added later rather than included earlier and dropped out. On the other hand, in the processes of copying it is not difficult to imagine this phrase being unwittingly lost. There is strong attestation in its favour in the manuscripts which include it. Most of all if, as seems likely, Mark is here providing the basis for his whole gospel, then 'Son of God' would occur most naturally. Just as the title 'Christ' will run through the story Mark tells (8:29; 14:61; 15:32), so also 'Son of God' is a major theme (1:11; 3:11; 8:38; 9:7; 7:12; 6:13; 32; 14:36, 61; 15:39). On balance it seems better to include it as intrinsic to Mark's intentions. He wishes us to know that the filial consciousness of Jesus in relation to God is well based in fact. He is, uniquely, Son of God. We need to know that from the outset. Most who met him during his lifetime did not recognize Jesus for who he was, but Mark wishes his readers to be clear about what the church now perceived and proclaimed about him. This contrast is in many ways the clue to the meaning of Mark's gospel.

g. Implications of Mark's opening

Before Mark's story develops we do well to reflect on what is implied by his first sentence.

(i) The good news is history

'Gospel' as a world-changing event points to the essential historicity of the Christian good news. Those who believe it, live by it, share it and proclaim it can count on the fact that it happened. Of course the events require interpretation, as the rest of Mark's gospel will make clear. But there is a basic 'givenness' in history which is fundamental to everything else. It happened long before we existed. We don't have to create it, imagine it, embellish it or subtract from it. Like the mountains or the landscape, the Jesus events are part of our historical terrain. We can look back and know that it is there. You may ignore or abuse historical evidence: you cannot erase it.

27

(ii) The good news is earthy

There is an earthiness at the heart of the message also. It is about God being committed to human affairs, being found alongside us. As Dr Lamin Sanneh put it, the earliest missionaries from the West, who went to Africa and Asia and translated Christian Scriptures into the native languages were asserting that 'God speaks to you in your mother tongue.'[3]

It is in the midst of the events of human history that God has made himself real, and continues to do so.

(iii) The good news is basic

Mark does not dwell on the detail of biography or events as his story unfolds. He writes nothing of Jesus' ancestry, unlike the other gospel writers. His interest in John the Baptist (1:2–8) will similarly be strictly limited to the part he played in the unfolding of the drama. It seems that Mark did not believe that Jesus could be 'proved' to be of divine origin – it had to be perceived by faith. So he does not build up steadily to awesome claims about Jesus. He simply states them baldly, clumsily, on a 'take it or leave it' basis. This sheds some light on, and is in turn illuminated by, the difficult verses in 4:10–12. Whatever else they mean, in their use of Isaiah 6:9–10, they certainly make clear that the real nature and meaning of God's presence in Jesus is not obvious – to anyone. It is perceived by God's grace through the gift of faith. The secret seems to be that only as you are willing to respond to Jesus do you perceive by faith the truth about him. Mark's gospel will make this process clear to us too – both positively and negatively.

(iv) The good news is challenge

This means that Mark is not writing just to inform but to challenge to faith. There is an urgency about his story. 'Immediately' is one of his favourite joining words. The gospel is not meant to entertain. It is much too serious for that. Life and death hang on it. In Mark, Jesus' opening words are crucial: *'The time has come . . . The kingdom of God is near. Repent and believe the good news!'* (1:15). Mark does not only testify to this urgent challenge to believe: he exemplifies it. We do well to hear him as we read his account of the good news 'about Jesus Christ, the Son of God'.

---

[3] Lecture to World Methodist Evangelism Regional Secretaries, London, December 1987.

2. An ancient prophecy (1:2–3)

It is written in Isaiah the prophet:

'I will send my messenger ahead of you,
who will prepare your way' –
³*'a voice of one calling in the desert.*
"Prepare the way for the Lord,
make straight paths for him." '

a. It is written . . . (1:2)

This expression regularly prepares us for a quotation. Mark is emphasizing that however new and awesome the gospel events are, they have been carefully prepared for by God, and that the Old Testament is the reliable witness to that patient preparation. He does not take away the sense of newness in the gospel: neither does he ignore the antecedent plan of God. They are all of a piece.

b. . . . in Isaiah the prophet (1:2)

The quotations which follow are actually from Malachi 3:1 combined with Exodus 23:20, and from Isaiah 40:3. Some think Mark was using a tradition which wrongly attached these quotations to Isaiah. Or they think he may be employing a form of grouped quotation used by followers of John the Baptist. It is more probable that this was a collection of Old Testament quotations brought together because of their common theme, and attached for purposes of recognition to the best-known author. Whichever is the case, Mark is not too tied to the literal text of the Old Testament Scripture as we know it. From Malachi 3:1, the 'way before me' becomes *your way*, and 'for our God' in Isaiah 40:3 becomes *for him*. Even the received Scriptures, it seems, were being seen in a new light because of the coming of Jesus. The way in which he fulfilled the Scriptures causes the New Testament writers to take statements about God and apply them to Jesus, as may have been happening here.[4]

Most important of all, Mark wishes us to know that John the Baptist, whom he is introducing through these verses, is part of God's preparation for the emergence of Jesus as the anointed one. After centuries of waiting, that hoped for day is drawing near.

---

[4] See, as a clear example, Paul's use in Phil. 2.10 of promises about God in Is. 45:23.

29

The need for patience

Reading the passage today we rush on to the main story, since we know that a moving moment for John the Baptist and for Jesus is about to be described. In our hurry, however, we may miss the significance of the long wait for the coming of the Messiah, and so ignore a vital spiritual quality – patience. The Bible in general does not make that mistake. The Psalmist often underlines the need to be patient (Pss. 37:7; 40:1; 43:5). Peter says that the prophets gave their messages but were unable to enter into the fulfilment of them because, 'they were not serving themselves but you, when they spoke of the things that have now been told you by those who have preached the gospel to you by the Holy Spirit sent from heaven' (1 Pet. 1:12). All the blessings of the gospel have come to Peter's readers. Spare a thought for the prophets who obediently spoke out but never saw the fulfilment of what they prophesied!

Patience in Christians is part of our response to the sovereignty of God. Only he knows the time, place and circumstance for things to happen in our lives. Often because we know some of the context we imagine we know it all. How often the moment must have seemed right to the prophet! But God knew better. The best answer to some of our prayers is 'wait', and sometimes 'no', not because God does not love us, but because the time and circumstance are not right just now. In a 'go-getting' instant culture we do well to cultivate the Christian quality of patience, over against the constant pressure for success, results and fulfilment.[5]

3. Enter John the Baptist (1:4–5)

And so John came, baptising in the desert region and preaching a baptism of repentance for the forgiveness of sins. ⁵The whole Judean countryside and all the people of Jerusalem went out to him. Confessing their sins, they were baptised by him in the Jordan River.

John the Baptist's ministry is now described, with minimal attention to biographical detail. Manuscripts vary as to the number and order of words at the beginning of verse 4, but the most likely translation would seem to be 'John the Baptist appeared, preaching in the desert', not least because it fits Mark's style of abrupt introduction of characters and events, highlighting the excitement and the unexpected nature of all that is taking place. God has planned it and is bringing it all to pass: men and women are taken by surprise.

[5] Col. 1:11; 2 Tim. 3:10; Heb. 6:12; Jas. 5:10.

a. In the desert (1:4)

As Stuart Blanch has pointed out,[6] the area referred to had a significant geographical location. It was a boundary between East and West, which the Romans would watch with particular care. It also had historical importance. Lot chose the Plain of Jordan when given the opportunity (Gn. 13). Jacob crossed the Jordan on his way to meet Esau (Gn. 33). Joshua led the people of Israel across the Jordan into the Promised Land (Jos. 3). The ministries of the prophets Elijah and Elisha had focused on the Jordan. In preaching and baptizing here, John was calling up many sacred memories. The desert had spiritual meaning, too. The people had wandered there for forty years, sustained by God's goodness. There was some idea that the Messiah would appear in the desert. Where better to preach and baptize than in the place where current political tensions, past sacred memories and cherished future hopes met?

b. Preaching . . . (1:4)

The word might be translated 'heralding'. In the Greek city-state the herald (a) preceded the king drawing attention to his coming, (b) called the citizens to the assembly which determined the city's life and, (c) told athletes at the games what the rules for participation were. To describe preachers as heralds is therefore an imaginative thing to do.

c. . . . a baptism of repentance for the forgiveness of sins (1:4)

The origin of John's use of baptism is complex. To be true to him we must seek a Jewish provenance. Jews had practised ritual washings since their time in the wilderness with Moses. Much of the provision of the law had used such washing to preserve sanitation and health. They were also familiar with the idea that washing made pure. The prophets had told them to wash themselves clean from their sins (Is. 1:16–18). Proselytes (those joining the Jewish faith from outside the race) were baptized, too. The surprise in John's ministry is that he calls on the Jews themselves to be baptized, so underlining the fact that their very religion may be the major hindrance to their readiness for the Messiah for whose coming they looked.

This is why he preached a baptism 'of repentance'. The word 'repentance' is best understood in terms of the Old Testament word

[6] Blanch, p. 18.

31

meaning 'to return' or 'to turn back'. The prophets had regularly called the people to do this, and they meant not just a change of mental attitude, but a total commitment to serving God, relying on his strength, doing his will and living as his people. Whatever fell short of that required repentance.

d. The whole Judean countryside and all the people of Jerusalem went out to him (1:5)

All of them? It must have seemed like that as the crowds came out. Why did they respond to John when their ancestors had so often ignored the prophets before him? They had now waited a long time for their Messiah. Four hundred years had elapsed since Malachi, the last recognized prophet, had spoken. The yoke of Rome chafed painfully and humiliatingly. And John evidently spoke with some vigour (even venom) and directness, if we put the witness of all four gospel writers together.[7] When he spoke of the coming judgment of God, they were inclined to believe him! So, confessing, they were baptized in large numbers.

e. Lessons for us from John

Our story so far draws attention to lessons for us today.

(i) The context matters
Christian truth and experience are not found independently of the history, social life and politics of the day. Neither the Jewish prophets of old nor the witness of John the Baptist will allow us to believe that. Precisely the opposite is the case. It is only as religious belief and practice truly engage with the affairs of everyday life that they can be seen to be authentically from God who is the God of all the worlds. John's role, location, manner and message interlocked Jewish history, contemporary life, future hope and God's presence in them all. True faith and mission always do.

(ii) Soul and body both matter
There is no room in Christianity for a 'spiritualizing' process which influences 'the soul' but not 'the body'; devotional life but not behaviour at work; church life but not home life. John the Baptist's call swept such distinctions away in one blast of divinely inspired preaching. Repentance relates to every part of life, as does forgiveness.

[7] Mk. 1:1–8; Lk. 3:1–18; Mt. 3:1–12; Jn. 1:19–28.

(iii) Readiness for new ways
There are ebbs and flows in history, as far as the impact of faith is concerned. Whether or not it should be so is a different question, but certainly history reveals it to be so. There are times when cultures, societies or nations seem to turn away from God, and the situation deteriorates steadily or dramatically. Then, so often at a very low point, revival begins, faith is renewed, and life is lived more according to God's will. In those moments it is for the people of God to be ready to respond and play their part. Sadly, too often the years of survival have witnessed the hardening of customs, attitudes and expectations till faith itself depends on them. When God does a new thing in the world, and most needs his people to testify to it and interpret it, too often he finds them resisting, resenting and even opposing it for being not precisely what they had hoped for, or still worse, being too disturbing of their long established ways. Sadly, even many of those who declared, in response to John the Baptist's preaching, that they were ready for the Messiah, proved unwilling to accept the anointed one when he came.

(iv) The vital importance of obedience
The test of true discipleship is on the one side openness to God's will revealed by his Spirit through Jesus, and on the other a life which expresses obedience to that will. The crowds were responsive to John, not least in view of impending doom: they were not ready to follow Jesus along the path of self-giving love, expressed in death and resurrection. The challenge is equally pointed, and the decision equally crucial, today.

4. The aim of John (1:6–8)

John wore clothing made of camel's hair, with a leather belt round his waist, and he ate locusts and wild honey. [7]And this was his message: 'After me will come one more powerful than I, the thongs of whose sandals I am not worthy to stoop down and untie. [8]I baptise you with water, but he will baptise you with the Holy Spirit.'

John's dress conjures up images of the prophets of the Old Testament, and Elijah (2 Ki. 1:8) in particular (6). His description of his own role is, however, specific rather than general (7). The slave tied the sandals for a master. To be willing to do that for another person is either to denigrate oneself beyond what is humanly reasonable or to elevate the other person beyond all normal

33

categories of work. John's aim is the latter. The reason follows in verse 8: '*I baptise you with water, but he will baptise you with the Holy Spirit*'. We must not assume that this is an easy verse to understand. It helps to hold firmly in mind the fact that the prime contrast is between two persons – John the Baptist and Jesus – rather than between two kinds of baptism. This is borne out by the fact that there is no evidence that Jesus baptized anyone. In any case, much of the contrast between the baptisms depends upon the difference between the persons. What John says Jesus will do is meant to heighten his hearers' awareness of the fact that Jesus is not simply another in the series of prophets of religion: he is the fulfilment of their dreams and visions. God is ushering in the end time through this anointed one who now comes.

Yet John does distinguish between the two baptisms, his own 'with water' and Jesus' 'with the Holy Spirit'. What then did he mean by the latter? Matthew and Luke add 'and with fire',[8] which has led to scholarly speculation about John's original words. The first suggestion is that he said simply 'he will baptize you with fire', alluding to the judgment the Messiah would bring. The second is that John spoke of Jesus baptizing 'with wind and fire', since the Greek, Hebrew and Aramaic words for 'spirit' can also mean 'wind'. In this case John was uniting two elemental forces, which were later identified as agents of God's power when the Holy Spirit came upon the disciples on the Day of Pentecost (Acts 2:2–4). If either of these reconstructions is correct, we then have to ask why in the gospels Jesus is described as baptizing 'with the Holy Spirit'. Some scholars answer that the evangelists included these words in order to harmonize John's statement with the later Christian understanding of baptism. Thus, if John had said 'with fire' they added 'and with the Holy Spirit', while if John had said 'with wind and fire', they substituted 'Spirit' for 'wind'. In both cases Jesus would be said to baptize 'with the Holy Spirit and with fire'.

But there is a third possibility, namely that John did actually say 'he will baptize with the Holy Spirit and with fire', and that either Mark did not have 'with fire' in the tradition or source he was using, or that he deliberately omitted the words, leaving only the reference to the Holy Spirit, in order to make it clear that Jesus' coming was primarily about grace, not judgment.

If we take seriously our task of understanding the Scriptures, we cannot simply ignore questions of the kind raised above, nor dismiss them as typical of an attitude of unbelief. Differences between gospel accounts must be faced, and reasons sought. Blanket

[8] Mt. 3:11; Lk. 3:16.

rejection of alternative suggestions may well prevent us from receiving new light on the meaning of the Bible. In any case we are often dealing with varying shades of likelihood or unlikelihood, and we do well to cross such territory with modesty and restraint about our opinions. It also serves to take the heat out of much debate on these matters, and enables us to reflect more soberly and clearly than might otherwise be the case.

Equally, however, I attach great importance to the principle of the General Editor of this series, John Stott, of seeking to interpret Scripture 'naturally' (as opposed to 'literally', 'figuratively' or other ways). If we approach this text in its context naturally we may note that the omission of 'and with fire' from Mark is less surprising, since he does not have in his account the passages from John's preaching which attack his hearers ('You brood of vipers! Who warned you to flee from the coming wrath?' Mt. 3:7; Lk. 3:7). Nor does he include the sections about God's judgment by axe and fire, ('The axe is already at the root of the trees, and every tree that does not produce good fruit will be cut down and thrown into the fire', Mt. 3:10; Lk 3:9). In Matthew and Luke it is immediately after these statements that John the Baptist promises that 'After me will come one who is more powerful than I . . . He will baptize you with the Holy Spirit and with fire' (Mt. 3:11; Lk. 3:16). Mark clearly omits this whole strand or did not know of it. Either way the reference to fire becomes less important.

If this is the case, then the 'wind and fire' solution is less rather than more likely. But could John have said 'the Holy Spirit'? There are perfectly good Old Testament reasons why he might have done. Ezekiel 36:25–28 provides a strong foundation for each of the points in John the Baptist's sermon as recorded by Mark. The context is God's determination to redeem his people from their bondage, 'It is not for your sake . . . that I am going to do these things, but for the sake of my holy name, which you have profaned among the nations where you have gone' (Ezk. 36:22). Israel clearly has much of which to repent, and the significance is beyond the boundaries of their own nation. What God is about to do will make clear his Sovereign Lordship, and will keep his covenant promises, 'I will show the holiness of my great name. . . . Then the nations will know that I am the Lord. . . . For I will take you out of the nations; I will gather you from all the countries and bring you back into your own land' (Ezk. 36:23–24). But how will God make his people worthy of such restoration? 'I will sprinkle clean water on you, and you will be clean; I will cleanse you from all your impurities and from all your idols' (25). Their renewal will have to involve a change of heart and mind (26), so closely related to

35

John the Baptist's call for repentance. Most of all (Ezk. 36:27–28), 'I will put my Spirit in you and move you to follow my decrees and be careful to keep my laws. You will live in the land I gave your forefathers; you will be my people, and I will be your God.' A prophet reflecting on those verses could well have said what the gospel writers record as the words of John the Baptist about the Holy Spirit. The same is true of Joel 2:28, which was so effectively used by Peter on the Day of Pentecost to account for the coming of the Holy Spirit on the early Christians (Acts 2:16–21).

There seems to be no intrinsic reason to doubt that the words recorded by Mark, suggesting that John the Baptist promised the coming of the Holy Spirit via Jesus, are authentic and accurate, as well as fully in harmony with the descent of that Spirit 'like a dove' (Mk. 1:10), rather than flames of fire or gusts of winds, as at Pentecost.

The fulfilment of John the Baptist's promise, baptism in the Holy Spirit via Jesus, is best understood historically in terms of Pentecost (Acts 2), and theologically in relation to Paul's affirmation in Romans 8:5–11, where those who 'belong to Christ . . . have the Spirit of Christ'.

Historically, the experience of the Holy Spirit on the Day of Pentecost is one in a series of God's bringing in the kingdom through Jesus Christ. The foundation of the kingdom was laid in the ministry, death, resurrection and ascension of Jesus. As to the spread of the kingdom, when his disciples asked him about its future (Acts 1:6) Jesus had told them to wait in Jerusalem for the power that the Holy Spirit would give, and then they would be witnesses in Jerusalem, Judea, Samaria and all the earth (Acts 1:8). Pentecost was the historic moment when the Holy Spirit came upon the new Christian community. Luke makes clear, in Acts 2:5, that those who received the Spirit in power on that Day of Pentecost were Jews. In Acts 10 he tells of another historic moment, when the Spirit came upon the Gentile believers gathered together by the Roman centurion Cornelius.

It would be wrong, however, to take these historical and historic occasions as patterns for individual believers ever after, and particularly to use them as a basis for a two-stage experience – first faith in Christ and then later the baptism of the Holy Spirit. It is here that the theological point has to be placed alongside the historical description.

Paul, in Romans 8, is seeking to encourage his readers in their submission to, and experience of the Holy Spirit. He suggests that they are not entering fully enough into the freedom which the Spirit gives (Rom. 8:2); they are not living 'in accordance with the

Spirit' (Rom. 8:5–8). He plainly feels they could be more controlled by the Spirit, but he never doubts that they have the Spirit. Indeed the basis of his encouragement to them to be more fully committed to the Spirit's ways is the fact that they are already indwelt by the Holy Spirit, since all who belong to Christ have the Spirit of Christ (Rom. 8:9). They can know God as Father only because the Spirit testifies to their spirits that it is so (Rom. 8:15–16). Paul puts the case in a different way in 1 Corinthians 12:3 when he asserts that no-one can say 'Jesus is Lord', except by the Spirit.

The coming of the Spirit at Pentecost was therefore the assurance for all time that those whose faith is in Christ receive the Holy Spirit with power. But in the rest of Acts, and in many other places in the New Testament, the question put to the believers concerns how fully they are living in harmony with the Spirit's presence within them. All who know Christ are already baptized in the Spirit. Our calling is to know moment by moment the fulness of the Spirit.

Mark's specific aim is to relate John the Baptist and Jesus to the kingdom of God. The contrast between John and Jesus is strikingly portrayed. John has played his part in announcing the kingdom: Jesus was the heart of that kingdom. John, as Jesus would later say, was the greatest of the prophets, yet the least in the kingdom introduced by Jesus was 'greater than he' (Mt. 11:11). In other words, John had a particularly honoured place. He announced the moment for which many other prophets had dreamed and longed. But it was also a limited place. Once his work was done he would pass from the scene as Jesus took over. John himself knew that (Jn. 3:27–30). His message was limited, too, as was his baptism. None of this is to detract from John's ministry. Quite the opposite, all these passages show how faithfully John played his limited part in God's larger plans.

Finding our limited place in God's overall purposes

John's place in God's larger plans is a lesson with broader implications for us all. We live in an age where to begin, continue and complete things is a dominating passion. Being 'in control of affairs' is taken as a sign of achievement. The Christian knows better than that. The gospel is meant to make us truly 'broad-minded', viewing the whole of life against the canvas of God's eternal plans for us and for his world. Worship week by week reminds us of that perspective, as ought our daily devotions and experiences of Christian fellowship. In that wider sweep of God's purposes we learn to play our limited – yet vital – part. History is his. The universe is his. The mission to the world is his. We are most fulfilled not when we seek fulfilment but when we seek to find our proper place in his never-ending purposes for this world. We are both less and more important than we think. In that on-going process, we belong to one another.

What would be the purpose of the prophetic longing had John the Baptist not been raised up to bring it to its point? And what would have been the meaning of John's words but for the prophets' faithful and painful work over the years? How would Jesus himself have begun without the milestone of baptism at John's hands? The intense individualism of our culture often cloaks the corporate implications of New Testament teaching. The failure of the English language adequately to distinguish between second person singular and second person plural is also a great hindrance. Not least it masks the fact that most of the great commands and promises of the New Testament are stated in the plural. We need some equivalent of the southern United States expression 'y'all'! In the language of the lovely NIV translation of Romans 12:5, 'In Christ we who are many form one body, and each member belongs to all the others'.

5. The baptism of Jesus (1:9–11)

At that time Jesus came from Nazareth in Galilee and was baptised by John in the Jordan. ¹⁰As Jesus was coming up out of the water, he saw heaven being torn open and the Spirit descending on him like a dove. ¹¹And a voice came from heaven: 'You are my Son, whom I love; with you I am well pleased.'

There is a strong link with the Old Testament in the story of John baptizing Jesus. Even the wording produced by the Authorized Version, 'And it came to pass in those days, that Jesus came from Nazareth of Galilee', recreates the mood of many Old Testament stories. So do significant elements in the story, like the opening of the heavens, the Spirit and the heavenly voice. It is permeated by the sense of a drama, composed and directed by an unseen hand, which is played out in a much broader context than that of John the Baptist and his hearers. The preparations have been centuries long; the implications can only be guessed at.

By contrast with the atmosphere of sensitivity to the divine presence, there is the simple allusion to Jesus' home town, Nazareth of Galilee. The contrast could hardly be greater, reflected by the words of Nathaniel in John 1:46, 'Nazareth! Can anything good come from there?' It is not that it was a particularly wicked place: it was simply unheard of, never mentioned in the Old Testament nor in those other Jewish sources where you might expect to read of the Messiah's home. We have to try to imagine the shock of this on first-century hearers of the gospel.

The second shock is that the story of the baptism of Jesus by John is included at all. That the one who came to be understood as sinless should submit to a rite directly related to repentance and cleansing is a sure sign of the authenticity of the event. We could well understand Matthew and Luke including in their account all those remembered or communicated elements which went as far as possible to explain the totally unexpected. Matthew, for example, records John as protesting at Jesus' request to be baptized by him (Mt. 3:14–15) but is persuaded to go on in order to 'do all that God requires' (GNB).

What the gospel writers cannot do is to omit it. We may only guess what it all meant to Jesus, but there is great sense in the suggestion that he dedicates himself to obey God's will through an event which symbolizes what the whole ministry will involve – making it possible for sinners to repent in order to find forgiveness and new life from God. In baptism he shares the circumstances in which people become aware of their needs, precisely in order to meet those needs. He was to do that again and again in his ministry, and supremely in his death and resurrection. 'To fulfil all righteousness' (Mt. 3:15) could hardly express it more clearly, and Paul's use of the same word 'righteousness' in the Letter to the Romans, (see especially Rom. 3:21 ff.) works the whole process out in detail.

But what actually happened when John baptized Jesus? It is not easy to reconcile the accounts given in the three synoptic gospels (Matthew, Mark and Luke).

All three synoptic evangelists say that 'heaven was opened', indeed 'torn open' (Mark). This was a common Jewish expression used to introduce a divine revelation. Isaiah 64:1 and Ezekiel 1:1 provide good Old Testament examples. But what was the revelation which the evangelists describe, and to whom was it made?

Primarily the revelation was made to Jesus himself. Matthew and Mark clearly say that '*he saw* . . . the Spirit descending on him like a dove'. Mark and Luke also say that the heavenly voice addressed him, saying 'You are my Son . . .'.

But was the revelation made to others too? According to the Fourth Gospel, God's purpose through the ministry of John was that Jesus might be 'revealed to Israel', and it was through seeing the Spirit descend on Jesus that John himself learned his identity (Jn. 1:32–34). The synoptists also appear to be saying both that the vision was seen by others (this is the natural interpretation of Lk. 3:22) and that the voice was heard by others, even though only

Matthew records it as declaring in the third person 'This is my Son'.

First and foremost, then, the revelation was made to Jesus that he was the Son of God, the Messiah, anointed with and bestowing the Spirit. In addition, however, as the baptism itself was a public event, so surely the accompanying phenomena (the vision and the voice) are meant to be understood as public signs. On the threshold of his ministry the private disclosure to Jesus of his identity and the public testimony to him took place simultaneously.

It is typical of our journalistic, televised age that we demand answers to these questions about the exact nature of the vision and the voice. In Mark's narrative, however, the emphasis lies elsewhere. We are fascinated by 'what?' and 'how?' questions, whereas the Bible is constantly answering the question 'why?' (The struggles over Genesis 1–3 may provide a parallel.) 'What?' and 'how?' questions are important. But if they are given priority status, they obscure what a story is about. This is not to deny the objectivity of the event (the Spirit came visibly and the voice was audible); but Mark's focus is on the significance of what happened.

The baptism of Jesus is about meaning. The rending of the heavens has apocalyptic significance, bringing out this meaning. It is about divine action to introduce the end times. The descent of the Spirit, unusually likened to a dove (John the Baptist must surely have expected at least wind and fire!) calls up memories of the Spirit brooding over creation in the Genesis story – not mildly brooding, but present with enormous creative force. The voice from heaven, also apocalyptic in character, despite lengthy scholarly discussion, still seems best understood as bringing together insights from Isaiah 42:1 ('Here is my servant, whom I uphold, my chosen one in whom I delight; I will put my Spirit on him'), and Psalm 2:7 ('You are my Son; today I have become your Father'). That they are not direct quotations is clear if one simply puts beside those two the text as we have it, '*You are my Son, whom I love; with you I am well pleased*' (1:11). There is no sense of God 'adopting' Jesus as son at the baptism. There does seem to be much in the combination of the lowly suffering servant of whom Isaiah wrote, and the royal prince of the Psalms. This gathers the Old Testament testimony together, focusing it on the high point of the baptism. It also provides the basis for Mark's account, which will concentrate on the way in which the divine authority of Jesus is finally expressed along the path of lowliness and suffering. And we may guess, though no more than guess, that, combined with John's words and recognition, all this was for Jesus a powerful affirmation of his act of self-dedication, and confirmation of his divine vocation. The next phase of Mark's story shows how necessary such affirmation and confirmation were.

Principles

(i) God constantly takes us by surprise

We cannot ignore the inherent unlikelihood of God's plan of salvation for the world beginning from Nazareth. We may equally have doubted the choice of so remote a prophet as John the Baptist. Were this an isolated case it could be so treated. In the Bible, however, there does seem to be a principle operating whereby God chooses the unlikely person or people to fulfil his purposes. Striking examples are Moses, the leader with the speech defect; Gideon, the youngest son of a poor farmer, chosen to be an army general; Jeremiah, a fiery reflective man too young for the task; and Amos, a farmer from the south chosen to prophesy in the court of the king in the north. The pattern follows through with John the Baptist, then the disciples, and is spelt out by Paul in the first letter to the Corinthians. In 1 Corinthians 1:26 he tells them, 'Not many of you were wise by human standards; not many were influential; not many were of noble birth.' Then, lest the strong should assume that this was a matter of chance, he writes, 'But God chose the foolish things of the world to shame the wise; God chose the weak things of the world to shame the strong. He chose the lowly things of this world and the despised things – and the things that are not – to nullify the things that are, so that no-one may boast before him' (1 Cor. 1:27–29). We must not jump to the immediate conclusion that the strong, noble and clever are not usable by God. How else would Paul have been included? But the clue is in verse 29. It is not the status which matters, but the attitude. The poor, weak and lowly are less likely (not necessarily unlikely) to boast before God than are the strong, noble and clever.

One remarkable thread running through Christian history is the way in which the church in times of revival has striven among the poor, the weak and the lowly. Recession of the revival has often coincided with control being taken over by the strong, the noble and the clever. They are not automatically boastful before God, but they have very much more resource for trusting in themselves. All the greatest human gifts have the greatest dangers of abuse built in. All the alleged disadvantages have compensations greater than are recognized. This is not to mount an attack on pedigree, human character, or learning. Nor is it to support the *status quo* with millions of poor people in the world. There are other Christian values which require us to struggle for human growth, ability and

41

learning to flourish, and for their fruits to be shared everywhere. But the greatest characteristic to be sought is humility before God, and to embody and communicate that God has again and again chosen unlikely individuals and groups who have been written off by the world. Let those who have ears to hear, hear!

(ii) *We are both inadequate and capable of being used by God*

A second principle here at work is at the heart of the baptism of Jesus by John. It is the way God takes what is there and uses it, despite its inadequacies. In this case the Jewish hopes for a Messiah were clearly far different from what God intended. The powerful soldier-king who could throw off the Roman yoke was a fair inference from the model of King David. How relevant that must have seemed to the Jewish people under Roman rule! We might even think that some of John the Baptist's view was also expressive of this picture. Images of axes hacking at roots of trees, and fire running across the floor burning up the chaff, would hardly be satisfied with the Spirit coming as a dove. No wonder John became impatient when Jesus left him languishing in prison (Lk. 7:18–23; Mt. 11:2–6). The Messiah he had predicted could easily have 'sprung a jail'! But it was not to be so, just as Jesus himself would not take an escape route from death on the cross (Mk. 8:31–33; 9:31–32; 10:33–34).

Yet, inadequate though Jewish popular expectations had become, and partial though John the Baptist's views were, God took that as the context for the ministry of Jesus, because the Jews were his chosen people, and because John grasped enough to be the messenger of repentance and forgiveness.

As Christians we need to be clear about such limitations, with regard to ourselves, our churches, and our culture. About ourselves, because at times we may feel useless to God, not knowledgeable or gifted or perceptive enough, and we will always be right in that judgment. The real danger comes when we forget that! But we are equally wrong to assume that because of our limitations God will not use us. Whoever we are, and however partial our knowledge and ability, God can use us.

Where churches are concerned, this lesson of God's willingness to use us applies in two separate areas. There is the context of Christians who constantly grumble about their local church or denomination, and long for something more informed, more pure, more sound, more biblical. All such longings are probably justified! But if the next step for them is to leave then that development is probably not justified. God has never had a perfect church with which to work, yet he goes on keeping his promises, as a covenant

God, and doing this work through inadequate human representatives. We need to be sure that when we leave a church it is for God's glory, rather than for our own comfort and convenience.

This same principle applies to the church in another arena, also, that of her influence in the affairs of everyday life. Christians often seem to be overawed by matters social, economic and political. We disguise our inadequacy by speaking of the 'inappropriateness' of church involvement in these matters, or we speak of individual commitment being acceptable, but not the church 'as church', as though that distinction was in any sense biblical, which it isn't. There is no such thing in the New Testament as a Christian behaving as an individual but not as part of the church, unless you can imagine a hand operating but not as part of the body to which it belongs. The stumbling-block seems to be that we feel we are defiled as a church by the participating, or that we do not know enough to do so.

Yet the worlds of social life, politics and economics, ecology and health, education and industry, need the Christian perspective, not just by Christians being engaged in them but by statements of Christian principles, values, insights and examples. The church does not need to have its own political party, or institutions, to achieve that. It needs, however, to be confronting the issues raised, at every level of its life, from individual study and prayer, through fellowship groups and meetings, to councils and synods and conferences, with appropriate comment and action at every level. The church of Jesus Christ has the right and the duty to comment, not least because her Lord is the Word of creation, the one through whom, in whom and for whom the universe was made (Jn. 1:1–14; Col. 1:15–17; Heb. 1:1–3). To fail to be involved and to make comment in this area of life is not to exercise an option, it is to fail in our witness. God will use us, despite our inadequacy and nervousness if, like John the Baptist, we are obedient.

6. The temptations in the desert (1:12–13)

At once the Spirit sent him out into the desert, ¹³and he was in the desert for forty days, being tempted by Satan. He was with the wild animals, and angels attended him.

By contrast with Matthew and Luke, Mark's account of the wilderness temptations of Jesus is blunt in its brevity. It is also characteristically raw – such as the assertion (in the Greek) that Jesus was 'driven out' into the wilderness, as opposed to the 'was led' of Matthew and Luke. There is a sense here not so much of the

43

unwillingness of Jesus to go, but of the urgency that he should do so. This word harmonizes well with Mark's frequent use of 'immediately', and also with the use by Jesus of the word 'must', especially when prophesying his death, and subsequent resurrection (Mk. 8:31). It has to do with the 'beloved Son' obeying the Father's will, under the true guidance of the Spirit. The natural trinitarianism of these verses, assumed rather than spelt out, is in itself convincing.

Despite his brevity, however, Mark has one puzzling piece of information not recorded by the other gospel writers. 1:13 simply says (Jesus) *was with the wild animals*. We are probably meant to understand this as meaning 'as opposed to human beings'. It is the loneliness and isolation which is here emphasized. Yet there is an element of harmony, too. The prophets had foretold that in God's coming kingdom there would be a remarkable unity among living creatures. 'The wolf will live with the lamb, the leopard will lie down with the goat, the calf and the lion and the yearling together; and a little child will lead them. . . . The infant will play near the hole of the cobra, and the young child put his hand into the viper's nest' (Is. 11:6, 8). Mark does not go into that detail, nor is he saying that this prophecy is now fulfilled. He may, however, be hinting that such possibilities are drawing nearer with the advance of the kingdom (1:15), and that Jesus' closeness to the animals is a sign of it.

He may not have had humans around him, but as well as animals he also had angels (1:13). It is easy for some to dismiss these as over-spiritualizing human experience, or as elements of superstitious imagery. We do well to recall that there is still much about human inner experience, and about what goes on invisibly around us, that we do not understand. If one ties in with that the experience of Christians over the centuries of being 'protected', 'guided', 'provided for', 'sustained', it seems well at very least to keep an open mind about angels. We may dispense with wings and feathers and much of the artistic creation across the centuries. Much of this depiction depended on visionary passages like Isaiah 6:2. Mark does not here describe the angels, nor the exact nature of their ministry. But if we accept the idea of the transcendent as fundamental to Christianity, then angelic ministry, whatever it means precisely, is a natural and acceptable explanation of those moments in our lives when God's hand seems particularly and unexpectedly on us.

For the rest of that section, the forty days period is full of symbolism. Moses (Ex. 34:28), Elijah (1 Ki. 19:8) or the forty years of Israel's wanderings in the wilderness all come to mind. Rather than seek to choose one, we are probably better advised to see the significance in terms of a recollection of places and experiences of spiritual warfare in Israel's history. These reminiscences, following the baptism of Jesus, speak powerfully of Mark's central theme of the costliness of commitment to God's way of salvation.

a. Following Jesus will not be an easy journey

Mark makes no attempt to explain the link between the baptism and the temptations. If the paragraph above is correct about his intentions, then the whole of the story Mark tells will serve to elucidate that link. To follow Jesus is both free and costly. We are accepted by God's grace, and experience it in our discipleship, but we live it out in a world where God's grace is neither applauded nor welcomed, for men and women are so often made uneasy by such a free offer of salvation, preferring to work things out for themselves. There is also a spiritual battle between good and evil into which the disciple of Jesus is drawn. In that context we survive by obedience to God's will and by drawing on the spiritual sustenance provided in worship and fellowship, Bible reading and prayer, preaching and sacrament.

Our evangelism fails our hearers if we give the impression that becoming a Christian is mainly a way of solving our problems and making life tolerable – even enjoyable – for ourselves. Certainly it is about receiving. Salvation by grace through faith makes that abundantly plain. But it is receiving salvation which brings us into the people of God, the body of Christ, the community of the Holy Spirit, whose calling is to serve God through Christ by the Holy Spirit in the world. That is anything but an easy route; it is the way of daily dying and rising with Christ. Our evangelism needs to make that clear, or what we call our 'follow-up' work will always be failing. The teaching of Jesus, and the preaching of the early disciples, never offered 'cheap grace'. Nor ought we.

b. Faithful discipleship is more about doing God's will than about feeling good

There is some puzzlement caused by Mark's omission of the details of the temptation of Jesus. By contrast, see Matthew 4:1–11 and Luke 4:1–13. It has been suggested that Mark knew that his hearers, or readers, had these details already. Yet this seems unconvincing, since he tells them other things they must have heard in the regular preaching and teaching of the church, not least about the cross. An alternative would be that Mark himself did not have these details, either in the traditions or the sources he had received. This is

45

equally unconvincing, both because of the fascination of the temptation stories and because of their relevance to the disciples' own
spiritual experience. It is more likely that Mark's purpose was not
to go into intimate personal details in writing his gospel. We have
seen that he showed little interest in the biographical details of
John and, more surprisingly, of Jesus. His emphasis is not upon
being concerned with one's internal state or circumstances, but
with getting on as an obedient disciple whatever the consequences.

After decades of the neglect of inner spiritual experience in much
of Western Christianity, we have now witnessed a swing of the
pendulum in both sacramental and charismatic circles. There is
much to welcome in both. There is also a danger of becoming so
taken up with one's own internal spiritual state – individually and
corporately – that we are almost obsessive about it. Before long
'how we feel' becomes the dominant consideration, determining
our judgments on our spiritual state and that of others; whether
or not some new idea is from God; even who should or should
not be in leadership. Mark seems to be pointing to much more
objective criteria, like costly commitment to doing God's will,
whether it produces comfort or not, happiness or not, fulfilment
or not. It is a 'driven-ness' to the urgent task of obeying God
according to the pattern of Jesus, in which there is no time for the
luxury of endlessly examining our spiritual state, individually or
corporately.

c. The animals and the angels broaden our vision of the kingdom

The animals and the angels provide a brief glimpse of the extent of
the kingdom shortly to be announced. However 'earthed' Mark's
picture of Jesus is, there is from time to time the hint of the 'cosmic'
Christ, so much more openly testified to by John (Jn. 1:1–18), or
in another way by Luke in the breadth of the people he records
Jesus as having met, taught and healed (Romans, women, children,
outcasts). Here in the wilderness, with the heavenly voice of affirmation ringing in his consciousness, as he struggles against temptation and its root in the soil of evil in the spiritual realm, he also
has the animals around him and the angels to minister to him. That
is probably, too, why Mark so unambiguously portrays Jesus as
Lord over nature in the miracle stories he tells.

What Matthew and Luke make clear in their record of Jesus
rejecting the temptation to pursue his goal by demonstrations of
miraculous power, or by spectacular physical escapes, or by ruling
the earth through worshipping Satan (Mt. 4:1–11; Lk. 4:1–13),
Mark hints at by including animals and angels in the context of the

46

temptations. The baptism is over; the temptations are resisted, heavenly and earthly beings are gathered into unity around him. The time is right for the declaration of the kingdom (1:14–15), and for hints of the cosmic proportions of the ministry of Jesus. John the Baptist had already warned his hearers that the way they were behaving in daily life was important for their readiness to receive the coming Messiah. We saw the social and political implications of that (pp. 32–33). We have noted the realities of the hidden spiritual world also (pp. 38–41). This bit of the story unites the proper use of the world's resources (as Matthew and Luke tell the temptation story), and the significance of the animals.

If the Spirit descending as a dove was reminiscent of the brooding over creation at the beginning, and if Mark's use of the word 'beginning' in Mark 1:1 also calls up memories of how it was at the beginning, then we must not miss the significance of the total picture, including the animals, for our Christian concern for ecology. The Lordship of Christ is over all creation. His disciples must not use that world as their possession, to be wasted at will. The wilderness, as a place of serious reliance upon what nature (not humans) provided, now witnesses with the animals to the intended ultimate harmony of all creation. We must not affirm that, then waste it.

d. The secret of Mark's gospel

In verses 1–13 Mark has revealed who Jesus is and what he came to do. We, the readers, now know what to look for. Yet in the story that unfolds he will be showing us how difficult people found it to accept what we already know. As Professor Morna Hooker puts it, '. . . we need to remember that here Mark is letting us into secrets which remain hidden throughout most of the drama, from the great majority of the characters in the story'.[9] In one sense, that is the story's inner meaning.

[9] Hooker, p. 6.

Mark 1:14 – 3:6
2. The ministry opens up

1. Jesus proclaims the good news (1:14–15)

After John was put in prison, Jesus went into Galilee, proclaiming the good news of God. [15]*'The time has come,' he said. 'The kingdom of God is near. Repent and believe the good news!'*

We race on again with Mark, his vague identifications of time and place allowing for other parts of the ministry of Jesus, witnessed to by the other gospels, to be fitted in conveniently. John's gospel, for example, suggests a shared ministry between Jesus and John the Baptist (Jn. 3:22–24). This is not important for Mark, however. His purpose, having carefully laid the foundations, is to introduce the ministry of Jesus.

We therefore begin with *After John was put in prison* (1:14). There are no details or explanations such as occur elsewhere. John has fulfilled his purpose and will be returned to in 6:14–29 when his tragic death will be described. Now, however, the spotlight is fully on Jesus, as John had himself foreseen (Jn. 3:30). In that, John is a model for all disciples, but not an easy one to copy.

Mark says that Jesus came into Galilee. For the implications of that statement Stuart Blanch contrasts modern visitors' sense of peace and quiet in Galilee with the realities of the time of John the Baptist and Jesus:

> Galilee was the centre of a humming political and commercial life. It stood at the crossroads of the nations of the ancient world, through which the armies and the traders and the diplomats passed. There some of the greatest battles of the world had been fought. . . . Galilee was the home of a thoroughly cosmopolitan population: Greek, Hebrew and Aramaic would all be heard in the markets; Syrian, Jew, Roman and Parthian mixed freely. It

was a land of passing excitements and dangerous fashions, of a barbarous dialect and offensive manners.[1]

He also draws attention to the tense political and religious scene there. We must resist the temptation to picture the beginning of Jesus' ministry as being centred in some gentle, quiet backwater (of the kind we often create in our churches!). He began at a place of conflict, threat, racial mixture and busy activity.

Jesus was *proclaiming the good news of God* (1:14). We are now into the content of the message. Mark is probably not saying that these are the sentences Jesus used wherever he preached. Neither should we therefore conclude that Jesus did not use these words at the beginning. There is everything to be gained by starting out with a striking statement of the 'good news'. For the rest Mark is encouraging us to see all the sayings, miracles, acts of Jesus, including his crucifixion and God's raising him from the dead, in the setting provided by the words with which Jesus began.

The good news

The good news contains two statements and two exhortations. Both statements concentrate on God's initiative. It is what God has done which calls for the responses demanded by the exhortations.

(i) 'The time has come' (1:15)

As with the story of John the Baptist's work, and of the baptism of Jesus, there is again a strong sense of God's sovereign control. A more literal translation 'The time is fulfilled' reinforces this sense. Not all the time ticked out by our clocks and watches is of equal value. Some minutes are filled with extra meaning. We know that from our own experience. The chronological measurement of my birth, conversion, services of ordination and marriage (in order of happening) would be a totally inappropriate way to estimate their significance. They were moments which, I believe, God filled with great meaning. In a way which far surpasses that, Jesus says God is now filling the time of the beginning of his ministry with immense importance. All the centuries of preparation and prophecy are reaching their fulfilment. This is a time heavy with eternal significance.

(ii) 'The kingdom of God is near' (1:15)

The second statement explained why that is so. It is now commonplace knowledge, yet needing constantly to be reiterated, that the

[1] Blanch, p. 31.

Aramaic term behind the Greek word for kingdom means 'kingly rule', 'sovereignty', or 'reign'. It is about the fact of someone reigning rather than about the geographical area of the reign. It is about 'rule' rather than 'realm'. In the Old Testament, extra-canonical writing, and rabbinic literature, two elements vie with one another. The first is that Yahweh is now king. Over Israel (Is. 41:21; 43:15), over the world at large (Je. 10:7; Mal. 1:14), he is the king now. Yet the other strand is equally present, namely that there will come a day when this will no longer be hidden, but will be seen by all to be the case (Is. 45:22–23; Zc. 14:9). They are not alternatives; for both are true and need one another.

The great new development at the outset of the ministry of Jesus is the identifying of a point where these two can (not automatically will) be seen as the focus of life-giving tension – in Jesus himself. His ministry will demonstrate in what way God is now sovereign. The particularity of that reign will now be spelt out, in a unique way, through Jesus. It will also provide the basis on which the future reign of God will be established. Many scholarly works have been written, identifying the moment at which the kingdom might be said to have come in Jesus. The words of John Stott remain a wise commentary on all that reflection:

> The controversy has been unnecessarily complicated by a tendency to forget that in the New Testament as a whole the conception of the Kingdom is not a static one. There was no one moment in the triumphant progress of our saving Lord from His cradle in Bethlehem to His final glory at the Father's right hand, at which it may be said 'the Kingdom came or will come then'. The Kingdom was coming all the time. It is still growing.[2]

At this time now introduced by the coming of Jesus, men and women will be able to perceive the kingdom of God come near.

(iii) 'Repent' (1:15)

The two exhortations indicate how this can come about, and no two words together have been used so much by Christian preachers – '*Turn away from your sins and believe the Good News*' (1:15, GNB). The more literal translation makes the point better '*repent, and believe in the gospel*,' RSV.

'Repent' has been not only much used, but probably also greatly misused, by being used too narrowly, not least by evangelical preachers! Fundamentally it means 'a changing of direction', 'turning back', 'change of mind'. It is certainly associated with turning

[2] Stott, p. 13.

away from wrong attitudes, words and deeds. The danger lies in narrowing its meaning down to an emotional sense of guilt, identified and acted upon at one particular time. This is where abuse in preaching takes place. In fact it has a much wider connotation. Hearing the stories of many who have become Christians makes the point effectively. For some there is an emotional sense of guilt at the outset. For others it is a discovery of the only source of true meaning in life. For yet others there is a call to radical discipleship in obedience to Christ. Yet all involve 'turning back', 'turning round', 'change of mind', 'change of direction'. Once the turn is made the other elements may come too. It is not the specific stimulus which is most important, it is the turning away from one's own path to that commended to us by God in Christ. Perhaps 'change of heart' is the best idiomatic translation to allow for depth and breadth. Not to recognize the larger meaning is to neglect both the meaning of the gospel and the variety of ways in which God enables people to respond to it.

(iv) 'Believe in the gospel' (1:15, RSV)
This is the only undoubted use of 'believe in' in the New Testament. Although this can be discussed as 'translation Greek', it could equally be a deliberate reinforcing of the idea that belief is more than credence or consent, and actually involves commitment. Certainly this is the implication of 'believing the good news', since the good news was that God's kingdom is coming, and God's kingdom means God's rule in the hearts and minds of men and women. One cannot truly 'believe' that without commitment.[3]

a. The good news has specific content

The way the story has now unfolded is a warning against accepting too easily the old adage that 'Christianity is caught rather than taught'. One understands the importance of not seeing it as either a 'classroom religion' (J. V. Taylor) or assent to a set of doctrinal propositions. It also stresses the importance of the quality of other people's lives as important in bringing us to faith. What it neglects, however, is that faith does have a content. What is more, the content was more clearly signalled to the first hearers or readers of the gospel by the particular words used, than it is for us. 'Time', 'kingdom', 'repent' and 'believe' are all examples of the content

[3] For a survey of the meaning of 'faith' in the New Testament, see Donald English, 'Faith in the New Testament' in John Stacey (ed.) *About Faith*: Preacher's Handbook New Series No. 3 (Local Preachers' Department, Methodist Church in Britain, 1972), pp. 28 ff.

which is important. The mind needs to be converted, too. An evangelism which teaches is one of our greatest needs.

b. The hidden values

We are under great pressure today to pay attention only to what is observable, and to measuring time particularly in those terms. The use here of 'time' by Jesus, as related to eternity and God's sovereign rule, shows how important it is to measure time not only by seconds, minutes and hours but also in terms of the importance of what is happening against the backcloth of God's purposes for the world. The modern commercial habit of 'costing' time can be very misleading here. How do you cost 'prayer time' for example? What about the important 'waiting time'? Even some of our church strategies need examining by this criterion.

c. It is always God who initiates: we who must respond

The basis of Jesus' call to repentance and faith was the announcement of God's initiative in bringing the kingdom near. The whole of life is based on that fundamental truth. We do not initiate, we respond, both in relation to life, by God's initiative in creation, and in relation to new life in Christ, by God's initiative in Jesus. Our sacraments celebrate that; as does the importance of preaching in our worship. The basic question of our daily life is how far we are responding appropriately to God's initiatives at every level. Since God is in all of life so should our responses be.

2. Jesus calls the first disciples (1:16–20)

As Jesus walked beside the Sea of Galilee, he saw Simon and his brother Andrew casting a net into the lake, for they were fishermen. [17]*'Come, follow me,' Jesus said, 'and I will make you fishers of men.'* [18]*At once they left their nets and followed him.*

[19]*When he had gone a little farther, he saw James son of Zebedee and his brother John in a boat, preparing their nets.* [20]*Without delay he called them, and they left their father Zebedee in the boat with the hired men and followed him.*

With John in prison Jesus could have decided to continue to exercise his ministry alone. He chose not to do so, with all the mixed results which the gospel will describe.

The details of the call maintain Mark's commitment to tell the story as briefly as possible, without dwelling on unnecessary elements nor drawing attention to the psychological reasons of those involved. The point is that Jesus called and they followed. Yet there is enough in the perspective chosen to suggest that this is a story recalled by Peter himself and told from the point of view of the fishermen. The promise in verse 17 that they will be *'fishers of men'* is odd since, according to Cranfield, its use in the Old Testament (Je. 16:16; Ezk. 29:4 f; Am. 4:2; Hab. 1:14–17) and in rabbinic literature is always in a bad sense. The point of using it therefore is that they were fishermen. But it may also illustrate the way in which New Testament writers were not afraid to take words and give them new meanings in the light of the good news in Jesus.

All this, however, is secondary to the main theme. Jesus, with authority (an authority to be demonstrated variously throughout the gospel) calls people to be disciples, and they follow. He embodies the divine initiative: they embody the appropriate human response.

He finds them where they are, speaks in language with which they are wholly familiar, but gives it an entirely different significance for them as they become apostles. The twelve had a special role, but Jesus did make clear to them what will be involved. He did this again and again throughout his ministry as he called others to follow him as disciples. Conversations begin in the terms which enable those addressed to be most at ease and secure. They 'know what he's on about'! Only as he indicates the implications of the ordinary elements of life by putting them into the context of God's purpose for their lives do they begin to see how much more is involved, and perceive the need to choose for or against the discipleship he offers.

By contrast we today too often expect unbelievers to make all kinds of adjustments – in dress, initiation into our ways of worship, language and thought form – before a proper conversation can begin. We build up our strength where we are, and invite outsiders in to our setting, one by one, so that they are at their weakest and least comfortable. In so doing we put so many obstacles between them and the simplicity of the gospel itself. We have much to learn about starting where people are.

3. Jesus displays his authority (1:21–31)

They went to Capernaum, and when the Sabbath came, Jesus went into the synagogue and began to teach. [22]*The people were amazed at his teaching, because he taught them as one who had authority, not as the teachers of the law.* [23]*Just then a man in their synagogue who was possessed by an evil spirit cried out,* [24]*'What do you want with us, Jesus of Nazareth? Have you come to destroy us? I know*

who you are – the Holy One of God!'
[25]'Be quiet!' said Jesus sternly. 'Come out of him!' [26]The evil spirit shook the man violently and came out of him with a shriek.
[27]The people were all so amazed that they asked each other, 'What is this? A new teaching – and with authority! He even gives orders to evil spirits and they obey him.' [28]News about him spread quickly over the whole region of Galilee.
[29]As soon as they left the synagogue, they went with James and John to the home of Simon and Andrew. [30]Simon's mother-in-law was in bed with a fever, and they told Jesus about her. [31]So he went to her, took her hand and helped her up. The fever left her and she began to wait on them.

We are now introduced by Mark to a series of events which demonstrate the nature of Jesus' ministry. The healing of the demon-possessed man in the synagogue (1:21–28) bears all the marks of an original reminiscence, told without embellishment or improvement because this is how it happened. Unusually, for Mark, a place name is given (21). Capernaum is as unknown as Nazareth in terms of Old Testament records. It is another unlikely setting for Messianic deeds.

There is a time element too (21) – the next Sabbath – though this helps more in terms of which day of the week it was (a feature not without significance in Mark's story as a whole, since it became a bone of contention with the religious authorities, Mk. 2:23–27), than which Sabbath it was in relation to any other Sabbath. That does not seem to be important to Mark.

What is important is what Jesus did in the synagogue, and what its effect was. He taught (21), and he cast out an evil spirit (23–27). Before looking at these it will help to notice the effect they both had. The people were amazed (22 and 27). Two different Greek words are used, but the overall impression is the same. Mark wishes us to know in his gospel, and he uses six different Greek words to communicate it, that Jesus constantly filled people with a mixture of wonder, awe and fear at what he said and did (1:27; 2:12; 4:41; 5:15, 20, 33, 36, 42; 6:50, 51; 9:6, 15, 32; 10:24, 32 (twice); 11:18; 12:17; 15:5, 44; 16:5 ff., 8). He was not the only person teaching, by any means, nor did he alone perform miracles. But Mark means us to understand that when Jesus did these things, people contrasted him with all the others because of his 'authority' (22, 27). Both his words and his works evoked attitudes and responses which befitted the immediate presence of God in what was happening. Such attitudes and responses did not, however, automatically produce repentance and faith.

a. Jesus' teaching

We are not told what the teaching content was. Since there is a contrast with the scribes (22), who were teachers of the law, we may be meant to infer that Jesus was not teaching about keeping rules but about being in harmony with God's kingdom now being established in Jesus. Mark does not include as much teaching of Jesus as the other gospel writers, but he uses the verb 'to teach' sixteen times of Jesus' activities, and the noun 'teacher' eleven times. Mark has already given us a summary of the kernel of the message (1:15). We will read different examples and applications of it as we follow Mark's account. But once again his interest is not in filling in every detail but in establishing the main constituents of the ministry of Jesus. His teaching clearly is one.

b. Healing by casting out demons

So is healing by casting out evil spirits (23–27). A man *possessed by an evil spirit* (23) may refer to some demon possession making him ritually unclean, or it may be a way of describing the source of a particular form of illness, mental or otherwise. Cranfield reminds us that the New Testament, by contrast with contemporary Jewish and non-Jewish material at the time, shows little interest in demons, except in relation to exorcisms. They are now seen as under Satan, not as independent: and they have met their match and been comprehensively defeated. Yet because, in the eyes of the gospel writers, they were there, Jesus is recorded as dealing with them authoritatively. R. P. Martin links the victory over evil spirits (1:23–28; 5:1–20; 7:24–31; 9:14–29) with that over disease (1:29–31, 40–45; 2:1–12; 3:1–6; 5:25–34; 7:31–37; 8:22–26; 10:46–52) and death (5:21–24, 35–43). This helpfully gathers the exorcisms into a larger category where they belong. The confrontation between Jesus and the evil spirit helps us also to understand the nature of the struggle in that whole area of conflict. The powers of evil recognize both who Jesus is and that the battle is one for survival. The two sides recognize one another in Jesus. *'Be quiet! Come out of him!'* (25), distinguishes the spirit from the man himself. The spirit identifies Jesus. *'What do you want with us, Jesus of Nazareth? I know who you are – the Holy One of God'!* (24) affirms both Jesus' earthly roots and his heavenly status, emphasizing either his Messianic standing or his being as Son of God. The battle is clear too. The spirit recognizes Jesus' purpose *'Have you come to destroy us?'* or *'You are here to destroy us'* (24). In return Jesus simply says, *'Be quiet! Come out of him!'* (25). The resolution of the struggle is in the shaking of the man and the loud scream (26). No wonder the news about Jesus spread quickly everywhere in the province of Galilee.

The question asked in our sophisticated day is, 'What actually happened?' We need to remember that the main emphasis in Mark is on the meaning rather than the event. He is telling us that Jesus, the Messianic Son of God, is fighting a struggle to the death against the powers of evil in every shape, and his authority ensures his victory. The struggle with demons is only one form of this larger battle, including healing and his triumph over death itself.

Do evil spirits exist? Restraint on both sides is needed at this point. There are those, particularly in branches of what is called the charismatic movement, who simply respond by saying that evil spirits do exist, and that they have cast them out. What is more important, there are many people who testify to the beneficial effect of being delivered from demon possession and whose lives are now transformed. Their personal testimony is important. On the other hand, there are many examples of what seems to be the attributing to evil spirits of what are identifiable physical ailments. Some have tended to seek a solution to almost all pastoral problems by the search for a demon, which often has the effect of reducing any sense of human responsibility, and makes future failure almost inevitable. Most of all we need to remember that even though an experience of God may be wholly valid, the description offered by the person undergoing the experience is not therefore necessarily correct.

To dismiss the idea of demonic activity is, however, too easy a solution. The gospel writers made a clear distinction between illness and demon possession. Moreover modern science makes less and less claim to be able to explain everything that happens in human life. Many people behave irrationally or wrongly in ways which are medically or psychologically explicable. In some cases, however, both the degree of uncontrol and the evil that results, particularly in religious contexts, raises questions of other than directly human sources. What is more, the whole area of psychosomatic medicine opens up the possibility of a relationship between spiritual oppression and physical illness. Difficult though that is for modern scientifically oriented cultures, we need to guard against the danger hinted at by Cranfield, that the greatest achievement of the powers of evil would be to persuade us that they do not exist.

(i) The authority of Jesus
To return to the detail of Mark's gospel, however, one must reiterate that the author's purpose is to underline the God-given

authority of Jesus. His words and his deeds alike cause wonder in the crowd. The evil spirit identifies him accurately: the irony is that the crowds do not yet take hold of the testimony they have heard from an unexpected source. Nor will they, and that is the tragedy, with the consequences which Mark will unfold.

(ii) Meeting people where they are

We seem far removed from such days and events, though not in missionary situations nor in some charismatic circles. Even if these particular examples did not apply today, however, the underlying challenge is unavoidable. Does Christian testimony and proclamation today answer the questions people are currently asking about the activity and the teaching of Jesus? Do we bother, individually and corporately, to work out what those questions and issues are, and to seek to deal adequately with them? Secondly, do our actions as Christians meet the felt needs of people, individually and corporately, as surely as Jesus' healing of the demon-possessed man did? Are we concerned enough to locate the areas of disease, pain and dismay in human lives and societies, and allow ourselves to be the agents of God's power to heal?

(iii) The large agenda of modern mission

The answer to those questions carries us far beyond the important realm of evangelism and exorcism. It raises issues of justice in our society, of peace in our world, of poverty, racism, sexism and starvation. It also calls us to the task of apologetics, of locating and dealing with those developments of thought and behaviour which are advanced as reasons for rejecting faith as a basis for life. The agenda is enormous, and requires all Christians to use their many gifts, experiences, abilities and commitments together to face the onslaught. We glimpse the size of the task by asking the simple question, 'What are the modern equivalents, at individual, family, society, national and international level of Jesus speaking about and embodying in his actions, with authority, the kingdom of God which was drawing near?'

c. Jesus heals Peter's mother-in-law

The healing of Peter's mother-in-law (29–31), is another example of the spread of the power of the kingdom. To an exorcism is added a straightforward healing. Reserve about detail is again noticeable, though with intimate reference to raising her up and holding her hand. It is well to note, in passing, the repetition of 'they', meaning the phrase 'Jesus and his disciples' (29, GNB; compare 21). They

57

then become partners in his ministry. Also significant is the fact that she got up and served them. If Mark is still establishing the main lines of his gospel at this point, then this feature is note-worthy. It is obedient service to God, at whatever cost, which characterizes Mark's picture of Jesus, and his hope for all Jesus' disciples. That these things happen while John the Baptist still languishes in prison is a reminder that disciples of Jesus are meant to find their peace and joy in being good disciples, not in their circumstances.

(i) Healing miracles

The question about exorcism is also raised, though with less sharp-ness, about healing miracles. The difficulty is a significant one, especially for those who take seriously the proposition that God made the world to respond to human observation, investigation, description and measurement, and that its consistency lies at the base of the entire scientific enterprise. Why would such a God interfere with his world, as miracles seem to require, thus raising questions about the consistency factor and confusing the whole system?

In response one may begin by observing that the effect of healing miracles is not to bring the scientific edifice to the ground. The work of healing medicine goes on, and Christians are wise to see it as an important part of God's plan for the world so clearly revealed in Jesus. Divine healing by miracle is neither alternative to nor opposed to divine healing by medicine – they are different routes from the same beginning in God's being to the same desti-nation in human health. Secondly, the stress in the gospels on the personal relationship between Jesus the healer and those who are healed must not be forgotten. In most cases the gospel writers record a conversation as well as a healing. Openness to be healed, honesty about the illness, faith in Jesus' power are highly personal elements present, often reflecting a move towards health within the ill person as well as the willingness and power of Jesus to heal. Modern medicine is learning to give more and more importance to these concomitants of scientific medicine, especially as attention is paid to medicine as being about health, rather than simply about curing diseases. Jesus' miraculous healings led the way along that road two thousand years ago. The interrelation of the power invested in Jesus, and the inner responses of the person being healed, are part of a proper understanding of the divine healing process.

The question about why God would do this brings the third and most significant point in favour of the authenticity of healing miracles. Grace is love in action. It is undeserved and unearned. It operates not because of the work of the recipient but because of the love of the one who exercises it. As such it lies at the heart of our salvation. As Paul reminded the Ephesians, 'For it is by God's grace that you have been saved through faith' (Eph. 2:8, GNB). Healing is also an activity of God's grace. And God's grace is extravagant. This is obvious to anyone who studies the natural world. It also constantly overwhelms the Christian, who knows only too well how undeserving of salvation she or he is.

(ii)   The company who belong to Jesus
The 'Jesus and his disciples' factor is now becoming a regular part of Mark's story (*they left . . . they went*, 1:29, 30). It developed in the theology of the early church in Paul's reference to the believers all together as 'the body of Christ'. Paul first had inklings about that on the Damascus road, when Jesus accused Paul of persecuting him (Acts 9:5). Paul might have replied, but for the shock of this experience, that it was not Jesus he was persecuting but the Christians in Damascus. To that Jesus would undoubtedly have replied, 'Precisely! Touch them and you touch me'. It is an awesome responsibility to be part of the body of Christ on earth; and an enormous privilege.

4.   Jesus leads the way (1:32–39)

That evening after sunset the people brought to Jesus all the sick and demon-possessed. [33]*The whole town gathered at the door,* [34]*and Jesus healed many who had various diseases. He also drove out many demons, but he would not let the demons speak because they knew who he was.*

[35]*Very early in the morning, while it was still dark, Jesus got up, left the house and went off to a solitary place, where he prayed.* [36]*Simon and his companions went to look for him,* [37]*and when they found him, they exclaimed: 'Everyone is looking for you!'*

[38]*Jesus replied. 'Let us go somewhere else – to the neaby villages – so that I can preach there also. That is why I have come.'* [39]*So he travelled throughout Galilee, preaching in their synagogues and driving out demons.*

We put together now two sections often kept apart by commentators (1:32–34; 35–39). Some scholars suggest that there might have been more ministry between the two. Each has a discrete content, but the two together teach a surprising lesson to the disciples which is an important part of Mark's story. It is the first open indication that who Jesus was and what he had come to do would remain 'a little beyond' the disciples right up to and on the other side of Jesus' death and resurrection. They could not perceive what was staring them in the face. There is more than a little symbolism in Mark's comment in 10:32 that 'They were on their way up to Jerusalem, with Jesus leading the way, and the disciples were astonished, while those who followed were afraid.' In one sense, in Mark's account Jesus is always going ahead of them because they never, not even Peter for all his words, could grasp the main purpose of his being among them. Jesus himself puts it more bluntly in 4:11–13, using Isaiah 6:9–10, in answering their question about the meaning of the parable of the sower, and hinting that they are as yet no clearer about his teaching than anyone else. The section 1:32–39 is the first of many examples.

The news of his healings has spread (28), so now all who can, bring their sick and demon-possessed for healing. There is pathos in Blanch's suggestion that since it was after the sun was set, Mark wishes us to understand that the Sabbath had just ended. When the synagogues were closed and the official business of worshipping God was over, then, in the open air, the real work of the kingdom began! None of us who belong to the church can feel easy in our consciences about the implication of that.

So far is Jesus from doing miracles as ways of demonstrating his power that he actually forbids the evil spirits from naming him (1:34). The theory of the 'messianic secret', that Mark deliberately built in the hiddenness of Jesus' identity to deal with the fact that the disciples had not grasped it throughout his ministry, is not really necessary. Much more natural is the insight that Jesus did not intend to *prove* who he was by his acts of authority and power. He healed out of love for the sufferer. He cast out demons because they had no right to occupy and spoil human lives. He taught in parables because these, like the healings and the exorcisms, required a response of humble faith. The disciples could no more understand that in their day than we can in ours. It is part of God's foolishness, as Paul described it (1 Cor. 1:18–31). It is Mark's version of 'it is by God's grace that you have been saved through faith' (Eph. 2:8). It is not the number of the healings and exorcisms, but their meaning, which matters.

This is even more heavily underlined, to the disciples' greater consternation, in 35–39. First there is Jesus' disappearance to pray (35). Lest his hearers or readers should assume, from the array of powerful happenings now being recounted, that Jesus' humanity is somehow insignificant (a common Christian error throughout the centuries) Mark reveals Jesus doing what any good disciple needed, and needs to do, praying to God and presumably receiving guidance and strength. Mark will record it again in 6:46, and 14:32–42, each at crucial moments in Jesus' ministry. It was no acted parable; Jesus needed that quiet communion with God. Was that a surprise to the disciples, one wonders?

What certainly was a surprise was his reaction when they found him. The verbs used for their search suggest some anxiety and not a little impatience. His response must have astounded them. Just when the crowds are growing, as well as his popularity, because of the healings and exorcisms, he tells them that this was not his major purpose. *'Let us go somewhere else – to the nearby villages – so that I can preach there also. That is why I have come'* (38). It seems clear from the significance in the Bible of the word translated 'came' that Jesus means more than 'came out of Capernaum' or even 'came on this ministry'. He means 'came from God', though whether the disciples yet perceived that is debatable. But the significance of the statement is that the preaching of the good news of the kingdom is fundamental to Jesus' God-anointed mission.

a. Faithfulness as well as relevance

We sense the dilemma for the disciples in this double story, a dilemma which we face today. We have already noticed that one of the reasons for Jesus' effective ministry was that he met the felt needs of the crowds. They wanted to be healed and he healed them. They had questions and he answered them, with authority. A church which fails to be relevant to the circumstances and needs of people around it can hardly expect to be effective in spreading the good news of the kingdom. And in our age of instant solutions, where politicians are expected to solve our social and economic problems in a three-minute television interview, we are under enormous pressure to 'be relevant'. True love will always predispose us to be so.

Yet Jesus' point to his disciples is the necessary corrective and the prior consideration. Everything that is done or said in the service of God must be in harmony with the good news of the kingdom. The proclamation is prior because within the message are the criteria for testing everything else. There is the centrality of love, the commendation of grace, the challenge to repentance, the invitation to faith. Above all there is the being of God himself, revealed in Jesus, witnessed to by the Spirit. Here is the truth by which all else is tested, and it would be true whether it were relevant or not! Forsake the truth, and the search for relevance becomes a journey without maps or compass, ending in a wilderness which destroys.

b. The crucial place of prayer

If Jesus needed the quiet time of communion and prayer, and especially before each new departure in his service of God, how much more do we?

c. Discipleship as following

For us, as for the earliest disciples, Jesus will always be 'walking ahead'. The journey of faith is always like that, with new truth to learn, new skills to develop, new experiences to go through, new closeness to God. It does not always take us through pleasant country, but the goal of the realization of the kingdom is fixed, and we know that ahead of us are the footsteps of Christ, and around us is the community of his people.

5. Jesus heals a man with leprosy (1:40–45)

A man with leprosy came to him and begged him on his knees, 'If you are willing, you can make me clean.' [41]*Filled with compassion, Jesus reached out his hand and touched the man. 'I am willing,' he said. 'Be clean!'* [42]*Immediately the leprosy left him and he was cured.*

[43]*Jesus sent him away at once with a strong warning:* [44]*'See that you don't tell this to anyone. But go, show yourself to the priest and offer the sacrifices that Moses commanded for your cleansing, as a testimony to them.'* [45]*Instead he went out and began to talk freely, spreading the news. As a result, Jesus could no longer enter a town openly but stayed outside in lonely places. Yet the people still came to him from everywhere.*

Mark's gospel is full of surprises! We have seen how the disciples were confounded by Jesus' disappearance to pray, and we have imagined their response at being told that they had missed the point in attaching such importance to the healings and exorcisms. Now it is our turn to be surprised by the turn of events.

It is the moment for a man with leprosy to be healed (40a). (The word 'leprosy' had a more general application than it would have today.) He, not surprisingly in view of the way people with leprosy were shunned at that time, asks for healing but expresses uncertainty about whether Jesus will want to heal him. He has no doubt that Jesus can do it (40b). The response of Jesus is clear, but surprising. His touching the man (41) would have shocked onlookers who knew of the ritual uncleanness of a person with

leprosy. We are more surprised by the original word Mark probably used of Jesus' attitude. Some early and reliable manuscripts
have a Greek verb which means not 'Jesus was filled with pity' but
'Jesus was filled with anger'. This must be the more original, since
one can see why scribes would insert the word used of the Good
Samaritan's attitude to the man on the road (Lk. 10:33), rather than
the other way round. But why was Jesus angry? Hardly with the
man, and least of all because of an interruption. Most likely it was
anger at the evil which spoils human nature in any shape or form.

He is willing to heal him, and does by a command. There is no
surprise in that, since Mark has already got us used to this kind of
authoritative kingdom act by Jesus. But two unexpected elements
follow. He tells the man to go to the priest and fulfil all that is right
according to the law in order to be declared clean. His teaching may
be less dominated by the law than that of the scribes (22), but he
is not opposed to the law itself, as Matthew's gospel makes clear
(Mt. 5:17–20). Mark does not wish his hearers to be so excited
with the new way that they neglect the essence of the old.

Before this instruction, however, we read that Jesus *spoke sternly*
(GNB) to the man, *and sent him away at once*. The rawness of
this account underlines its authenticity. A variety of attempts at
translating the word behind 'spoke sternly' include 'groaned', 'mur-
mured against', 'growled at', 'upbraided', 'roared at', or even
'snorted'! It is a word representing deep emotion expressed inarticu-
lately. The word for 'sent away' really means 'drove out'. Jesus
was deeply moved by the presence of human suffering. His inarticu-
late groan is part of his reaction.

The other part must tie in with what follows. He instructs the
man not to tell anyone about how his healing has happened (44a).
Linked with verse 34 where he forebade demons to speak because
they would have identified his status, we conclude that this is part
of Jesus' determination not to have a following because of the
miracles, which are performed primarily in the struggle against evil,
and partly to set people free. They are not tricks to gather a
following.

However, the opposite happened, and as so often, the well-
meaning enthusiasm of the healed man to tell his story curtailed
the ministry of Jesus at that point (45).

a. The primacy of love

The ease with which Jesus crossed social and religious boundaries
is breathtaking. One has to put together the panic and fear incul-
cated by the early news of Aids, and add to it strong religious

ritual revulsion, to begin to understand what touching a person with leprosy meant to orthodox bystanders in Jesus' day. Yet this was fundamental, not to his *strategy* but to his *being*. A life dominated by divine love does not need to work out the comparative influence, or prospective success or failure, of a particular word or deed. Love says or does what is necessary and works out the consequences later. People were attracted by the crossing of the boundaries to reach the outcast and the needy. But what they are meant to discover is the love at the heart of it. Sadly, too often they stay with the sign and miss the reality. Even more often we Christians expect others to find the reality when we have not, in love, manifested the signs. It is here that Christian in-fighting about the priority of evangelism, or social caring, or the struggle for justice, reveals our near fatal lack of truly loving incentive. If we loved those around us enough we could not make such distinctions since the decision about which is needed, and when, is determined by love's responses to their condition, not on theological or experiential preferences.

b. The cost of spiritual perception

The unusual concern of Mark about Jesus' inner state, reflected by Jesus' manner and utterances, is a necessary reminder to us of the cost of true discipleship and service. The degree to which we both perceive what God intends for the world and are committed to it, is the degree of spiritual anguish we will experience when confronted with anything different from that purpose of God. Light-hearted discipleship is a contradiction in terms, according to Mark's account of Jesus.

c. The 'results' syndrome

Jesus' reticence about having followers on any grounds other than personal faith provides a stern test of our evangelism and witness. Our concern to impress or get results too often takes priority over a determination to help people to true faith in God through Jesus which will stand the test of daily life. The 'numbers game' is a distinct snare for the Christian church leader.

6. Jesus heals and forgives a handicapped man (2:1–12)

A few days later, when Jesus again entered Capernaum, the people heard that he had come home. ²So many gathered that there was no room left, not even outside the door, and he preached the word to them. ³Some men came, bringing to him a paralytic, carried by four of them. ⁴Since they could not get him to Jesus because of the crowd, they made an opening in the roof above Jesus and, after digging through it, lowered the mat the paralysed man was lying on. ⁵When Jesus saw their faith, he said to the paralytic, 'Son, your sins are forgiven.'

⁶Now some teachers of the law were sitting there, thinking to themselves. ⁷'Why does this fellow talk like that? He's blaspheming! Who can forgive sins but God alone?'

⁸Immediately Jesus knew in his spirit that this was what they were thinking in their hearts, and he said to them, 'Why are you thinking these things? ⁹Which is easier: to say to the paralytic, "Your sins are forgiven," or to say, "Get up, take your mat and walk"? ¹⁰But that you may know that the Son of Man has authority on earth to forgive sins. . . .' He said to the paralytic, ¹¹'I tell you, get up, take your mat and go home.' ¹²He got up, took his mat and walked out in full view of them all. This amazed everyone and they praised God, saying, 'We have never seen anything like this!'

This is the first of five stories in 2:1–36 where a new element is brought to the fore – the growing opposition to Jesus from the religious authorities. These five incidents may not all actually have happened at the same time, but they are so gathered by Mark to describe and account for the unusual fact that when God's Messiah had come, those who might have been expected to receive him soon began to oppose him.

We must also note that in terms of the action 2:1 may not follow directly on from 1:45. Mark's *a few days later* is suitably vague. His aim is to get Jesus back to Capernaum where the next story is located. It may be significant that Huck in his Synopsis (a harmonization of Matthew, Mark and Luke into one sequence) fits the Matthew account of the Sermon on the Mount between these two verses. The incidents and their meaning are what matters to Mark.

Commentators have noted various difficulties in understanding the composition of 2:1–12. Some claim that there are two discrete topics, healing and forgiveness, covered by two distinct sections (1–5, 10–12 and 5–10). One contains many practical details while the other is dominated by theological debate. The end of the section, if it is taken as a whole, seems to refer only to the healing. It is also argued that the linking points (at 5 *Jesus . . . said to the paralytic* and 10 *But . . . he said to the paralytic*) are awkward interpolations which show the joining points.

Strong rejoinders to these literary difficulties are possible, however. Whether or not there are two distinct themes, healing and

65

forgiveness, depends on one's view of what Mark was seeking to do in telling this story in the first place. If he was trying to insert the thought of forgiveness into the setting of a healing miracle, then separate origins for the two sections may have existed. But supposing the point being made, by Jesus originally rather than by Mark, as Cranfield suggests, that disease and sin are organically connected, and that 'Jesus' healing miracles are sacraments of forgiveness'. Then a unity is much more likely. Questions of original meaning must take precedence over those of literary form, especially if the shape of the passage itself leads to a particular meaning, as in this case.

The crucial point of confrontation between Jesus and the teachers of the law comes with the question in verse 9, 'Which is easier: to say to the paralytic, "Your sins are forgiven," or to say, "Get up, take your mat and walk"?' The thrust of the question is surely that it is easier to say the former, since no-one will know whether or not the forgiveness has taken place. But to say the latter is to submit oneself to the immediate test of whether or not the man will actually be healed. Jesus therefore takes the argument one stage further and suggests that he will do the one (demonstrably difficult) act of release in order to show that he can do the other (more difficult spiritually) act of release also. The two themes not only can belong together, they do so vitally in order to make the point at the heart of Jesus' ministry, that physical and spiritual healing are not worlds apart, but belong together fundamentally in his understanding of people and of his ministry. The so-called joining sentences therefore become necessary comments by the story-teller, and the fact that verse 12 refers only to the 'taking up of the mat' is wholly appropriate, for this was the outward part of the total healing which Jesus had performed. That the first half of the story, and verse 12, contain vivid practical details and the centrepiece theological discussion is also fitting, since on this construction that is exactly how it would have happened.

As to the detail, Jesus is portrayed by Mark as doing what he had said (1:38) he had come to do, namely, preaching (2). The fact that he allows a case for healing to interrupt the preaching (3–5), shows that he was not rejecting the latter in order to do the former. The preaching was prior, but not exclusive to all else.

Mark says that Jesus offered forgiveness, when he *saw their faith* (5). The text does not make clear whether Mark refers to the faith of the four bearers or of the five including the paralysed man. In view of the circumstances it seems more likely that the ill man also had faith, bearing in mind all that he went through simply in order to be where he was!

The offer of forgiveness by Jesus (5), is a source of understandable offence to the teachers of the law since forgiveness comes only from God (Ex. 34:61; Ps. 103:3; Is. 43:25; Dn. 9:9). His words bring him within the range of the accusation of blasphemy. He answers it with the puzzling question (9) dealt with above.

Here another problem is presented. Would Jesus use the bodily healing of the paralysed man as a proof of who he was (10)? Does this not run contrary to the imposition of silence about his status, on both the demons and the man healed of leprosy? The difficulty has to be faced, but the issue is not precisely the same. There the question related to the identity of the one performing the healing; here it concerns the nature of the healing itself, both spiritual and physical. In order to justify that meaning he had to reveal more of who he was. Yet even here there is no compelling proof. Anyone in the crowd would have to take Jesus' word for it that the man was forgiven as well as physically healed. It was still a challenge to faith, not a compulsion imposed by the force of the raising of a paralysed man. That this is so is made plain by the progression through the stories in this group, finishing at 3:6 with, not a plan to follow him, but a plot to kill him.

'*Son of Man*' in verse 10 could mean simply 'this man' as in the Hebrew background of Ezekiel 2:1 and Psalm 8:4. But it is more likely to be derived from Daniel 7:13 where one, 'like a son of man . . . was given authority, glory and sovereign power; all peoples, nations and men of every language worshipped him. His dominion is an everlasting dominion that will not pass away, and his kingdom is one that will never be destroyed.' In this confrontation about the extent of his authority over sin and disease such a reference would be appropriate, though we must not assume that everyone present would immediately perceive the total significance which measured study reveals. The use by Jesus of the title Son of Man concerning himself will be discussed more fully under 8:31.

a. The danger of good people being on the wrong side

Mark is now identifying the presence of evil in places which make us uncomfortable. The battle with Satan in the wilderness (1:12–13), or with evil spirits (1:23–27; 32–34), is somehow predictable. The possibility of religious leaders being the agents of evil is harder to bear, especially for those who are religious leaders! Yet the combination of rigidity in teaching, narrowness of expectation about the Messiah, prejudice about the unpromising pedigree of Jesus (see 2:7 *this fellow*) and, sadly, maybe more than a little jealousy at his success, causes serious, religious men to be on the side of evil not good, Satan not God. It is a chilling experience to test our attitudes and actions by such criteria.

b. Good action, and evil reaction

However one identifies the struggle, Mark does describe a development which seems to be universal, that the doing of good will not go unresisted. At the individual level there seem always to be those who will resent, criticize, suspect or oppose it. At the corporate level there will be some vested interests challenged by those who seek, out of love and for no gain, to set others free. The idea that if the church 'got her act right' society would embrace her may well be illusory. Persecution and opposition might be more likely, and we must be ready for that.

c. The breadth of evil and the health of humanity

The intrinsic unity between the forgiveness and the healing in this story is crucial to our understanding of mission. This is not in some scientific category of how much sin produces how much disease, or even (in relation to this passage) which sins lead to which diseases. It is rather that both sin and disease are harmful to and destructive of human life, and Christians are called to oppose everything which threatens full humanity, and to do so in the name of the kingdom of God. Evangelism, social caring, justice issues, bodily health, ecological concern, racial harmony, affirmation of women as well as men in our society are all issues for the Christian. To limit our perspectives is to miss the point of this passage and to fight only half-heartedly for the kingdom in the struggle against evil.

7. Jesus calls a tax collector (2:13–17)

Once again Jesus went out beside the lake. A large crowd came to him, and he began to teach them. [14]*As he walked along, he saw Levi son of Alphaeus sitting at the tax collector's booth. 'Follow me,' Jesus told him, and Levi got up and followed him.*

[15]*While Jesus was having dinner at Levi's house, many tax collectors and 'sinners' were eating with him and his disciples, for there were many who followed him.* [16]*When the teachers of the law who were Pharisees saw him eating with the 'sinners' and tax collectors, they asked his disciples: 'Why does he eat with tax collectors and "sinners"?'*

[17]*On hearing this, Jesus said to them, 'It is not the healthy who*

need a doctor, but the sick. I have not come to call the righteous, but sinners.'

Jesus' ministry now takes yet another turn which surprises those who follow him and annoys those who do not. He enlists a tax collector among the apostles. In 3:18 he includes James, son of Alphaeus, as well as Matthew. But Matthew tells an almost identical story and identifies the tax collector as Matthew (Mt. 9:9–13). What is more, Matthew's list of the twelve apostles also includes both Matthew the tax collector and James, son of Alphaeus (Mt. 10:3)! In terms of identification, the most likely solution is to identify, as is traditionally done, Levi in Mark as Matthew in Matthew. Why Mark has, in that case, two 'sons of Alphaeus' in his story, Levi and James, remains a puzzle. One senses, however, that this would have troubled Mark less than it troubles us. The point he is making is far bigger than matters of detail. He is reporting that the one for whom messianic claims are being made took a tax collector into his intimate circle. Remembering that the tax collector worked for the cruel Herod Antipas, who would not have been in power but for the Romans; that tax collectors mostly extorted more tax than was required, even from the poor; and that meeting with Gentile traders who were ritually unclean was frowned upon by the Jews, it is hardly surprising that those who expected the Messiah to free them from Rome were greatly shocked by this action. As Hargreaves puts it, 'He sat near the lake at a table. Around him were piles of money, and account books, and fish, but few friends.'[4] Whatever did Jesus think he was doing?

Our surprise should not cause us to miss the way Levi evidently got up and followed at once. This is, of course, Mark's style. But it also says something about Levi. He may already have heard Jesus, and almost certainly had heard about him. But he must in any case have been a person willing to take hard decisions and live by them – his job involved that. Jesus met him where he was, and challenged him along an avenue with which he was familiar. 'Take a risk, make your mind up *now*, and come.' Levi did.

For the critics, and maybe even more for the supporters, of Jesus, worse was to come (15–16). Jesus now eats with Levi and his friends (*tax collectors and 'sinners'*) and Jesus' disciples (they uneasily?). Was it at 'his' (Levi's) house (as NIV), or 'his' (Jesus', on loan from Peter?) house? We do not know, but whichever it was would have a particular stigma attaching to it. Mark records the critical presence of the teachers of the law again, with a question which is a mixture of genuine surprise and understandable offence

---

4 Hargreaves, p. 40.

(16). Jesus' reply requires time to digest (17). Put bluntly, Jesus is saying that you would expect to find a saviour among those who need to be saved. You would not look for a doctor among the well but among the ill.

The test is whether or not we are willing (and here it is raised again) to put our trust in God through Jesus. Some people, by the very condition of their lives, will find that a more obvious thing to do than will others.

Moral standards and mixing with others

Mark touches Christians on a sensitive spot with this story of Jesus going into table fellowship with Levi and his friends. Christians do, after all, have a duty to uphold moral standards derived from their belief in God through Jesus. It is natural, therefore, that the church defends such standards and the members embody them in their life style. This sets clear boundaries to the extent to which we can mix easily with those whose life styles are very different from ours. We quickly feel not only uneasy, but actually compromised. What is more we sense that the atmosphere in such settings may be inimical to our spiritual growth.

Yet if that becomes our dominant attitude, then we find ourselves increasingly cut off, especially in social rather than work contexts, from those who are different from us in not believing. The church develops an entire subculture of its own and is increasingly insulated from 'the world'. To that extent its witness and missionary effectiveness are diminished.

The example of Jesus is again our model. He was sustained by his prayers to the Father, and in his fellowship with his disciples (despite their inadequacy). From these, and his deep knowledge of the Scriptures, he drew sustenance to go into the most unlikely company and not only survive in it but actually win others to faith within it. We are called neither recklessly to risk ourselves nor timidly to secure ourselves, but to find the point of life-giving tension between the two. In that way our worship and fellowship have more point and our witness more depth.

8. A question of religious practice (2:18–22)

Now John's disciples and the Pharisees were fasting. Some people came and asked Jesus, 'How is it that John's disciples and the disciples of the Pharisees are fasting, but yours are not?'

¹⁹Jesus answered, 'How can the guests of the bridegroom fast while he is with them? They cannot, so long as they have him with them. ²⁰*But the time will come when the bridegroom will be taken from them, and on that day they will fast.*

²¹*'No-one sews a patch of unshrunk cloth on an old garment. If he does, the new piece will pull away from the old, making the tear worse.* ²²*And no-one pours new wine into old wineskins. If he does, the wine will burst the skins, and both the wine and the wineskins will be ruined. No, he pours new wine into new wineskins.'*

The struggle with the religious authorities becomes fiercer over a religious practice which marked the piety of the Pharisees – fasting. Only the fast on the Day of Atonement (Lv. 16:29) was enjoined by the law, but the Pharisees fasted on Mondays and Thursdays throughout the year. Reference to disciples of John the Baptist is understandable, and may be crucial to an understanding of Jesus' references to the bridegroom being present or away (19, 20). Reference to disciples (18) of the Pharisees is unusual, since disciples related to teachers of the law, which the Pharisees, in general, were not, though scribes who were Pharisees were teachers. Anderson[5] mentions evidence of an extremist group among the Pharisees who would have had much in common with the disciples of the Baptist. The reference could therefore be original and authentic.

The question about fasting (18) is another indication of the gap developing between the expectations of the Messiah and the actuality in Jesus. The answer they receive, as Mark tells the story, operates at two levels. The specific response uses the picture of the wedding feast and deals precisely with fasting (19–20). The twin parables of the patch (21) and the wineskins (22) raise questions about the whole structure of Jewish ceremonial in the light of the arrival of the kingdom.

The use of the bridal feast to respond to a question about fasting is itself unusual. The point Jesus is making is that the coming of the kingdom through his ministry is a time for joy. His hearers loved marriage feasts. Reference to fasting when the bridegroom is taken away (20) is strange if only a marriage is the focal point. People did not fast just because the bridegroom had gone away (and presumably the bride too!). But if the inclusion of John the Baptist's disciples is significant, then of course their teacher had been taken away. A projection of this to Jesus' being taken away, on which this gospel concentrates heavily, would be altogether appropriate. Why disciples of the Pharisees would have any particular reason like that for fasting is not clear from the text, but

[5] Anderson, p. 107, referring to J. Bowker, *Jesus and the Pharisees* (Cambridge University Press, 1973), p. 40.

then they did not need any extra reason anyway, since it was their regular custom.

The objection that this is too early in the gospel to be introducing the shadow of the cross depends entirely on one's perception of what Jesus knew. If his baptism by John had the significance suggested earlier (pp. 40–41), then it would not be odd for this reference to occur here. The fundamental question is not what Mark intended now, but what was the case with Jesus' understanding of the future. James Denney's treatment of this remains extremely valuable reading.[6]

There is, of course, another possibility. In the Old Testament the bridegroom is an image of Yahweh himself (Ho. 2:19; Is. 54:4 ff.; 2:4 ff. and Ezk. 16:7 ff.). The image was used in the New Testament with messianic implications (Jn. 3:29; 2 Cor. 11:2; Eph. 5:32). Its use by Jesus therefore could carry strong hints about his own nature and role but again, not directly or obtrusively. Only the eye of faith would at this point perceive its significance.

The double parable of the patch and the wineskins now broadens out the issue. There is a glad freedom about belonging to the kingdom of God proclaimed by Jesus. The old way is simply not able to take it in as an adjunct or a new element. The new patch tears the old garment, the new wine bursts the old wineskins. Jesus is not saying that the old should be discarded. He is affirming that what has now come far surpasses all that went before. The old should not hold back the new, however, by making it conform to its shape.

a. Hints about the costliness of discipleship

Already Jesus is saying enough to indicate that the struggle of the kingdom against the forces of evil will be a costly one. In Mark's gospel itself, as R. P. Martin has cogently argued,[7] the costliness of obedience is the crucial theme, and John the Baptist is not just a forerunner of Jesus, he is a prototype. As John served and suffered for it, so will Jesus. And, Mark is already preparing the ground for saying, so will the disciple. This will become crystal clear later (8:34–38). For the moment it is no more than a matter of mood.

b. Discerning which new developments are from God

The danger of the old constraining or crippling the new is a peren-

---

[6] James Denney, *The Death of Christ* (1902; revised and abridged by R. V. G. Tasker; Tyndale Press, 1951).

[7] Martin, *Mark: Evangelist and Theologian*, pp. 66–69.

nial problem in Christian, as in all human experience. Those who have sustained the vision, or laid a foundation for the future, or simply survived in difficult days, can so easily find that what they have waited for is not what they had expected. People at the centre of great new adventures, are often in their day treated as dangerous rebels or iconoclasts. Some are later revered and honoured for the value of their work, like Luther or Wesley, Bunyan or Carey, Gladys Aylward or Florence Nightingale, who were not welcome in their day, to put it mildly. Yet others who attempt new ways do later prove to have been misguided, or worse! How does one make the distinction, or is it impossible, except in retrospect (following the wheat and tares (Mt. 13:14–30) or sheep and goats (Mt. 25:31–46) principle)?

There is a question of pedigree, to put it bluntly! If what is done can be shown to have its roots in the ministry and teaching of Jesus, not simply in some indirect way, but deep into the heart of what he did, then a positive response is indicated. Then there is the question of how it relates to Scripture, again not just to some verse or section but to the whole of the scriptural panorama of salvation. A third question would involve what the church has learned through the ages. A fourth would be how it meets the real needs of people today. It is clear that these guidelines may seem so general as to be unhelpful, but they are better than nothing! What is more, it is amazing how often they are forgotten.

9. A question about the Sabbath (2:23–28)

One Sabbath Jesus was going through the cornfields, and as his disciples walked along, they began to pick some ears of corn. ²⁴*The Pharisees said to him, 'Look, why are they doing what is unlawful on the Sabbath?'*

²⁵*He answered, 'Have you never read what David did when he and his companions were hungry and in need?* ²⁶*In the days of Abiathar the high priest, he entered the house of God and ate the consecrated bread, which is lawful only for priests to eat. And he also gave some to his companions.'*

²⁷*Then he said to them, 'The Sabbath was made for man, not man for the Sabbath.* ²⁸*So the Son of Man is Lord even of the Sabbath.'*

Mark's version of the confrontation over the Sabbath is bare by contrast with Matthew (12:1–8) and Luke (6:6–11). Nor does he link up with what has gone before or what follows. Its place here, however, is a logical one. It identifies one more step in the

73

escalation of the struggle between Jesus and the religious leaders, pointing towards their initial conference in a plan to kill him (3:6). We need now to be asking what it is in these accounts which would produce such violent opposition.

The initial complaint relates to something the disciples had done (23–24). There is no need to see this as a sign that the early church was using this account to defend its Sabbath practices by finding defence from Jesus who was not here accused. It makes as much sense to take seriously what has already emerged in Mark's gospel, that Jesus and his disciples are now seen increasingly as a unit. To criticize them is to produce response from him.

The criticism concerns their plucking (equivalent to reaping) ears of grain on the Sabbath (Luke, 6:1, adds that they ground them in their hands, also). There were thirty-nine forbidden activities on a Sabbath ('forty save one') and the third was reaping. This was all built on the injunction in Exodus 34:21 forbidding Sabbath work.

The reply of Jesus, couched in rabbinic style, asks a question in relation to the story in 1 Samuel 21:1–6. David had taken the 'presence-bread' – the twelve newly baked loaves that were laid in two rows on a table before God in the tabernacle every Sabbath, and were later eaten by the priests (Lv. 24:5–9). As he had given it to his hungry soldiers, on the Sabbath, so now the disciples were taking food on the Sabbath also. There is here a conjunction of human need being more important than ritual requirement, and of this happening on the Sabbath. Jesus challenges his critics to choose between David's practice and their complaint, and between human need and religious reputation. He does not defend the breaking of the Sabbath, as such, on the basis of either example. He simply suggests that there is a more important principle at stake, human need.

Jesus' reference to Abiathar as high priest is difficult here on two counts. One is that the reference in 1 Samuel 21 is to the priest, not the high priest. The second, and more formidable, is that Ahimelech, Abiathar's father, is the priest named in the story. Abiathar became priest after Ahimelech was killed by Saul for his part in this very incident quoted by Jesus. Reasons suggested include a copyist's gloss, a midrashic exposition of the story based on 1 Samuel 21:1–6, or that someone somewhere was working from memory and got it wrong. It is a mistake, and some manuscripts omit it because they knew so. Did Mark know so? If he did then here, as in other places (e.g. concerning Levi in relation to the list of the apostles, 2:13–14; 3:16–18), he faithfully recorded what he received. He may be an 'arranger' of the material, and a 'selector' also, but he shows reticence about being a 'creator' or 'changer' of

74

what he had before him in written or spoken form. We should not attempt far-fetched explanations to exonerate him, nor overestimate the degree of his creativity. The evidence points to his faithfully recording what he received, as being from the mouth of Jesus himself.

Jesus now extends the point, much as in 1:18–22 he went from the specific issue of fasting to the larger question of the old and the new in God's kingdom. Here the spectrum is widened from a particular incident of Sabbath breaking to the wider issue of Sabbath regulations and human need (27), and to the even larger question of how all that relates to *the Son of Man* (28).

In one sense the general point can be found in rabbinic teaching also. 'The Sabbath is delivered unto you, and you are not delivered to the Sabbath', is an example from rabbinic teaching. This general point alone would hardly therefore lead to such vehement opposition as Mark records in 3:6. Tied in to the idea of the coming of the kingdom, however, when ordinary people (like the disciples) feel free to do these things, the threat would be greater. Discipline and the exercise of power and control would now seem to be threatened.

Even greater would be the offence if Jesus actually said what Mark records in 2:28. Some commentators feel either that it would be too early in his ministry for Jesus to be making such a claim for himself, or that for him ever to have made such a claim would have been out of keeping with the 'secret' of his identity which he seems determined to preserve (as in 1:33 and 44, for example).

Much depends, however, on how that 'secret' is construed. As opposed to treating it absolutely, it may fit the evidence better if we see it as Jesus' unwillingness to enforce faith by miracles, exorcisms or other demonstrations of power. Where, however, he is called upon (as here and in 2:1–12) to *justify* his teaching or claims, the use of this phrase 'Son of Man' would be understandable. This is even more the case when one recalls the ambiguity of the expression. Even today, after decades of the most detailed study, it is not always clear whether the Greek words denote an ordinary person (a 'man', a 'fellow', a 'chap') or the heavenly figure in Daniel 7, or some other figure from the past. If it lacks such clear distinction now, we can understand how it might be used in Jesus' ministry with a significance which he understood because of his deep sense of vocation, but which the hearers did not fully grasp, or believe, at the time, yet which also the disciples came to recall as significant later when the whole ministry of life, death, resurrection and ascension was complete. As such it would be part of Mark's portrayal of Jesus as the one who invites, yet never compels, faith, knowing how slowly people were likely to come to it (4:10–12).

If there was in his hearers, particularly those who were 'theologically trained', any glimpse at all of what 'Son of Man' might mean (and they probably had more than a glimpse but were unwilling to accept its implications), then the strength of their opposition as set out in 3:6 becomes more intelligible. The issue was very serious indeed, threatening so much that they held dear. Added to John's testimony at the calling of disciples, there had already been healing, exorcism (when the demons said very strange things about the man Jesus), teaching with authority, the offer of forgiveness and now an onslaught on their views on fasting and Sabbath. Such a beginning held very great threat not just for their authority but for what they considered to be crucial to the faith as they understood and defended it.

a. Rules and spirit

The issues are becoming sharper, not only for the religious authorities of Jesus' day, but also for us. Whether we are aware of it or not, much of our spiritual life is sustained by rules, regulations, practices and rituals which give shape to our daily existence, not least in difficult and dry days. They become like boundaries and goal posts to a playing field, or white lines down the middle of a road. Our dependence upon them becomes so great that when anyone begins to alter the boundaries or move the goal posts or paint new lines, our whole spiritual life seems to be threatened.

b. Principle and application

The difference between the principle and the application becomes vital at this point. We need it in relation to our understanding of Scripture. Problems about meat offered to idols do not trouble us where I live and worship (1 Cor. 8:1–8) but care about how my behaviour influences the consciences of brother and sister Christians is a vital principle (1 Cor. 8:9–13). It is true about our practices. Baptizing and taking Holy Communion are basic sacraments instituted by Jesus. But is one or other particular way of doing it so very crucial? We are right to seek high and holy moral standards for our lives and for that of society, but does that require a high judgmental attitude to those with Aids? The principle and the application need careful distinction if we are to face the constant challenges of change and variety around us. Sadly, the religious leaders of Jesus' day found that as hard to do as we often do.

76

10. The opposition grows (3:1–6)

Another time he went into the synagogue, and a man with a shrivelled hand was there. ²Some of them were looking for a reason to accuse Jesus, so they watched him closely to see if he would heal him on the Sabbath. ³Jesus said to the man with the shrivelled hand, 'Stand up in front of everyone.'

⁴Then Jesus asked them, 'Which is lawful on the Sabbath: to do good or to do evil, to save life or to kill?' But they remained silent.

⁵He looked round at them in anger and, deeply distressed at their stubborn hearts, said to the man, 'Stretch out your hand.' He stretched it out, and his hand was completely restored. ⁶Then the Pharisees went out and began to plot with the Herodians how they might kill Jesus.

The distinction between the perceptions of different listeners to Jesus in relation to 1:28 now takes on a new sharpness when we learn that 'some people' (this section is no more specific than that) were watching him. The verb suggests close, adverse scrutiny, as given to a potential wrong-doer, which makes it most likely that they were his constant opponents throughout this section, the Pharisees, which 3:6 appears to confirm. Mark says they were no longer simply following, they were now searching for grounds of accusation. As one follows the story through one can feel the tension and confrontation growing. That it happened in the synagogue (1), simply serves to increase the friction. And it was the Sabbath (2).

The man has become a test case (3), and Jesus has again sensed their criticism (compare 2:8) – he not only teaches and heals more authoritatively than others, he evidently also perceives what others think they are concealing. Jesus (4) poses the question they would rather not face. Choosing their ground – what the law required – he asks on that ground what the best direction for this situation would be. Should they help, by healing; or harm by refusing? Is the law salvific or destructive? This seems preferable to the idea that Jesus is contrasting what he is about to do, namely to heal, and what they are currently planning to do, namely to kill him. This latter idea would be premature in relation to verse 6 anyway. But it would also bifurcate the vision at a time when Jesus is keeping sharp focus on the disabled man in their midst.

When the question is put to them like that, what are they to say? Rabbinic teaching allowed for Sabbath healing if life was in danger, but that is not so here. Having narrowed the focal point to one man, Jesus now widens the question to a general principle. The question is not 'to save life or not to save life?', it is 'to do

77

good or not to do good when it is possible and therefore to do evil?', and this in the context of human need. How could they say that any purpose of the Sabbath, or of their regulations about it, was for evil not good? Yet if they allowed his point, the narrowness of their legislation, when placed in the setting of genuine human need, became all too obvious. So they said nothing (4).

Jesus looked round at them with mixed emotions. He was angry (compare 1:41). If their dulled human perception had led to apathy about needs around them, his divine-human perception quickened his awareness of what was happening. Religious rules offered to God were hindering the liberation offered in the kingdom of God. How could he not be angry at that? On the other hand he was, says Mark, sympathetic towards them because they could not see the truth. Are there preparations for 4:10–12 here? The barrier of misunderstanding and unbelief seems almost impenetrable. Yet his emotions are not allowing him to write them off yet, by contrast with their apparent attitude to him (3:6). He would give them the benefit of the doubt long after they had ceased to do so for him.

He could at least act out the kingdom before them one more time, and that he does (3:5). The man obeys the command given, joins in the healing process and is made well.

By contrast with this co-operation for good, Mark now describes an unusual combination for evil. The Herodians, supporters of Herod Antipas, tetrarch of Galilee, would have little in common with the Pharisees, since they differed so strongly about relations with Rome and about religious ideals in general. On this occasion, however, the Pharisees would need Herodian support to get rid of Jesus, which has now become their purpose.

a. Keeping close scrutiny of our guiding principles

One cannot but feel sorry for the Pharisees here. They were on the whole good religious men, but the very foundation on which they stood – the understanding of religion in terms of obedience to the law – was now being threatened. What made it worse was the fact that their opponent was not rejecting the law. He was rather looking behind it to see what principles lay there, and then applying those principles anew in the context of perceived human need around him. It was hard for them to take, not least because their authority and status in society so strongly depended on their general position being right.

We all need opportunity, regularly, to review in fellowship as well as in private, those guiding principles, even religious rules, by which we live our lives. Do they truly reveal the nature of God?

Are they still life-giving stimuli to new departures and discoveries in spirituality, or are they steadily becoming a restrictive code? And do they still enable us to meet the needs of those around us, whom we seek to serve in God's name? In times when we are up against it, and survival is the order of the day, the dangers set out above are all the more prevalent. We may feel that this has been the case with Western Christendom during most of this century, and that we need therefore to be vigorous with ourselves in facing these questions. Apparently even as loyal a servant as John the Baptist found that difficult (Lk. 7:23; Mt. 11:6).

b. Holding on to power

There may be here, too, a problem about not being willing to see someone greater – or even newer, younger and more enlightened – sent by God to carry forward the work we have been doing. So often in the history of the church good leaders have been unwilling to move over and hand over to those following on, usually in the interests of preserving important truths the 'young people' do not understand, or defending methods and systems with which the 'new leadership' is not so sympathetic, or simply holding on to power so long as they are fit and well. Let those who are still young, and new, and 'upwardly mobile' learn the lesson now, and pray not to forget it!

c. Good people beware!

Even harder to bear is the conclusion which emerges from an attempt to avoid the stereotypical way in which Christianity has presented the Pharisees. As Stuart Blanch puts it,

> They were not necessarily 'Pharisaic' in the way in which we use that pejorative term; they were genuine believers in God, who were concerned for the spiritual renewal of their people, and enjoyed a huge reputation for piety of life and uprightness of conduct. There were honourable men among them like Joseph of Arimathea, looking eagerly for the Kingdom and diligent in prayer for it. It was their very proximity to the ideals which our Lord himself held dear that made the confrontation between them particularly painful.[8]

We should be neither hard on them nor easy on ourselves.

d. Who is this Jesus?

Hidden within these four pronouncement stories are claims of Jesus about himself which must not be missed. In the story of the paralytic it is his claim to forgive sins which so offended the teachers of the law (2:7). They know that only God could forgive sins. Just so! In 2:17, to explain his presence among the acknowledged sinners of Levi's company, he uses the doctor-patient analogy which shows that he is the soul doctor who comes to heal the sick – sinners. In 2:19, 20 he is the bridegroom, an Old Testament picture of God in relation to his people. In 2:25 he is the lord of the Sabbath. Since God gave it, who else could be lord of it? The points are so subtly made by Mark's presentation, though they would be so offensive to the religious leaders of the day, that we might miss them. We mustn't, for Mark's point is that one group after another was missing the real understanding of who it was who stood in their midst. When will they see? (And when will we see?!)

[8] Blanch, p. 45.

Mark 3:7 – 6:13
3.   Words and deeds in Galilee

1.   The ordinary crowds welcome Jesus (3:7–12)

Jesus withdrew with his disciples to the lake, and a large crowd from Galilee followed. ⁸When they heard all he was doing, many people came to him from Judea, Jerusalem, Idumea, and the regions across the Jordan and around Tyre and Sidon. ⁹Because of the crowd he told his disciples to have a small boat ready for him, to keep the people from crowding him. ¹⁰For he had healed many, so that those with diseases were pushing forward to touch him. ¹¹Whenever the evil spirits saw him, they fell down before him and cried out, 'You are the Son of God.' ¹²But he gave them strict orders not to tell who he was.

By contrast with the resistance, and now the plotting of the religious leadership, the crowds in Galilee welcome the teaching and the miracles of Jesus. The numbers are large (7, 9), and the area from which they come is extensive (8). It offers Mark's unspoken comment on the implications of verse 6. Matthew (12:15) puts the move away down to the fact that Jesus knew about the plot against him, or at least he puts the two side by side. The fact that the word translated 'withdrew' in Mark 3:7 is sometimes used of escaping from danger is not conclusive evidence that this was Jesus' (negative) motive for the move. Taylor shows adequately that the verb is also used with less defensive implications. In either case the contrast between Jesus' commitment to do God's will wherever he could, and the religious leadership's (in Mark's view) opposition to it remains stark. In that sense Jesus' move is symbolic. He leaves the synagogue, and the learned religion of that place, and goes to where the ordinary people receive him gladly and are enriched by his ministry of word and deed.

Another reason for seeing Jesus' move as a more positive one is the way in which Mark introduces new regions from which the

81

people come. This is an extension of the ministry, not an escape from danger (7–8a). And their reason for coming is clear (8b). From Jesus they hear and receive what they know themselves to need.

The other contrast of irony and pain in this story is the repeated fact that while religious authorities cannot see who Jesus is, or will not even begin to consider the possibilities, the evil spirits recognize at least his power and seem to know his name (11). Again they are commanded to silence – faith needs firmer ground than that, and the ingredients for the final revelation are not yet all in place.

Mark's story is complex. Jesus sought to deal with the Pharisees' objections on their own ground. He dismissed neither their concern to be faithful to what they knew, nor their seriousness in testing what he was doing. The obstacle was in them. Their ideology, based on their use and interpretation of the law, got in the way of true theology, knowledge of the living God.

Yet just as Jesus did not dismiss their serious questions, neither did he wholly support what the crowd was doing. They wanted to hear the teaching and to be healed. It would have been made so easy simply to have attached the idea of Son of God to that, making the teaching and healing the basis for the title and the response of faith. Mark knows, and suggests that Jesus made clear, that there was much more to the meaning of his ministry than anything they had seen yet. If there is a 'messianic secret' it is because Jesus' right to be known as Son of God will be based on evidence much deeper than the parables, healings and exorcism.

a. Finding the way to saving faith

'The clever missed it but the crowds saw it', is too simple a conclusion to draw, though in essence that is what Mark appears to be saying. The danger is that we end up making the wrong contrasts such as between quiet reflection and immediate response; between testing new things out and receiving them without hesitation; and worst of all, between knowledge and experience, or truth and relevance. All are necessary and all are justified, but above all openness to Jesus himself is the key.

b. Authentic evangelism

Popular evangelists, whether of the predominantly 'power' or 'preaching' type, are given pause for thought here. In one sense Jesus was engaging in both kinds. This is one of the reasons why evangelists ought properly to be honoured and used. We also know that Jesus commanded faith no larger than a grain of mustard seed, and that many who came to him must have had little idea of who he was in any theological sense. Yet, on the other hand, as R. P. Martin[1] has argued, one major purpose of Mark's gospel was to make sure that readers and hearers understood that the most important thing about Jesus was neither the parables nor the miracles but the obedient acceptance of the way of the cross, and that this is the prime model for discipleship. In this sense 'popular' will always be an inappropriate description of true evangelism. The teaching and healing by Jesus rightly attracted the crowds and met their full needs. But those alone would have provided an inadequate basis for understanding the meaning of 'Son of God' as shouted by the evil spirits. They are also an inadequate basis, on their own, for the understanding and experience of discipleship.

2. Jesus appoints the Twelve (3:13–19)

Jesus went up on a mountainside and called to him those he wanted, and they came to him. [14]He appointed twelve – designating them apostles – that they might be with him and that he might send them out to preach [15]and to have authority to drive out demons. [16]These are the twelve he appointed: Simon (to whom he gave the name Peter); [17]James son of Zebedee and his brother John (to them he gave the name Boanerges, which means Sons of Thunder); [18]Andrew, Philip, Bartholomew, Matthew, Thomas, James son of Alphaeus, Thaddaeus, Simon the Zealot [19]and Judas Iscariot, who betrayed him.

Mark now accounts for the appointment of the apostles, 'the Twelve'. His loyalty to what he 'received' (see Paul in 1 Cor. 15:3, 'what I received I passed on to you'), leads to difficulties he could have avoided had his attitude been more 'creative', but that was not his purpose.

Certainly Mark begins by setting out three characteristics of discipleship (13). *Up on a mountainside* is vague and does not attempt any geographical location, but it does communicate the sense of away from ordinary life and work. There is a separation involved in being a disciple. Secondly, they became disciples because Jesus *called to himself those he wanted.* The initiative and the choice came from Jesus. The third is that they came. There is an immediacy and urgency about the response which characterizes Mark's insight into the whole gospel.

Was a larger group called, from whom twelve were chosen? Mark's text allows that interpretation. Matthew refers simply to

[1] Martin, *Mark: Evangelist and Theologian*, pp. 208–209.

the call of twelve (Mt. 10:1). Luke (6:13) clearly intends us to understand that a larger group were invited from whom twelve were particularly chosen and appointed. This seems to be the best interpretation of all three versions, since Matthew's account does not preclude it. Since later in the gospels we read of seventy-two (or seventy) being sent out, we are wise not to attach exclusive importance to the Twelve, as we sometimes tend to do. They are different from the other disciples in a specific vocation and privilege of being always with Jesus and later to bear witness to that time. But the faith and commitment expected of them is expected of all disciples.

For the symbolism and the historicity of the appointment of the Twelve, see Cranfield.[2] Their task was threefold, to be with Jesus, to preach and to cast out evil spirits; witnessing, proclaiming, setting people free.[3] That word and deed, proclamation and action, are both seen as emerging from being with Jesus, and both are authentic witness to him, is extremely important, especially if one transposes them to our late twentieth century corporate as well as individual context of human need.

What is also clear is that the rejection by the Pharisees is now matched by the firm identification of the Twelve, with all the overtones of the twelve tribes of Israel. The identification by nicknames was not new. Rabbis with the same name were also distinguished in this way. In one sense the nicknames are more descriptive of their activities than their characteristics. 'Rock-like' hardly describes the overall New Testament picture of Peter, even after Pentecost. Yet in practice he was often the rallying point for the others, and especially during the early days of the church after Pentecost.

Reference to James and John as Boanerges is complicated, but of the various suggestions 'Sons of Thunder' seems most likely, as Mark's text suggests, and no doubt relates to the events described in Mark 9:38 and Luke 9:54.

'Iscariot' is not explained by Mark (19), though Judas' best known deed is alluded to. Anderson makes the valuable point that a group of special disciples whose list of names begins with Peter who denied Jesus, and end with Judas who betrayed him, make it

[2] Cranfield, p. 127.
[3] Some reliable manuscripts include 'and healing the sick', but the majority do not. It is more probably a scribal addition in harmony with Mt. 10:1 which includes it. Since Mark has consistently linked healing and exorcism in his general accounts of the ministry of Jesus so far, the omission may be another example of his faithfulness to the tradition he had received. In any case, the two parts of the healing work were closely related, though distinct.

abundantly clear that they were not a collection of the immediately perfect. Discipleship, like apostleship, is also a long hard road of temptation and trial.

a. Apostleship and discipleship

Mark is now getting down to the sharp focal point of what it means to be a disciple, with the apostles as a clear example. Choice, call, obedience, appointment, and separation are all involved. The task means drawing on Christ's presence and being sent out to preach and cast out demons.

The balance is not easy to keep in lively tension. Many Christians seem to spend much more time 'being with Jesus' (if that *is* what happens in our plethora of church meetings and fellowships, committees and services), and much less in proclaiming and casting out demons. Much training for ordination also seems to concentrate on the pastoral concerns of caring for the church community. All of that is necessary, but if dominant it provides a largely inward-looking perspective on church life. It can also lead to a narrowing down of our perception of the gospel as we adapt it to our needs. The missionary perspective of proclamation and casting out evil spirits forces us to test our understanding of the gospel in the setting of those who do not believe. There we are much more vulnerable and at risk, and there, for that very reason, we can prove the extent and the power of the message we proclaim and the authority it carries. If we hold back from the risk, we shall never discover how great and many-sided the gospel is.

b. Demonic forces

We are prone to apply 'casting out of spirits' individually. There is much however, both in Paul's widening of the picture (Eph. 6:12 for example, and Col. 2:15), and in our observation of world history, to show the reality of the demonic in groups and institutions, in systems and hierarchies. At very least it explains how groups of humans made in the image of God can behave as destructively towards others as they sometimes do. It also helps us to understand the relentlessness of the wiles and pressures of evil in the world. Exorcism, in this context, is not just about individual spiritual liberation therefore. It is about setting the world of institutions and structures free also, from injustice, cruelty and neglect; from extortion, corruption and greed, from the lesser gods of profit at all cost, and beating down the rest whatever it takes. The charismatics and radicals are nearer to one another than they think when they get down to the action – and they need one another too. It is tragic to see, in parts of our world, strong pentecostal churches largely supporting governments wielding demonic power, while the congregations practise individual exorcism regularly. It is equally sad to see Christians struggling in politics and other public areas of life who are largely ignorant of the Spirit's power to heal.

3. A contest with unbelief (3:20–35)

Then Jesus entered a house, and again a crowd gathered, so that he and his disciples were not even able to eat. [21]*When his family heard about this, they went to take charge of him, for they said, 'He is out of his mind.'*

[22]*And the teachers of the law who came down from Jerusalem said, 'He is possessed by Beelzebub! By the prince of demons he is driving out demons.'*

[23]*So Jesus called them and spoke to them in parables: 'How can Satan drive out Satan?* [24]*If a kingdom is divided against itself, that kingdom cannot stand.* [25]*If a house is divided against itself, that house cannot stand.* [26]*And if Satan opposes himself and is divided, he cannot stand: his end has come.* [27]*In fact, no-one can enter a strong man's house and carry off his possessions unless he first ties up the strong man. Then he can rob his house.* [28]*I tell you the truth, all the sins and blasphemies of men will be forgiven them.* [29]*But whoever blasphemes against the Holy Spirit will never be forgiven; he is guilty of an eternal sin.'*

[30]*He said this because they were saying, 'He has an evil spirit.'*

[31]*Then Jesus' mother and brothers arrived. Standing outside, they sent someone in to call him.* [32]*A crowd was sitting around him, and they told him, 'Your mother and brothers are outside looking for you.'*

[33]*'Who are my mother and my brothers?' he asked.*

[34]*Then he looked at those seated in a circle around him and said, 'Here are my mother and my brothers!* [35]*Whoever does God's will is my brother and sister and mother.'*

We come now to a painful section – painful because its theme is the inability of people to see who ought to be able to do so, in the spiritual sense. They include Jesus' own family (21, 31–35), some members of the crowds who followed (reading *they said*, 21, as 'people were saying'), and teachers of the law (22–30).

The initial reference to the family of Jesus (20–21) is not found in Luke or Matthew. Was it too daring and bold? It certainly is not an invention. The bringing together of unbelief, whether expressed in concern for Jesus' psychological state (21) or given a more sinister setting (22); whether from casual onlookers, or family or religious leaders, has the effect of identifying the battle lines in the epic struggle.

The family had heard reports that Jesus was mad (21), curiously because he was attracting such large crowds, though probably they had heard about what caused the large crowds, namely the teaching, healing and exorcism. Mark says they came *to take charge* of him, a word used for taking hold of someone's hand or for arresting a person. As Taylor puts it, 'Deep personal concern for Jesus is combined with a want of sympathy for His aims and purposes.'[4] There is strong evidence in favour of taking 'people were saying, "He's mad" ', to be really 'They (his family) were saying . . .' If so, their lack of sympathy was even stronger, in Mark's view, at this point. We may begin to imagine the pain of that for Jesus.

In 3:22–30 the theological ground of accusation is crossed by teachers of the law. They not only affirm his madness; they know its origin (22). Mark's information that they had come from Jerusalem adds a new twist to the story (Matthew simply says 'Pharisees', 12:24), while Luke more generally has 'some of them' referring to the crowds, which could possibly incorporate either or both of the other two). Mark's point is to show how Jesus' fame, and therefore the mounting opposition, has spread to Jerusalem. It may also be to make it clear at this point that Jerusalem will be the place for the final contest.

It is not absolutely clear whether their accusation was a single one or whether it contains two parts, a lesser and a greater. Since 'Beelzebub' ('Lord of the dwelling', most likely, not least because of references to 'house' in verses 25 and 27, or 'Lord of the flies' or 'Lord of the demons') is not used in Jewish literature as another name for Satan, it has been suggested that it must be an attempted identification of a lesser demon. On the other hand Jesus, to judge by verse 23 onwards, takes the accusation as relating to Satan only (not even mentioning Beelzebub), and since Matthew and Luke (Mt. 12:24; Lk. 11:15) take the two to be synonymous, it seems wiser to see them as such. In any case the lesser would probably have been seen as under the power of the greater. The point of importance is that the learned religious opponents of Jesus are not neutral about what he is doing: they ascribe its origin to Satan, *the prince of demons* (22). Here, as in so many places in the gospel story, neutrality was rarely possible. To see and hear Jesus was to put oneself into the dangerous situation of having to choose.

[4] Taylor, p. 236.

Only Mark has the next bit of the story. Jesus *called them and spoke to them in parables* (23). In fact Mark is significant for giving less of the content of Jesus' speaking ministry than the others. He has drawn attention to its importance (1:38), and indicated its basis (1:15). But he is sparing with detail. As with the healings and particularly the exorcisms (in the repeated injunction of silence about his identity), even Jesus' teaching will not in the end be the reason for discipleship, nor its model. That will lie in his death, towards which the story rushes and on which Mark spends so much time, and the assurance, though not the ultimate proof, of resurrection.

The phrase *in parables* uses a Greek word found in the New Testament only in the synoptic gospels. From a Hebrew word meaning 'a wise saying or story', it both introduces Jesus' answer to the present criticism and points towards his use of the story of the sower in chapter 4.

Jesus' argument employs the pictures of a human grouping (country or family) (23–26), and a house being broken into (27). Since he is casting out demons, and his enemies have not questioned that, then if Jesus casts them out by Satan's power, it is like a nation or family engaging in internal warfare. The end will be disastrous and so their hypothesis seems unlikely. By contrast (27), if what they have seen is a contest, then they know well that a strong man's house can only be burgled by a stronger man who can bind the other and steal his goods. Is that not a much more plausible scenario? There is a realism here, not only about what Jesus had actually done, but also about what both those witnessing the event and those receiving Mark's gospel know to be the case, namely that Satan might be a defeated foe but he was not yet a powerless one.

Mark makes very clear here what will become even clearer in 4:10–20, that alongside the deeds *of* God there have to be the explanations *from* God. It is not self-evident what God is doing, least of all, it seems, to those who were trained theologically. Action and word together are not only necessary in our mission in the world; they are necessary first in God's mission in Christ to us.

This is seen clearly in what follows. In verses 28–30 Jesus now interprets what has happened, not in the exorcism but in the attitudes and words of his critics. These are amongst the most awesome words he is ever recorded as having uttered. Matthew's version of this whole sequence supports the unity of this section (see Mt. 12:31 for example). The link between verse 28 in Mark's account and the things his opponents have said, is clear. So is the sharpening of the argument by direct reference to the Holy Spirit, also supported by Matthew (12:31–32) and Luke (12:10), though in a different form.

Whatever the construction of the text, however, it is the meaning which matters. Its seriousness is evidenced by the beginning of verse 28, literally 'Amen, I say to you.' 'By its use he (Jesus) solemnly guarantees the truth of what he is about to say' (Cranfield). Jesus uses this form of speech often, but it is no less important for that. He says there is only one exception to the universal principle that in God's universe sins can be forgiven (28). That exception is in general called blaspheming or saying evil things *against the Holy Spirit* (29).

The context has never been more important for a saying to find its true meaning. The critics of Jesus have watched God's grace freely given in the casting out of demons. Their offence is not that they asked questions. In the gospels it is occasionally the questions, even the sharp questions which lead to some of Jesus' most profound statements. (See, for example, Thomas and Jesus in Jn. 14:5–6.) Nor is their crime that they doubted. Thomas, again, is a good example (Jn. 20:24–29). Nor is it that they did not understand. The disciples of Jesus will find themselves in that situation in the very next chapter of Mark's gospel (4:10–12). Least of all have the religious leaders unthinkingly, or ignorantly, or unknowingly, used hapless words constituting 'blasphemy' or 'bad language'.

Their sin is that, in the presence of God's grace in action, they have not only rejected it but ascribed it to the devil. This is their fixed position. No wonder they will not find forgiveness.

They are set on calling the Spirit's work the activity of Satan. It may be that Jesus means that they have not yet reached this point of no return, and that he is warning them against hardening their current attitude into a permanent stance. Either way, the sin against the Holy Spirit is portrayed as resolute attribution of God's gracious work to satanic origins. There is no forgiveness here because such an attitude is incapable of seeking it. What makes it worst of all is that these are the informed and educated religious leaders.

The next section (3:31–35) is not as dire as its warning, but must have been extremely painful for all concerned. First, there is the making public of a family tension (31–32), and then a statement by Jesus with far-reaching consequences.

In the first half Jesus' *mother and brothers* are mentioned. This and 6:3 are the only two places in Mark's gospel where Mary is directly referred to, though 3:21 probably includes her, since they must have come some twenty miles from Nazareth to see him. Reference to Jesus' brothers has caused embarrassment to those in

89

the church who feel it inappropriate for the virgin Mother of the Saviour. 'Cousins' or 'children of Joseph by another marriage' have been suggested, but this is a most unnatural way of reading the text. Mark means natural brother to Jesus, borne by Mary. The general absence of reference to Joseph suggests that he was by now dead.

A more difficult problem is how Mary who, according to the stories in early chapters of Luke and Matthew, had gone through such unforgettable experiences, should now be with those trying to take him home. Such difficulties, however, arise only if one is determined not to let her be what she probably was, a simple Hebrew maid 'engraced' by God. How could she understand all that was involved? Why should she not have shared the view of those around her about who Jesus was, and be equally upset at the unexpected turn of events, with such crowds and teaching and healings and exorcisms, and the pretentious claims implied – and occasionally blurted out at the height of excitement or controversy – about who he was? How could she have known that he would be in opposition, as it seemed clear he now was, to the religious leaders of the day whom she regarded with deep respect and awe? And if Joseph was now gone, how much more anxious about Jesus she would be. (If only his father had been here!) This attitude, of itself, neither detracts from the authenticity of belief in a virgin birth, nor shows Mary as in any sense unworthy or out of character in her behaviour. Many mothers can no doubt identify with her, if at a lesser level, in the anxiety and disappointment when a son's life does not go as expected.

What follows must have been almost crushing for her. The crowd seems to take the side of Jesus' family, and the implication is that Jesus will either go out to them or make room for them to come in (32). In effect Jesus, as so often, in the words of T. W. Manson, stood normal human values on their heads. A new situation has developed. Stronger ties even than blood are now being forged. In the perspective of the kingdom 'the family' consists of *whoever does God's will* (35).

There is of course no ground whatever here for those sects who seek to take people, especially young people, away from their unbelieving families (or even from those believing, but not in the same way). That is unscriptural, since God placed human beings into families, and there is much New Testament teaching on the importance of the family unit. It is also inhuman and contrary to God's creative purposes. But it is a warning that even so deep, precious, and basic a relationship as that of human family is superseded by the fellowship of the new family of God, which will continue into eternity. This can be seen simply as a 'hard saying', but like all such there is a rich promise on the other side of the coin, as Peter discovered in Mark 10:28–30.

For the moment Mark has brought us to the point where Jesus is opposed by those from whom a casual onlooker might have expected him to get strongest support: and ardently followed by those who might have been thought likely to listen once and never return. The kingdom of God continues to surprise!

a. The kingdom gathers momentum

One senses, reading this section from Mark 3:20 onwards, that the movement of the kingdom is gathering a momentum of its own. More and more are playing their part, and the disciples themselves must certainly have felt increasingly the danger of things getting out of hand. They have come a long way since those early, though thrilling days, when first they were called. Did Jesus feel this too? References to the Holy Spirit (3:29) and to doing God's will (3:35) suggest a clarifying of points of reference as the pressure builds up. There is an excitement about being launched out into deep and choppy waters in God's service. Sadly so many churches and Christians miss it by playing safe.

b. Saving faith requires more than a keen mind

Church leaders and theologians do well to pause over these last stories. Intellectual grasp and academic ability are not of themselves signs of saving faith or perceptive spirit. They can equally provide ample skill to deflect the challenge of gospel truth. Similarly, uninformed conviction related to long experience can produce prejudice of the most stubborn kind. And none of us likes being disturbed or having to change established views or ways. Perceiving the Spirit's work and doing the will of God, centred in Jesus, are not as easy as they sound, but they provide a permanent set of correctives to the pressures which are at work in the lives of leaders in any walk of life.

c. Which 'family' should the church emphasize most?

The words of Jesus about 'family' have implications for our church life today. They may raise questions, for example, about making family the major point of emphasis in church programmes. There are many who do not have natural family around them, or have no family at all. It asks questions, too, of rigorist views in paedobaptist churches about which babies should be baptized. If the church is more significant and enduring a family than blood families then our attitudes and programmes should show it. And there is a loving word for those whose families reject the faith. Your family is much, much larger than that!

4. The parable of the sower (4:1-20)

Again Jesus began to teach by the lake. The crowd that gathered round him was so large that he got into a boat and sat in it out on the lake, while all the people were along the shore at the water's edge. ²He taught them many things by parables, and in his teaching said: ³'Listen! A farmer went out to sow his seed. ⁴As he was scattering the seed, some fell along the path, and the birds came and ate it up. ⁵Some fell on rocky places, where it did not have much soil. It sprang up quickly, because the soil was shallow. ⁶But when the sun came up, the plants were scorched, and they withered because they had no root. ⁷Other seed fell among thorns, which grew up and choked the plants, so that they did not bear grain. ⁸Still other seed fell on good soil. It came up, grew and produced a crop, multiplying thirty, sixty, or even a hundred times.'

⁹Then Jesus said, 'He who has ears to hear, let him hear.'

¹⁰When he was alone, the Twelve and the others around him asked him about the parables. ¹¹He told them, 'The secret of the kingdom of God has been given to you. But to those on the outside everything is said in parables ¹²so that,

' "they may be ever seeing but never perceiving.
and ever hearing but never understanding;
otherwise they might turn and be forgiven!" '

¹³Then Jesus said to them, 'Don't you understand this parable? How then will you understand any parable? ¹⁴The farmer sows the word. ¹⁵Some people are like seed along the path, where the word is sown. As soon as they hear it, Satan comes and takes away the word that was sown in them. ¹⁶Others, like seed sown on rocky places, hear the word and at once receive it with joy. ¹⁷But since they have no root, they last only a short time. When trouble or persecution comes because of the word, they quickly fall away. ¹⁸Still others, like seed sown among thorns, hear the word; ¹⁹but the worries of this life, the deceitfulness of wealth and the desires for other things come in and choke the word, making it unfruitful. ²⁰Others, like seed sown on good soil, hear the word, accept it, and produce a crop – thirty, sixty or even a hundred times what was sown.'

Mark now introduces us to a section (4:1–34) wholly taken up with parables. It therefore begins (1–2) and ends (33–34) with the description of the context and the report of Jesus' commitment to parables as a teaching method.

It is difficult to improve on Vincent Taylor's definition of parables as used by Jesus. 'A metaphor or story connected with the affairs of daily life is used as an illustration of moral and spiritual truths, on the assumption that what applies in one sphere is relevant also in the others.'[5] It is important to notice that the definition leaves room for variety within the category, a point separately reinforced by Taylor. It is also important to notice that the category itself may have become more widely interpreted in New Testament times, a development wholly in harmony with its Hebrew origin. The purpose of Jesus in using parables becomes a point of some contention when we deal with 4:10–12, indeed a point of puzzlement, too, but here we suggest that one aim in using this method is to encourage serious, persistent, perceptive faith. Each of those adjectives is important. The emphasis on *seriousness* was necessary because 'hearing Jesus' seems to have become 'one of the things to do' at the time. Crowds begat crowds, and there was enough excitement, in the healings, exorcisms and controversy, to keep them coming. The parable requires seriousness if we are to begin to grasp its meaning, hence, *'Listen!'*, in verse 3. *Persistence* was also important. There were plenty of wandering teachers and miracle workers around. The parabolic method of teaching did not pander to the casual, half-hearted listener. The hearer had to work at it and continue with it. *Perception* was needed, too, since at face value the stories were about things that just about everybody in the crowd knew already. Unless there was some veiled meaning, they were innocuous, even shallow tales. Yet the perceptive saw more than was obvious.

The story of the sower (1–9 and 13–20, with the comment on the purpose of parables, 10–12) seems engaging enough as a story for most of his hearers. What he described probably happened to some of them regularly. Certainly they would know about it. The economy of the language and the Semitisms reflecting closeness to the Aramaic in which the parable was told witness to the authenticity and suggest that we are dealing with an accurate account of the words of Jesus himself. The practical details also fit the setting as it would have been. The point of emphasis is in verse 8, with the mounting excitement of the verbs and their tenses celebrating the remarkable harvest of thirty, sixty and even one hundred-fold.

[5] Taylor, p. 249.

That *would* be a good harvest for a sower around Galilee in Jesus' time.

But what is it really about? The 'explanation' in 13–20 simply justifies the story in terms of its possible detailed application to a crowd or group listening to the message of God being preached.[6] It does so, however, like most commentaries on an original event or story, in a rather flat and prosaic way. 'For seed, read gospel message. For sower, read preacher. For soils, read people.' One wants to add, 'For meaning, work it out for yourself'! For the meaning seems still to be left to the serious, persistent, perceptive listener.

The central clue in the parable is found in the various types of receptivity in the ground. Neither the sower nor the seed (and certainly not the weather!) are determinative. Everything depends on the state of the ground. If, as Julicher asserted as long ago as 1899, a parable has one major meaning, then this is it. The receptivity of the ground determines the harvest. If C. H. Dodd was right in claiming that the meaning of a parable will be a 'kingdom' meaning, that is, a truth related to the kingdom of God, then the parable of the sower is explaining why some respond and enter, while others do not, when the grace of God is freely available to all. And if Harald Reisenfeld accurately claimed[7] that the single meaning of a parable will have a variety of applications, as evidenced even in the New Testament, then we may offer conjecture about the intention here. Jesus may himself have been reflecting on this question. We must never assume that he was indifferent to the rejection of his work and words, so long as some responded (Mt. 23:37–39; Lk. 13:34–35). Why would they not all respond, if the offer was to all? We may be sure that his disciples were already wondering this, not least about the religious leadership (3:22–30), and perhaps even more personally about Jesus' own family (3:21, 31–35). Equally, we may guess, those who received this gospel of Mark would be facing that mystery, as Christians do today. Neither the parable (1–8), nor the explanation (13–20), *explain* why it is so. But they do identify the source of the problem – human hardness, shallowness and self-indulgence. There is a sense in which the preacher of the message is limited by these factors, since God will not force his grace on to people (see again, for example, Mt. 23:37–39 and Lk. 13:34–35). We touch here on a mystery of divine providence, where triumphalism both misses the point and stores up frustration for young Christians.

[6] For a balancing of the case for and against the authenticity of this section, see Cranfield, pp. 158–161.

[7] Lecture in Cambridge Divinity School, 1980.

The section 4:10–12 is amongst the most difficult passages in the New Testament, first to understand with any degree of certainty, and secondly to accept if we get near to an understanding. The apostles are puzzled, and come to Jesus for help (10), in itself a praiseworthy thing to do. In doing so, however, they reveal that they are hanging tenuously on to their role as chosen disciples of Jesus. He reminds them of this special position in verse 11, which we must not forget. The secret (mystery) is not a reference to mystery religions, but to an Old Testament idea of something hidden until revealed by God, which cannot otherwise be perceived. Here the mystery relates to the kingdom of God and must refer to the declaration of 1:14, 15, now filled out in the teaching, healing, and exorcisms, but perceived only by those who see the something that is different about Jesus. This they have at least *begun* to do, in that they have left all and followed him. Their struggle with the parables is not surprising, and reveals how far they have to go. As Cranfield puts it, 'The incarnate word is not obvious. Only faith could recognise the Son of God in the lowly figure of Jesus of Nazareth. The secret of the Kingdom of God is the secret of the person of Jesus.'[8]

The parables alone, not responded to by faith in Jesus, will evidently not be enough (12). Like the seed on hard, shallow or thorny ground, the parables will be stultified in their influence by the unresponsiveness of their reception. Jesus uses Isaiah 6:9–10, evidently from the Septuagint, the Greek version of the Old Testament. The problem concerns the *so that* of verse 12. Suggestions have been offered, such as the possibility that 'with the result that' would be better. It would certainly be easier! Matthew and Luke seek to soften its sharpness, but sharp it remains.

Putting it all together, the most likely meaning seems to be that parables alone will not produce faith, otherwise all who hear would believe. Parables are an invitation to faith as (taking 4:14 at its face value) is the gospel itself. Neither parables in particular, nor the gospel in general, enforce or ensure faith. What is required is the secret of the kingdom of Jesus. Without that, the parables will simply go on frustrating the hearers, for they mistake the signpost for the destination, the shadow for the reality, the metaphor for the truth. How God deals, and expects his people to deal, with this situation is referred to elsewhere in Scripture. For the moment we must accept an awesome limitation, and learn not to become ourselves like *those on the outside*. We should be as surprised as Jesus plainly intended his first hearers to be, that in such adverse

---

[8] Cranfield, p. 153.

circumstances the harvest is as great as it is.

a. Faith is not easily come by

For the disciples this may have been a low point in their experience of Jesus so far. After the initial excitement of John the Baptist's ministry (assuming that at least some of them witnessed it), the call and the early miracles, things seemed to have turned for the worse. Religious leaders move into opposition. Jesus' family worry about his sanity. Maybe some of the crowd did, too (see the GNB translation of 3:21 'people were saying, "He's gone mad!" '). What is more, they, his own disciples, listen to his little stories (which Mark calls parables) and yet do not understand them. They know the stories cannot be taken at face value, but they are not sure how to take them. Why would the Master not make it all easier, or say more openly who he is?

'Faith made easy' is what we would all like. But the kingdom is not built on impressive speakers nor powerful performances. See Paul making exactly the same point in 1 Corinthians 2:1–5. Interestingly enough Paul also used the word 'mystery' (God's secret) at this point (1 Cor. 2:1). For Paul, too, the focal point was to know 'Jesus Christ and him crucified' (1 Cor. 2:2). One could scarcely have a better comment on Mark's picture of what Jesus was trying both to communicate and to do.

This restraint about what we might call evangelism needs careful reflection today. Paul's expressed aim to 'save some of them by whatever means are possible' (1 Cor. 9:22), clearly does not mean 'at any price'. On the other hand, neither is it right for us to presume to tell people whether or not they are ready to become Christians. We can, however, do two things. One is to avoid trying to push people into believing on an inadequate basis. The other is to be sure that we make clear what it means to be a Christian disciple. It has more to do with taking up our cross and following him than with an endless round of spiritual excitement. Jesus, in Mark's gospel, is clearly doing all he can to avoid that mistake. So, evidently did Paul. So should we.

b. The servant of the good news is never in control of it

There is also something here which may appear to fly in the face of the previous section, and yet which lives alongside it in New Testament teaching. It is that the servant of Jesus is also the servant of the gospel in the sense that he or she never controls either the gospel or its effects. Even Jesus is here reflecting on the unpredictability of the response when the message is made plain. The use of metaphors from nature, especially where sowing and reaping are concerned, reinforces this insight. The farmer knows that though he must plan, labour and enable growth, there are other forces at work which may be more determinative of the results than all his skill and industry. The preacher, evangelist, and witness must remember that too. He or she plays a part, but it is only a part. To play that part is to risk oneself every time, with the possibility of frustration and failure or fulfilment and success. Paul's comment is again helpful: 'Your faith, then, does not rest on human wisdom but on God's power' (1 Cor. 2:5). All our Christian work should be periodically measured by that test.

5. A lamp on a stand (4:21–25)

He said to them, 'Do you bring in a lamp to put it under a bowl or a bed? Instead, don't you put it on its stand?

[22]For whatever is hidden is meant to be disclosed, and whatever is concealed is meant to be brought out into the open. [23]If anyone has ears to hear, let him hear.'

[24]'Consider carefully what you hear,' he continued. 'With the measure you use, it will be measured to you – and even more. [25]Whoever has will be given more: whoever does not have, even what he has will be taken from him.'

In this passage two sayings are put together; they both fit well into Mark's scheme here and are used in different settings by Matthew and Luke. Of course Jesus, like any busy public speaker, would reproduce similar statements and ideas on different occasions. Luke 8:11–18 reproduces the same sayings in the same context related to the sower. But some of these sayings also appear in many places.[9] At this distance we have to do the best we can to determine whether we have here faithful records of different incidents when on each occasion Jesus used these words, or whether the evangelists, faithful to the words of Jesus, set them out differently in order to make separate, theological points within the overall context. Neither involves their unfaithfulness to the message of Jesus, but our conclusion should be lightly held, and will reflect our attitudes to Scripture and its origin at a much wider level.

In Mark's account the logic of 21–25 fits not only internally but also into the development of the story so far. On the one side a light is to be used to illuminate everything about it, and nothing

[9] Lk. 6:38; 11:33; 12:2; 31; 14:35; 19:26, and also in Mt. 5:15; 6:33; 7:2; 10:26; 11:15; 13:9, 12, 43; 25:29.

remains hidden forever. Jesus is saying that there is a mystery (seen still as something hidden which only God can reveal) but that it will not remain hidden forever. The implication is that God is now revealing the hidden secret, in Jesus. Therefore (23–25), they should pay attention all the more carefully. They who hear his teaching, see his miracles, are all the more under obligation to make the proper response. (Note again the important point that neither the teaching nor the miracles automatically produce the true response. Somehow he is calling on them for that. We are into the area of 'serious, persistent, perceptive faith' again.) The background of 24 and 25 is as homely as anything one finds in the teaching of Jesus. They could see how true that was in terms of everyday life. Jesus says it operates in the hidden spiritual realm, too.

a. The nature and interpretation of the parables of Jesus

A point is also being made with the use of these homely metaphors, about the deeper significance of Jesus' use of parables. Are they simply metaphors, or more than that? Even if they are metaphors only, on what does their value as metaphors lie? Traditionally it has been normal to see them in the category of illustration. Yet if that is all they were, then Jesus spent most of his teaching ministry illustrating, with very little indication of what it was he was illustrating. On that construction the majority of his 'sermons' contained no theology at all! They were, as we might say, pleasant little children's addresses.

We take one step towards investing them with more significance if we follow what has been suggested as Mark's approach in this gospel, namely to see Jesus as the clue to all that he said. The stories do not have within themselves the force to persuade or convince. They were not intended so to do, any more than the miracles. But they are pointers, signposts, avenues which, if followed, point to the one who does convince and persuade, namely Jesus himself, and the attitude which helps one to follow the pointers and signposts along the avenue is serious, persistent, perceptive faith. The 'explanation' of Mark 4:14–20 is an example of the invitation being given, since in that context he was casting the seed of the gospel on to the various kinds of soil.

We take a second step of understanding the parables in general if we affirm that, contrary to the usual interpretation, they *are* theological in character, in the sense that they affirm the unity of nature and grace. Jesus, on his construction of the parable, is not saying that this homely story happens to illustrate that spiritual truth. He is saying that his heavenly Father so created everything that there is a direct correspondence between nature and grace – a oneness between the two which enables him to stand astride the two. For a clear example we may take the saying of Jesus recorded by John in John 12:24. John has made much of the hour of the Son of Man having arrived (23). The disciples are ready for the manifesto of the kingdom. It turns out to be a simple lesson in gardening! 'Unless a grain of wheat falls to the ground and dies, it remains only a single seed. But if it dies, it produces many seeds.' How trivial! Everybody knew that to be the case with horticulture. What could it mean?

John spells it out in the words of Jesus, but first he tells us it is Passover time (Jn. 12:1, 12); so there were fifty days to Pentecost, the Jewish Harvest Festival. Gardening talk was probably frequent, therefore the 'grain of wheat principle' was on the agenda. But Jesus says that this principle applies to him (Jn. 12:27, 31–32, 33). He will be the grain of wheat dying and being buried to produce the harvest. And, even more graphically, it applies to his followers also (25–26). The dying and fruit-bearing principle is fundamental to Jesus' disciples, too.

Now the main point here is that one principle applies in all three spheres – nature, Jesus' work of salvation, and discipleship. God has written the dying and rising principle *into all three areas*. At this point there is continuity between nature and grace, for the same principles are meant to apply. And (as we know from Jn. 1:1–14), Jesus Christ is the clue to the meaning of all three worlds.

If this is a principle to be generally applied, then the parables are more than homely illustrations. They are theological statements about how life is, because God made it so. They also imply that they reflect God's way of working in every area of experience – nature and grace. The same principles apply because God is the originator of both.

The implications of this exciting truth tumble out one after another. It means, for example, that Christians are not called to be 'world-renouncing' in the sense that everything 'outside the church' is somehow suspect. Art and science, music and philosophy, economy and ecology, politics and pastimes are all part of the gift of the one God to his creatures, and are meant to operate according to the *same principles*. The tragedy that human beings have spoiled all these areas of life goes as far back as the story at the beginning of Genesis of man and woman's disobedience and fall. But that should cause Christians to have all the more reason for becoming involved in the world's life, since we in Christ have *some* understanding and experience of how the world is meant to work. To retreat into the safety of an ark-like church is to miss our way. It is our privilege and responsibility to be fully involved in the world's affairs. Jesus said that the meek would inherit the earth (Mt. 5:5): but his church has spent most of its life trying to avoid doing so!

It also follows that if the same principles of operation are meant to apply to nature as to grace, then we can *begin anywhere* in our evangelism with the hope of *ending* at the feet of Christ. The wise men, the Magi, of the gospels are surely there for that purpose. Following their normal pursuit of knowledge they got as far as the king's house, and were met by a revelation out of the Scriptures.

Following it they found the baby they sought (Mt. 2:1–12). This principle is also clear in Jesus' own ministry. He began where people were, talked to them in words and with concepts they understood, seeking to lead them to faith. The story of the woman at the well in John 4:5–41 is a classic example, where 'water' means both the elements in the well to meet Jesus' need (7–8) and the spiritual life God would give her within her own inner being (10–14). From a most unpromising start (see 9) the story ends with large numbers of people believing because they had tested for themselves the witness she had given (39–41). It all began because Jesus talked to a woman at a well – about water!

A third conclusion from this principle is that the apologetic task of the church is a vital one. Apologetics means hearing and understanding the objections raised against Christianity at the intellectual and moral level, and seeking to answer them. The link between nature and grace in God's creative purpose means that it not only can, but must be done. C. S. Lewis was probably the last well-known apologist in Western culture. Maybe now we need schools of apologists, since the extent of knowledge is burgeoning at such speed. It is all the more necessary, perhaps crucially necessary, if the meaning of the parable of the sower is that the state of the soil is crucial to the harvest. To ignore soil preparation, on the basis that the sowers are good and our seed of highest quality, is to leave our evangelistic witness in a very exposed situation and to ignore our Lord's own teaching.

b. The imperative to choose

The seriousness of the occasion is now being communicated to the crowd (and to the disciples, indirectly). To hear the message is not a neutral affair. Hearing puts them under great obligation, not least because they are hearing just at the time when God's kingdom has drawn near (1:15). The time has come, not just for Jesus to preach and heal, but also for them to make up their minds. This theme also recurs in the spread of the early church, as in Acts 17:30–31.

It means that those who preach or witness to others must realize how awesome a task they perform. They put their hearers under great obligation and responsibility. How important to do it with all the sensitivity, care and preparation possible!

6. Other parables of sowing (4:26–34)

*He also said, 'This is what the kingdom of God is like. A man scatters seed on the ground. *[27]*Night and day, whether he sleeps or gets up, the seed sprouts and grows, though he does not know how. *[28]*All by itself the soil produces corn – first the stalk, then the ear, then the full grain in the ear. *[29]*As soon as the grain is ripe, he puts the sickle to it, because the harvest has come.'*

*[30]*Again he said, 'What shall we say the kingdom of God is like, or what parable shall we use to describe it? *[31]*It is like a mustard seed, which is the smallest seed you plant in the ground. *[32]*Yet when planted, it grows and becomes the largest of all garden plants, with such big branches that the birds of the air can perch in its shade.'*

*[33]*With many similar parables Jesus spoke the word to them, as much as they could understand. *[34]*He did not say anything to them without using a parable. But when he was alone with his own disciples, he explained everything.*

In 4:26–29 Jesus now extends the teaching of the sower parable. His hearers, especially the disciples, must have felt somewhat discouraged by the sower. If the condition of the ground is so significant, what chance have they? Now Jesus reminds them of another factor in farming. The reason for the limitation of the farmer's control is a hidden power at work in the process of gestation and crop-bearing. The clue is in the word translated 'by itself', the word from which we get the English word 'automatically'. There could be no harvest without this constant element in nature. Without human assistance there is a power for new life and growth at work.

Jesus does not define it here, but he is drawing attention to the divine provision which meets their limitations. If they wonder how they will achieve anything, if the soil is so dominant, they must remember that they are not the only ones at work. Paul, in 1 Corinthians 2:10–12, expounds this same truth theologically in terms of the work of the Holy Spirit. For the moment, here in Mark, Jesus is encouraging his disciples in this, as in everything else, not to judge only by what is observable on the surface, any more than they would judge a harvest just after the seed has been sown. There is hidden energy at work below the surface, as the

101

gospel message is preached and enacted. They must put that along-side the truth of the parable of the soils. Part of their task will be, like the farmer, to recognize the signs of harvest and play their part in gathering it in. There may be here an historical reference, too. At this stage of Jesus' ministry there may not be for them the clarity or power for which they had hoped. At hidden levels, however, things were moving forward. They would one day need to be ready to play their part then.

The next passage (4:30–32), adds another piece to the jigsaw of the disciples' understanding. The reference is still nature. As they might be tempted to feel that the task was hopeless in view of the disappointing response from Jewish leaders and even family (to which the idea of hidden growth was a reference), so they might also be inclined to contrast the smallness of their whole enterprise (organization would be much too pretentious a description) over against Rome and Jerusalem. Nature, which they know, again pro-vides a clue – or rather, a principle of divine operation. Jesus asks them now to consider the mustard seed (31). It was not the smallest seed, but proverbially it seems to have been the typical small seed (see Mt. 17:20; Lk. 17:6). The details are not the same in Luke or Matthew's version (Mark calls it a garden plant, or shrub (RSV), they a tree. Mark says the birds perched *in its shade*, while Luke and Matthew have them perching 'in its branches' Lk. 13:19; Mt. 13:31). Yet they all draw attention to the contrast in size between the original seed, from which at face value little would be expected, and the eventual shrub or tree, which the birds were glad to use.

As they are invited to see, via the parables and miracles, the hidden presence of the Son of God, and behind the difficult work of sowing the hidden energy of gestation and growth, so they are also bidden to see in these small beginnings the potential for the future of the kingdom which is greater than they can easily imagine.

The concluding section of this collection of parables is not as straightforward as it seems, particularly in relation to Jesus' words to the twelve apostles recorded in 4:11–12. One part of it is clear. It reinforces the differences between the inner band of the disciples and the crowd at large. The distinction in 4:11 is now spelt out in verse 34 with the description of the method of Jesus in telling parables to the crowd but also explaining them to the Twelve. When the crowds could hear, they heard; what the apostles needed further, in view of their insight into the mystery of the kingdom, was given in private. The verb translated 'explain' literally means 'untie', a nicely pointed word. We may imagine some of the knots into which they got themselves while they listened to him in public! The unravelling was necessary.

The difficulty concerns the point of Jesus' dealing with the crowds in this way. The description is clear enough. He taught them in parables *as much as they could understand* (33). This was, in any case, evidently a basic principle in this ministry (see Jn. 16:12, for example). The method is clear, but what was the purpose? Surely not simply to keep them entertained and therefore keep them coming, since some of his stories were more calculated to send them away permanently.[10] If, as has been suggested, the parables did not produce faith but provided an avenue along which a person travelling might find faith in Jesus as Son of God, veiled though that identity was, then the crowds heard what interested them, and were willing to hear more along that line. They could not see any full exposition of who Jesus was because, as Mark's gospel makes clear, the death and testimony to resurrection were necessary for that. Yet some might perceive it and respond. Did they then join the band of disciples, defined more widely than in terms of the apostles alone? However we understand it, the focal point is dependence on Jesus as the teller and interpreter of the parables, and as the destination to which they invite the listening traveller.

Finally, it is worth noting Mark's reference to Jesus, using *many similar parables* (33). He is offering us a selection, not the entirety.

The appeal to spiritual curiosity

Before moving on to describe some striking miracles, Mark has recorded the major direction of Jesus' teaching ministry. The 'reserve' about openly identifying himself is here. Yet it is reserve, not total secrecy. The teaching, like the miracles, point in a clear direction, but the destination cannot be seen from the vantage point of the hearing or the seeing. That destination is found only by perceiving that there is more to the ministry than meets the eye or the ear, and by following that perception through to the one who stands at the centre of all that is happening. The Twelve have taken steps in that direction, largely because they were called. The religious leadership refused to contemplate that possibility and are now moving in the opposite direction. For the moment Jesus' family, and maybe some in the crowd, are inclined to resist the ministry, believing him to be psychologically disturbed. There is a clear impression that all is by no means yet revealed, and that the struggle between good and evil has yet a long way to run. But the elements in the struggle are evident, as is the mounting sense that

[10] See Lk. 14:28–30, for example, with the teaching on either side, in verses 25–27 and 31–33.

to get anywhere near the action is to be fascinated and challenged by it.

7. The calming of the storm (4:35–41)

That day when evening came, he said to his disciples. 'Let us go over to the other side.' ³⁶*Leaving the crowd behind, they took him along, just as he was, in the boat. There were also other boats with him.* ³⁷*A furious squall came up, and the waves broke over the boat, so that it was nearly swamped.* ³⁸*Jesus was in the stern, sleeping on a cushion. The disciples woke him and said to him, 'Teacher, don't you care if we drown?'*

³⁹*He got up, rebuked the wind and said to the waves, 'Quiet! Be still!' Then the wind died down and it was completely calm.*

⁴⁰*He said to his disciples, 'Why are you so afraid? Do you still have no faith?'*

⁴¹*They were terrified and asked each other, 'Who is this? Even the wind and the waves obey him!'*

Mark now introduces two new developments in his story. The first is a straightforward 'nature miracle'. The second is a sharpening of the relationship between Jesus and the disciples on the issue of faith.

The story carries clear signs of eye-witness origins. There is the detail of when the miracle happened (35); then in the first part of verse 38 we read the particular reference to Jesus sleeping in the back of the boat with his head on the helmsman's pillow. There is also stark language, such as, *'Teacher, don't you care if we drown?'* (38), followed by *'Do you still have no faith?'* (40). Added to all this is the delightful though largely unnecessary reference to other boats being there (36); unnecessary since they play no further part in this story. Mark says they were there because an eye-witness knew they were there!

The first new element, the nature miracle, has raised difficulty in a scientifically oriented culture. There is a sense in which the exorcisms disturb us less because psychiatric medicine struggles both to describe adequately and to locate and address effectively those destructive forces which are evident in human lives. Descriptions and diagnoses are neither so precise nor so irrefutable as to exclude another set of terms from a different perspective. But what of stilling a storm? (The idea that Jesus' words in verse 39 are really addressed to the disciples carries little weight. Mark clearly believes that Jesus addressed the wind and the waves.) In modern scientific investigation there seems now to be a less rigid understanding of how things happen, how universal any scientific 'law' can be, and how much in the upper reaches of research can be unquestionably proven in any case.[11] At least there is room acknowledged by many for openness to a variety of possibilities where the 'miraculous' is concerned. Nor should we forget the careful work of the late Ian Ramsey, suggesting the possibility that what we view as two worlds, the material and the spiritual, are truly parts of the one world, and that we may one day, by perceiving more fully how both work, see also how much closer they are to one another.[12]

Our response to this issue both influences and is influenced by the larger question of how we view the incarnation, and our belief about the power exercised by Jesus anyway. If Jesus' relationship to God is as unique as the New Testament writers suggest, we should expect miracles of every kind, including nature miracles. The incarnation is the greatest miracle; all else follows.[13]

Before leaving this point, we must pose a sharper problem for our understanding of Mark's presentation of the ministry of Jesus. If, as we have suggested, neither the parable nor the miracle can in themselves induce faith, why would Jesus perform such a miracle at this stage? Would it not be likely to produce a faith that was inadequately based, the very thing he seemed to be avoiding?

The answer lies along the line of harmony with what has been so far suggested. Jesus does not believe that the crowd should hear in concrete terms who he is, lest they 'believe' in him for inadequate reasons of parable or miracle. Only his death and risen life will be firm enough foundation for the demands of discipleship. There are, however, three observable exceptions to this principle. One is his debate with the religious leaders, who by their position, experience and training ought to be able to perceive what is going on (Mk. 2:1–12, 27–28). The second concerns the Twelve, to whom he seeks to communicate the meaning of the kingdom ahead of all the evidence being available (Mk. 4:10–12). The third relates to situations of human need, as when the demon-possessed are brought and it was better to risk being named.[14] In the face of informed opposition, questions by disciples, and extreme human need, the

[11] John Polkinghorne, *One World* (SPCK, 1986). See, for example, p. 12, 'If you wish to give an experimental physicist an uneasy moment, look him in the eyes and say . . .'.
[12] I. T. Ramsey, *Our Understanding of Prayer* (SPCK, 1971).
[13] For the question of divine intervention, via miracle, in a consistent universe, see pp. 58–59.
[14] Mk. 1:23–24 where the spirit cried out; and Mk. 1:34, where they were evidently kept silent. Marginally the same is true of the leper of Mk. 1:40–45, where the ordinary healing miracle included a stricture against spreading the news, an injunction ignored by the man who was healed.

105

divine power was revealed and sometimes the divine nature named. Even in these situations, however, more than observation and hearing was required for true discipleship. The perception of faith was not automatically communicated.

The nature miracle of 4:35–40 fits into the third category of extreme human need. It would have fitted all the more naturally if the disciples could have perceived that, with Jesus resting in their midst, they were perfectly safe in the storm. Their waking him shows how far they yet have to go.

This leads us to the second new element here, the sharp exchange between the disciples and Jesus over the issue of faith, an exchange much less obviously sharp in Matthew 8:23–27 and Luke 8:22–25. Our sympathies must be with the disciples. Some of them were, after all, fishermen. They knew Lake Galilee very well. Contrary to publicly held views on the matter, it is usually the experts who recognize the need to panic! Was it all the harder that it was a carpenter who was ignoring the obvious signs of extreme danger? Whatever their stimulus, including their fear, their question undoubtedly reproaches Jesus for neglecting their safety by sleeping during a dangerous storm.

They could hardly have been ready for the reply. '*Why are you so afraid? Do you still have no faith?*' The crux of discipleship is located here. They needed him to *do things*: he wanted them to trust *him*. His very presence amongst them was all that they needed to survive.

a. Nature, grace and the miraculous

The nature miracles raise the question of the relation between nature and grace. Catholic theology in general has stressed the continuity between the two, Protestant theology – particularly since Barth – its discontinuity. In the nature miracle there is a particular focusing of the relationship. If God is sovereign Lord over all that is made then his presence in Jesus could be expected to reinforce what we understand to be the normal working of nature. Yet it could also be expected that he would show a distinctive relationship to nature, as Son of God. This is clear in his teaching. He uses ordinary everyday experiences and incidents in his parables, but in so doing assigns to them considerable theological weight (see p. 38). They are more than sheep and goats, sons and daughters, houses and lands, mustard seeds and birds. They have a theological significance as part of the world God has made, a world which in itself displays fundamental principles like death and resurrection, forgiveness and new beginnings, patience and respect. He sees in it 'as much as' everyone else and 'more than' anyone else, without disturbing the 'as much' which most of us see. It is the same with his deeds. The part he plays in the ordinary natural developmental pattern of life is 'as much as' everyone else's in that he was born, grew up, could be tired, lonely, hungry, thirsty, disappointed, overcome with emotion, and in the end died. Yet there is a 'more than' here too. There are the descriptions of unusual circumstances of conception and surrounding events at birth; high moments in his progress as a wandering rabbi such as his baptism, temptation, transfiguration, prayers in Gethsemane; and finally the story of the witnesses to his resurrection. These all suggest a 'more than' the rest of us in relation to nature, a 'more than' which brings sharp focus to his redemptive action within the setting of nature. It is here that the miracles fit best in our overall understanding of Jesus.

b. With Christ is enough

At the personal spiritual level there is a deep lesson to be learned from the stilling of the storm incident. For the disciple it should be enough to be with the Lord, whether life's seas are running smoothly or not. Forms of Christianity which encourage and promise a life of continual success, excitement and growth will not only lead to frustration and despair; they actually point the disciple towards the wrong goal in the Christian pilgrimage. It is enough that Christ goes with us on our journey. We do not judge his care for us, nor the state of our discipleship, by the roughness of the seas over which we sail. We 'rejoice in the Lord', not in our current circumstances, as Paul made clear to the Philippians (Phil. 3:1).

8. Jesus heals a demon-possessed man (5:1–20)

They went across the lake to the region of the Gerasenes. ²When Jesus got out of the boat, a man with an evil spirit came from the tombs to meet him. ³This man lived in the tombs, and no-one could bind him any more, not even with a chain. ⁴For he had often been chained hand and foot, but he tore the chains apart and broke the irons on his feet. No-one was strong enough to subdue him. ⁵Night and day among the tombs and in the hills he would cry out and cut himself with stones.

⁶When he saw Jesus from a distance, he ran and fell on his knees in front of him. ⁷He shouted at the top of his voice, 'What do you want with me, Jesus, Son of the Most High God? Swear to God

107

that you won't torture me!' [8]*For Jesus had said to him, 'Come out of this man, you evil spirit!'*

[9]*Then Jesus asked him, 'What is your name?'*

'My name is Legion,' he replied, 'for we are many.' [10]*And he begged Jesus again and again not to send them out of the area.*

[11]*A large herd of pigs was feeding on the nearby hillside.* [12]*The demons begged Jesus, 'Send us among the pigs: allow us to go into them.'* [13]*He gave them permission, and the evil spirits came out and went into the pigs. The herd, about two thousand in number, rushed down the steep bank into the lake and were drowned.*

[14]*Those tending the pigs ran off and reported this in the town and countryside, and the people went out to see what had happened.* [15]*When they came to Jesus, they saw the man who had been possessed by the legion of demons, sitting there, dressed and in his right mind; and they were afraid.* [16]*Those who had seen it told the people what had happened to the demon-possessed man – and told about the pigs as well.* [17]*Then the people began to plead with Jesus to leave their region.*

[18]*As Jesus was getting into the boat, the man who had been demon-possessed begged to go with him.* [19]*Jesus did not let him, but said, 'Go home to your family and tell them how much the Lord has done for you, and how he has had mercy on you.'* [20]*So the man went away and began to tell in the Decapolis how much Jesus had done for him. And all the people were amazed.*

After a major nature miracle Mark now moves to an equally important healing miracle involving the casting out of demons but going into considerable detail about it. Again there is strong evidence of eye-witness account, probably from Peter.

There is a further new element in the story relating to the question of where it took place. There are at least three options. The main text of Mark has *Gerasenes* (which Luke, in 8:26, also chooses). An alternative in some reliable manuscripts of Mark has *Gergesenes* – a version at least as early as Origen. Matthew, though evidently using Mark's gospel as a guide, opts for *Gadarenes*. The possibility of errors by copyists is obvious. But so is the alternative that the later gospel writers, or the copyists, were trying to correct what they viewed as a mistake. Gergesa was a place of little significance, while Gadara and Gerasa were sizeable towns. On the other hand both Gadara and Gerasa were several miles from the shore of the lake, making the descent by the pigs (in 11–13, assuming this to be part of the original story) very unlikely, unless strong emphasis is placed upon the events taking place in the region of whichever place seems most likely. On these grounds Gergesa seems to be the best placed geographically for the story to be enacted in full. The site of a small unpretentious location may be significant in itself.

Perhaps most likely of all is Cranfield's conclusion that scribes took Mark's reference to Geresenes to necessitate the well-known Gerasa, whereas he meant the smaller town, reflected in modern names Kersa and Koursi, right by the shore.[15]

The real importance of this whole development, in the ministry of Jesus and in Mark's account of it, is that it probably is a deliberate step into Gentile territory. Mark, typically, makes no attempt to explain any inner reason of Jesus for the move. He simply states it, maybe expecting his readers, like the very first witnesses of Jesus, to learn how to perceive the meaning of Jesus' actions. Serious, persistent, perceptive faith is required from the readers also. The reason might be once again to get away from the crowds or to have space to wait on God. In terms of what follows in the story and its significance, however, a deliberate excursion into Gentile territory, at this point of opposition and doubt from his own people, might seem the most likely reason. It also helps us to understand some of the more difficult elements in the story.

As to the story, verses 3–5 need to be seen as an explanatory commentary on verse 2, since verse 6 could lead straight on from verse 2. It does not require the solution of a later insertion. The detail of verses 3–5 is accurate as far as the treatment of the demon-possessed was concerned. It also prepares the way for the contrast described so briefly and powerfully in verse 15 (*sitting . . . dressed and in his right mind*). Something dramatic evidently took place.

The confrontation between Jesus and the demon-possessed man is full of insights. The man, for all his wild and unpredictable behaviour (3–5), is irresistibly drawn to Jesus (6). It is not a meeting of hope however. He fears the worst (7) once Jesus speaks a word of exorcism (8). We should remember that the knowing of the name, accurately, was believed to give one power over the person named, since the name stood for the nature of the person (hence Jesus' giving of extra, typical, names to some of the disciples, as in Mk. 3:16–17). The demons resist Jesus' first command, in which he did not name them, by crying out his name and identity. This plainly fails to overpower Jesus, who now asks for the man's name (9). The response enables the man to describe his condition (9). Since a legion consisted of upward of 6,000 soldiers, the answer does not provide names but it graphically describes his condition, and he seems unable to distinguish himself from the army which

[15] Cranfield, p. 176.

occupies his territory. Yet neither can he break their hold over him, even to asking for them to remain (10). The spirits, however, know they have met a superior power. They (note the use of the plural now in the communication coming from the wretched man) dissociate themselves from their human abode in a bizarre negotiation about where they will go (11–12). Even here Mark draws attention to the power of Jesus. He not only casts them out but also controls their destination. The resultant action proved disastrous for the pigs (13) but entirely liberating for the man (15).

Such a story is, of course, strange territory for scientifically oriented readers to cross. Some readers may regard the section about the pigs as an addition from folklore, noting that Jews would in particular enjoy the selection of pigs, to them unclean animals.Or they may see this as a way of accounting for the upset to a herd of swine, caused by all the commotion of this confrontation. The question there is how well the story holds together as it stands. But Mark, as elsewhere, plainly tells the story as something that happened, from start to finish. If we trust his account as guided by God's spirit we will accept this story too.

Whatever conclusions we reach, we do well to hold it tentatively and humbly. We are considering areas of human life which are largely strange to many in the West (though not to all); but which are still part of the lives of other cultures. We should by now have learned not to dismiss such things as superstition, since our Western civilization is nowadays constantly shown to fall short by contrast with the deeply spiritual perceptions of other cultures. One thinks of the struggle of our medical scientists to re-establish medicine as being not about healing diseases, which we do increasingly well with our advanced technology; but about health and wholeness of the person, including spiritual dimensions, which some African and Asian cultures have known for centuries. It is not difficult for us to perceive the personal nature of much evil in the world: the wholly untypical way that some humans behave under the influence of evil, and the dramatic and sudden way in which some people are set free from such behaviour patterns. At very least we do well to keep an open mind in such matters, recognizing that the conditions described certainly are still with us today, in corporate as well as individual forms. At most we can recognize that we have not found better ways of understanding human evil behaviour which adequately accounts for its bestiality and unexpectedness. Nor have we seen power greater than that of Jesus to deal with it.

In Mark's developing story it is the next verses (14–20) that contain the most telling material. First there is the surprising account (except to those who have learned what the parable of the sower meant, Mk. 4:3–20) of the reaction of the local inhabitants. The swineherds spread the story, the people come running, they see the man at the centre of the story totally cured, and they are awed in the presence of a supernatural happening (14–15). Those who had been present now tell the detail (16).

We are ready for an outburst of faith and discipleship as we reach this point in the story. The opposite happens! They ask him to leave. Mark could hardly spell out more clearly his conviction that even the most powerful of healing miracles cannot, do not, of themselves induce faith or provide a foundation for it. Everything hangs on the openness of the observers to seeing beyond the miracle to the person at its heart. Gentiles, if such they were, are no different from Jews at this point. They too fail to see beyond the sign to the reality.

By strong contrast then, Mark now tells of the response of the healed man. Not only does he believe, he wishes to follow physically, joining the line of disciples to get into the boat (18). Now comes another surprise. Jesus, who plainly does not yet trust his disciples to go out alone preaching, since they barely yet have what he calls faith (4:40), sends 'Legion' straight back home to preach the good news. Is it too much to suggest that this man has already been to the heart of the gospel, in that his experience of exorcism is a dying and rising one? Certainly he has known what the disciples have not yet been willing to discover (4:35–41), namely what it means for one's life and future to be wholly in Jesus' hands and at his disposal, and to have emerged at the other end a 'saved' person. Such, evidently, in the mysterious economy of God, are to be trusted with the message while those with much more background are stumbling forward on a voyage of virgin discovery. The man's message is how the good news has liberated him (5:19). This is the content he promptly delivered (20).

One remaining issue concerns the inconsistency between, for example, 1:34 and 44 on the one hand, where healed people are bidden to be silent about what has happened, and 5:19 in this story where Jesus positively commands the man to preach. We can, of course, simply observe that Jesus is not bound to any rigid patterns of ours, particularly since different circumstances and people require different treatment. Yet we are surely obliged to look for patterns if any should be discernible; and one possibility is that this story of Legion probably happened in Gentile territory. The people who would hear this cured man had none of the presuppositions of Jesus' own people about the shape of the task of the Messiah. They would be free, if they could hear about and respond to a man into whose hands you could place your life absolutely, and feel the force of transcendent power. It is at least a possible explanation. If it is accurate then Mark adds another category of exception to Jesus' reluctance for his work and his status to be spread abroad. Not only religious leaders, disciples and those in dire need may learn the secret. Gentiles too may know, not yet from Jesus' apostles but from one of their own who knows that a total entrusting of your life to Jesus is at the heart of the kingdom's meaning.

Our need to be there where 'Legion' is

This stirring drama, once generalized and applied to our day, may come as a challenge to our Christian witness. In how many ways are people, individually and corporately, living lives which in one form or another reflect the particular elements or the overall state of the man called Legion? Jesus was exposed to such people and needs by his wandering presence. He was ready for the necessary confrontation between good and evil that a captive might be set free. At political, social and economic structural levels, as well as in cultural, family and individual areas of life, the demonstration of the power of Jesus to set free through his disciples is still awaited while too often the disciples are hidden away in our churches or comfortable subcultures. The sense of God's transcendent power in the midst of society, expressing itself in lowly liberating love, is not known because his disciples, the chosen avenues of that powerful love, are largely absent.

Faith means ultimate risk

What is more serious is that such absence from the world's stage may reflect failure on our part truly to live out the heart of discipleship as Mark portrays it (and as Legion experienced it), the total commitment of life, the risking of everything, in trusting ourselves to God in Jesus Christ. Much of our search for more secure ways of being Christian may in fact be escapes from the raw reality which Mark communicates.

9. The nature of true faith (5:21–43)

When Jesus had again crossed over by boat to the other side of the lake, a large crowd gathered round him while he was by the lake. [22]Then one of the synagogue rulers, named Jairus, came there. Seeing Jesus, he fell at his feet [23]and pleaded earnestly with him, 'My little daughter is dying. Please come and put your hands on her so that she will be healed and live.' ²⁴*So Jesus went with him.*

A large crowd followed and pressed around him. ²⁵*And a woman was there who had been subject to bleeding for twelve years.*

²⁶*She had suffered a great deal under the care of many doctors and had spent all she had, yet instead of getting better she grew worse.* ²⁷*When she heard about Jesus, she came up behind him in the crowd and touched his cloak,* ²⁸*because she thought, 'If I just touch his clothes, I will be healed.'* ²⁹*Immediately her bleeding stopped and she felt in her body that she was freed from her suffering.*

³⁰*At once Jesus realised that power had gone out from him. He turned around in the crowd and asked, 'Who touched my clothes?'*

³¹*'You see the people crowding against you,' his disciples answered, 'and yet you can ask, "Who touched me?" '*

³²*But Jesus kept looking around to see who had done it.* ³³*Then the woman, knowing what had happened to her, came and fell at his feet and, trembling with fear, told the whole truth.* ³⁴*He said to her, 'Daughter, your faith has healed you. Go in peace and be freed from your suffering.'*

³⁵*While Jesus was still speaking, some men came from the house of Jairus, the synagogue ruler. 'Your daughter is dead,' they said. 'Why bother the teacher any more?'*

³⁶*Ignoring what they said, Jesus told the synagogue ruler, 'Don't be afraid; just believe.'*

³⁷*He did not let anyone follow him except Peter, James and John the brother of James.* ³⁸*When they came to the home of the synagogue ruler, Jesus saw a commotion, with people crying and wailing loudly.* ³⁹*He went in and said to them, 'Why all this commotion and wailing? The child is not dead but asleep.'* ⁴⁰*But they laughed at him.*

After he put them all out, he took the child's father and mother and the disciples who were with him, and went in where the child was. ⁴¹*He took her by the hand and said to her, 'Talitha koum!' (which means, 'Little girl, I say to you, get up!').* ⁴²*Immediately the girl stood up and walked around (she was twelve years old). At this they were completely astonished.* ⁴³*He gave strict orders not to let anyone know about this, and told them to give her something to eat.*

One of Mark's literary stratagems is the device of fitting one story inside another and interrelating them. We saw it in 3:13–35 where Jesus' confrontation with the scribes from Jerusalem over exorcism (3:22–30) is slotted into an account of the attempt of Jesus' family

113

to get him away from there and take him home (3:20–21, 31–35). We shall find it again in 6:13–30. In Mark its main purpose seems to be to set side by side two or more comparable elements such as the religious leaders' belief and that of Jesus' own family; or two contrasting attitudes, as seems to be the case here.

Jairus and the woman with the haemorrhage could hardly be more different from one another, in sex, status, public recognition, identification in the story itself, approach, and manner of ministry by Jesus. Her simple (even superstitious) faith also contrasts strongly with the attitude of members of Jairus' household once his daughter has died (contrast 5:28 with 5:35 and 5:40, for example). The central element of believing or not believing, in the sense of implicit trust in Jesus himself and the power he bore, is sharply focused once again in these two, interwoven, stories.

In 5:21–23 Mark lightens a little the load of disappointment at the failure of Jewish leaders to welcome Jesus. A synagogue official, Jairus by name, not only welcomes Jesus but physically casts himself on his mercy (22–23). Somehow he has discovered the secret of discipleship. (For a helpful and fascinating account of the significance of the synagogue, and of a synagogue official like Jairus, see Blanch.[16] Enough here to notice the link not only with worship and teaching but with a whole range of community activities, and the high profile of laymen in these activities.) In this story, at last, there is a Jewish leader who in desperation sees that everything depends on trusting himself to Jesus, bearing in mind the possible consequences. There is again plenty of evidence of eye-witness contribution to the account, not least in the number of Semitisms in the language, and the use of Aramaic words at its high point (5:41). The request to lay on hands introduces a practice familiar in Mark's gospel (6:5; 7:32; 8:23, 25). It occurs in the contemporary Jewish contexts of blessings and sacrifices and authorization, but not for healing. The word translated *be healed* in verse 23 could also mean 'be saved'. The former use is common, and we must not make too much of the link, but it is good to note the fact. Some commentators are willing to acknowledge both meanings in this verse.

The crowds set off with Jesus, no doubt fascinated by this unexpected union of the young (largely rejected) rabbi and the synagogue official. It is in this setting that the second story is told.

The plight of the woman is twofold. Her illness is chronic and has cost her all her money. Mark is sharply critical of the doctors. Perhaps as bad, however, was the fact that her particular form of

---

[16] Blanch, pp. 71–73.

disease rendered her ritually unclean (Lv. 15:25–30). This may account in part for her furtive approach (27), coming up behind him. The touching of the garment was related to a common belief at the time that the clothing carried the power of the person (see Acts 19:12).

Her place in the narrative at this point harmonizes with that of the synagogue official. For all the differences between them she, also, has perceived on the basis of reports she had *heard about Jesus* (27, literally 'the things concerning Jesus'), that Jesus will be able to meet what she sees as her basic need physically and ritually. Again the word used could mean 'I will be saved'. Unlike the synagogue official, however, she had to be brought by the two stages to a proper understanding of what relating to Christ means.

Her touch achieves what she had hoped for (28–29), but she had not allowed for the effect on Jesus himself. He knows that power has gone out of him and asks by whom (30), to the amazement of his disciples, in such a crowd (31). But he will not be gainsaid. The woman now comes up in front of him, greatly afraid, and tells him the whole saga (32). Her commitment is complete. She had received *power* already (29): she now receives *peace* (34). And the clue is her *faith* (34).

As the Jewish leadership plots against him, some of his family doubt him, his disciples stumble along more or less perceiving in isolated flashes what is going on, and a synagogue ruler is on his way to discovering what trust in Jesus can mean, this unnamed woman has cut through all the barriers, impelled by need, and by two steps has found the secret of faith – trusting Jesus and telling him all. What he accused the disciples of still not properly having (4:40) he now praises the woman for possessing (5:34). The crescendo of Jesus' miraculous deeds is rising still. It is also another response of faith to encourage Jesus himself, and Mark's readers.

We now return (35–38) to the procession towards Jairus' house. But the delay over the woman has evidently proved disastrous for Jairus. News comes that his daughter is dead and, by contrast with the whole-hearted trust of the woman so recently healed, Jairus' messengers discourage him from allowing Jesus any further (35).

The response of Jesus is somewhat surprising. Unhindered by their remarks he offers a potential reason for failure to believe. '*Don't be afraid; just believe*' (36). The tense suggests that Jairus has already begun to fear the worst. We may well imagine his feelings concerning the delay over the woman with the haemorrhage. 'Believing', however, probably means here what it meant in 4:40. If Jesus remains with you, there is no ground for fear. Trust the person, not the circumstances. Jairus had just witnessed a lonely, sick and shunned woman manage to do this very thing. He must also believe, because Jesus had shown his intention to make the girl well. It is significant that the tense for believing means 'keep on believing'. The sense is, 'Don't go on fearing the worst, but do keep on believing for the best'. The bridge from the one to the other is Jesus' presence to heal the girl. Jairus had begun well (5:22–23). He must not lose faith now.

The by now familiar process of preventing shallow responses by large numbers begins again. Jesus halts the crowd and takes only three of the disciples with him (37), something he would repeat from time to time (9:2, 14:33). The mourners at the house simply mock when Jesus tells them that the girl is sleeping (39–40). The most likely interpretation of the words *'The child is not dead but asleep'* (39), is not that she was in a coma (he had not yet seen her to offer such a diagnosis!) but that if, as reported, she was dead, then it was like sleep for he was on his way to raise her up. This is borne out by his words to the girl, reported by Mark by transliterating the Aramaic used, *'Little girl, I say to you, get up!'* With remarkable restraint and coolness, Mark records that the girl, and he gives her age as twelve years, got up, walked around, and was evidently in a position to eat (42–43). A raising from the dead is the highpoint of this series of miracles, showing the power of Jesus over nature, evil spirits, disease and death. Yet still, on the one side people in large numbers do not believe, and on the other side, Jesus seeks to prevent the spread of the news of these things (43), as though he knew they were not an adequate base for discipleship and so did not wish them to encourage a shallow form of following.

Concerning the question of whether this was a raising from the dead, and whether such things happened in Jesus' ministry, reference should be made to Cranfield's[17] treatment of the question. Over the more general issue of miracles like the four in this section of Mark, two comments by Stuart Blanch are worth pondering. 'The miracles are not the product of a fevered imagination: they are recorded with the utmost restraint and with vivid, circumstantial detail.' 'If, as we believe, God, the creator of the universe and the Lord of all history, is in Christ, then we ought not to be surprised other things happen which transcend what we like to call normal and defeat our efforts to explain them.'[18]

[17] Cranfield, pp. 190–191. [18] Blanch, p. 74.

a. What having faith means

It becomes increasingly clear that the central theme emerging from our examination so far is the nature of true faith. Parables, miracles and exorcisms do not ensure it. Religious education and background does not automatically discover it. Family ties are not enough to create it. Demons, in a curious way, know its basis and oppose it. People in deepest need and desperation seem to find it, by a variety of routes. The disciples are moving towards it, because they have responded to a call and are travelling close to Jesus. Yet their failures show that they are so near yet still not, apparently, there; or not permanently so. For true faith is self-risking trust in Jesus himself. He seeks to restrict the use of names of exaltation for him, usually, ironically, by demons, presumably lest people mistake the signs (parables, healings, exorcisms, raising from the dead, nature miracles) for the reality. Such a mistake will be much less likely later, when the wonder-worker goes to Jerusalem to trial and crucifixion. Then other, and deeper, reasons will be needed for commitment to him. For the moment he is met by opposition from the authorities, by doubt within his family, by a shallow but willing following from the crowd, and by a tenuous commitment from his bewildered disciples. Yet some, out of their utter need, have grasped it – the demon-possessed now free, the diseased woman now well and at peace, the synagogue official whose daughter has been raised from the dead. The secret, once hidden but now revealed, is that God's kingdom is being established in Jesus. The criterion for being in it or out of it is trust in him as a serious, personal continuing commitment.

b. Triumphant, but not triumphalist

Mark is also making plain the fact that Jesus is Lord, over nature, evil spirits, illness and death. Yet triumphalism is absent, both from the language used and the mood described. He is Lord in lowly service of those in need – frightened disciples, fearfully possessed human beings, timid sufferers in the crowd, and beloved children for whose healing faith pleads. Even in the ascription of power and triumph to Christ, Mark is preparing for the story to unfold as a journey of obedience and lowly suffering. This is why belief based on observed miracle and heard parable would not be adequate. It has to be belief in him, a belief which will survive the vicissitudes of the road to Jerusalem, via Gethsemane and Pilate's Hall to the cross and beyond.

c. The power of love and the power of evil

The model for believers today, as we engage in God's mission to his world, points to ways in which we, like Jesus, should be his instruments today for taking on and defeating those forces which terrify, oppress and imprison human beings. They extend from those forces which deliberately aim to destroy moral standards based on God's laws, through all that cheapens, demeans and warps human life, to those who through the structures at their disposal assign individuals and groups to subhuman existences. Working behind all that, and the sinfulness in individual human lives, are the forces of evil in the world. Our Lord's pattern is one of bringing the power of love to bear on all such situations and relationships, loosening the grip of evil, and setting people free. The path for that victory is the lowly one of self-giving as he gave, risking ourselves as he did, dying and rising daily with him. A church so committed is set to be used to establish God's kingdom by his power. Mark wishes us to know that this journey can only pass, in obedience to Christ, via Calvary and the empty tomb, in the footsteps of the Master. But that last sentence is, for the moment, to jump too far ahead.

10. 'Isn't this the carpenter?' (6:1–6a)

Jesus left there and went to his home town, accompanied by his disciples. [2]*When the Sabbath came, he began to teach in the synagogue, and many who heard him were amazed.*

'Where did this man get these things?' they asked. 'What's this wisdom that has been given him, that he even does miracles! [3]*Isn't this the carpenter? Isn't this Mary's son and the brother of James, Joseph, Judas and Simon? Aren't his sisters here with us?' And they took offence at him.*

[4]*Jesus said to them, 'Only in his home town, among his relatives and in his own house is a prophet without honour.'* [5]*He could not do any miracles there, except lay his hands on a few sick people and heal them.* [6]*And he was amazed at their lack of faith.*

The unlikelihood of true faith emerging as response to Jesus now becomes even plainer. One might have expected that even if strangers misunderstood or resisted him, his own local people would support what he was doing. On the contrary, his own people are now added to the impressive list of those who do not accept him or the validity of his claims and activity. Anderson links this passage with 3:6 as being crucially placed, and comments, 'In each case we may perceive the shadow of the cross already falling upon Jesus' ministry'.[19] What is worse, in this case they hear the teaching and see (or know of, 2) the miracles, and not only fail to be led by them to faith in Jesus, but rather use the dismissal of the miracles as their ground for rejecting the teaching and miracles (3). This must have been a very low point indeed for Jesus (4). Low also for his disciples. He does no miracle there, not because a certain degree of faith in people wanting to be helped is 'part of the cure', but because the atmosphere of faith is an essential part of the kingdom being established. Jesus is not free to be a 'magic worker'. As the word will not produce spiritual growth where the capacity for response is barren, choked or scorched (4:1–20), so the presence of Jesus will not produce miracles in the atmosphere of total unbelief and resistance. Yet even here, it is the need of some, perhaps, that produces in them an attitude he would not refuse (5).

The authenticity of this story seems well supported by its more daring characteristics. There are the uncomplimentary references to his kinfolk, the description of him as '*Mary's son*' (3),[20] alluding to his birth as from Mary, with no mention of Joseph, and the self-identification of Jesus as a prophet when by the time the gospel was written he was known to be so very much more. Then there are the breath-taking (for the gospel writers) statements that Jesus *could not do any miracles there*, and that he was amazed at their unbelief (he who had known when goodness passed out of him through his robe when a woman touched his clothing from behind in the crowd! 5:25–34).

As to these details, Mark has already been frank about the failure of natural connections to ensure faith (3:31–35). The linking of Jesus with Mary and not Joseph, even if Joseph was, as seems likely, dead, was a derogatory way of writing about a person, but may have had the point of defending the belief in the virgin birth of Jesus, to which both Luke (Lk. 1:26–38) and Matthew (Mt. 1:18–25) give strong testimony. Jesus' reference to himself as prophet certainly uses familiar sayings of the time, but they do not include the person of a prophet. Was Jesus choosing as modest a self-description as he believed they might be capable of perceiving and accepting on the evidence? If so, they showed themselves not to be capable even of that. They not only did not accept him, they were scandalized by him (the force of *took offence at*, 3). Something about his being one of them became the ground not for supporting

[19] Anderson, p. 157.
[20] The best attested and most likely because most difficult of the variations in this text and in the synoptic gospels.

119

him but for being offended by him.[21]

This leaves only the remarkable frankness of verse 5, softened by Matthew (Mt. 9:58), about Jesus not 'being able' to perform miracles, and about his marvelling at their unbelief. On the 'inability' Mark plainly does not intend that to be taken absolutely, as 5b shows. Rather he is underlining the way in which Jesus does not stand apart from individuals and groups, 'throwing miracles at them'. He becomes deeply involved in relationships with them, and the miracle is performed within the context of the relationships, both corporate and individual. Where that relationship is one of near total animosity on the part of the crowd, the setting is not right for healing intended to provide an opportunity for perception of who he was. This, clearly they were not ready for.

The attitude of amazement occurs only here and in the account of the faith of the centurion in Matthew 8:10 and Luke 7:9. In that case faith was unpredictable, as was the rejection by his own folk at Nazareth. We may see Mark here underlining both the humanity of Jesus, and the total indefensibility of the response of his people.

a. Choosing the right way forward

We may reflect that the human mind is virtually able to find reasons for defending any attitude, word or action. Rather than perceiving the depth of his teaching, the compassion of his actions to the needy, and the significance of his having come home to them again, Jesus' kinfolk chose to belittle him by reference to his background, and to their familiarity with him and his family. All life's coins are two sided. The better informed carry greater responsibility to make a proper response, but they also have more detail with which to manufacture their resistance. The learned can find reasons for dismissing forms of spirituality which offend or even threaten them. The untrained can use their experience as grounds for rejecting the results of rational thought. Alternatively the learned can find their understanding enlivened by a spirituality with resources which include but are more than the purely rational, and the unlearned can find a firmer content to their spirituality through the proper use of reason. Yet trained minds cannot just accept every spiritual claim that is made, and the unsophisticated must not fall for every idea offered. So how are we to proceed?

In Mark's gospel those who 'got it wrong' (which means most of the people in the story) did so because they based their judg-

---

[21] See 1 Pet. 2:6–8 for the significance of this idea with the root meaning of 'stumbling' or 'tripping' over something.

ments on too narrow a foundation. In this story before us the people of Jesus' own area reached conclusions based only on his home and family background (2–3). The gospels as a whole show this same narrowness of criteria in almost everyone Jesus meets.

John the Baptist, in the tradition of Elijah, is expecting a heavily judgmental ministry from the one whose coming he announces (Mt. 3:7–10; Lk. 3:7–14). No wonder he later has doubts about whether Jesus was God's anointed one (Lk. 7:18–20; Mt. 11:2–3). The reply of Jesus (Lk. 7:22–23; Mt. 11:4–6) shows that it is not he who is falling short of God's purposes, but that it is John the Baptist whose presuppositions are wrong – too narrowly determined by the prophetic past. In the same way the scribes and the Pharisees set limits to what the anointed one should do (see Mk. 2:1–12 as an example, and 3:22 as the only conclusion left to them on the basis of their preconceived notions).

Jesus' own family tested him by ordinary standards of behaviour and feared for his sanity (Mk. 3:21). The disciples are well-founded enough to follow him when called (Mk. 3:13–14; Mt. 10:1; Lk. 6:13), but not enough to perceive the meaning of his teaching (Mk. 4:10; Mt. 13:10; Lk. 8:9), nor to believe that to be with him was to be safe (Mk. 4:38; Mt. 8:25; Lk. 8:24). Even the demons who know who he is are not able to adopt the proper response (Mk. 1:23–24; Lk. 4:33–34; Mk. 1:34; Lk. 4:41; Mk. 3:11; Mk. 5:6–8). The desperate who are healed come nearest to understanding but do not yet grasp all that he is (Mk. 2:1–5; Mt. 9:1–2; Lk. 5:18–20; Mk. 5:21–24, 35–42; Mt. 9:18–19, 23–25; Lk. 8:41–42, 49–56). What help are we to derive from that?

The answer is not a fixed one, but will be a continual source of new challenge and therefore new growth. The religious leaders were right to be led by their knowledge of history and prophecy from their past, but wrong to interpret it too narrowly and to be unwilling to be open to the new things God was doing among them now. Jesus' family were right in their concern for his health and reputation but wrong to have forgotten the likely implications of his birth and its attendant circumstances. The disciples were right to be bold enough to follow him but wrong not to see that he was the secret of everything God was doing to establish his kingdom. The evil spirits were right to perceive who he was and wrong not to bow down and worship. Those who came aware of their need were right to risk themselves by trusting him. They, at least, are not to be faulted for their limited assumptions. As with the disciples, the basis on which they began could prove adequate for the future. They knew their need. They believed in his ability to meet that need. They took the step of trusting to the limit of

121

their understanding in relation to their need, and were healed.

The secret seems to be not to choose any one of the good responses listed above, still less simply to avoid the errors. It is somehow to hold together all that is positive, but to do so in healthy tension. A knowledge of what God has done in the past, and of what he has promised to do for the future is obviously important, since he is not inconsistent. What he does now and in the future can be expected to have continuity with what he did before. Our theological beliefs and perceptions are important here, also. Yet our interpretation of his actions and promises needs to be constantly tested and reviewed, not least in the light of what he seems to be doing now, and also in view of the changing circumstances around us. Our own experiences, and the experiences of others provide helpful insight by which to judge this matter. The interplay of all these factors, at an individual and corporate Christian level, provides the basis for Christian judgment and growth. Its point of reference is Jesus, who is better understood through our knowledge of Christian history and doctrine, and by our faith experiences and cultural perceptions today. Jesus, however, is also larger than them all, and will constantly shatter all our categories and formulae, because he is greater than them all.

Had all the people in the gospel stories paid more attention to Jesus, as the unique focus of God's revelation, they would have fared much better. They judged him by their history, theology, tradition, experience, culture and expectations. The message of the gospels is that all those areas of life are to be tested by him. This is why the needy and the disciples came nearest to understanding, for their circumstances pointed them in that direction; and why the religious leaders were further away, because they were not willing to allow Jesus to be the focal point for God's revelation. They wanted all new patches to fit old coats, any new wine to fit into old wineskins (Mk. 2:21–22). Jesus said it was not possible in the kingdom of God. It is never possible, as both Christian history and experience make clear. So many of our divisions within Christianity relate directly to this problem, both as to structures and practices. So much of our dulled spirituality is caused by constraints from the past upon the present. Sadly, the result is too often for us, as for those before us in the passage, that he is 'not able to perform miracles' among us, because of our unbelief.

b. Problems of witness in our culture

Christians today may have difficulty both in holding on to faith, and in communicating it, because of obstacles in the present state of our culture similar to those in Jesus' time. There are certain 'canons of acceptability' which influence people subconsciously, and make it harder or easier for them to accept our ideas presented to them. Such untested impressions include, 'If you can't prove it you can't know it', 'Only this life matters', 'You have to put yourself first if you want to survive', and 'Life is what it appears to be'. These and many other assumptions stand in the way of people accepting and believing the good news about Jesus.

Another phase of Mark's story thus reaches its end, with heavy concentration on the single issue of how people do or do not come to faith in the presence of the ministry of Jesus in establishing the kingdom of God. Now the work of missionary outreach must be stepped up.

11. Jesus sends out the Twelve (6:6b–13)

Then Jesus went round teaching from village to village. [7]Calling the Twelve to him, he sent them out two by two and gave them authority over evil spirits.

[8]These were his instructions: 'Take nothing for the journey except a staff – no bread, no bag, no money in your belts. [9]Wear sandals but not an extra tunic. [10]Whenever you enter a house, stay there until you leave that town. [11]And if any place will not welcome you or listen to you, shake the dust off your feet when you leave, as a testimony against them.'

[12]They went out and preached that people should repent. [13]They drove out many demons and anointed many sick people with oil and healed them.

It seems best to include verse 6b in this section. A case has been made out for linking it to 6a, as though Jesus' response to rejection in his home town was to go to the surrounding villages. There is no hint of this in the wording, however, and it harmonizes better with the overall theme of discipleship to see Jesus now preaching in the villages around and then sending the Twelve out in twos as an extension of his ministry and their experience. Hargreaves suggests that the theme of Mark 1–5 is 'He called them', and of 6–16 is 'He sent them'. In general terms that clearly depicts the change of direction at this point, as long as we remember that he will increasingly take time to teach them specifically, and that there will be times for them to be alone (see 6:31 as the expression of that aim).

Mark's version of verse 6b is much briefer than the apparent parallel in Matthew (Mt. 9:35–38). Mark stresses the teaching, consistent with this report of Jesus' words in 1:38.

He sends the Twelve out (6:7–9), as he had promised to do in 3:14–15. The time of initial teaching is over. Now, despite all their limitations, they are to put it into practice by telling others. They go out in twos (a Jewish custom reflected in Lk. 7:18, Jn. 1:35 and 37, and later in Mk. 11:1 and 14:13). Later, in Acts, we read of Paul working with Barnabas and with Silas.[22] It is no more a law for Christian activity than anything else in the list which follows, but it was a reminder of their frailty and humanity and of the importance of fellowship in Christian mission.

He *gave them authority* (7). Again their appointment as apostles (3:13–15) is in the background. Whatever they do will be effective only in so far as it is an extension of his work. They had no natural authority over evil spirits. He had. Mark assumes (following 6b, and prior to 12) that readers understand that the Twelve were to proclaim as well as to cast out evil spirits.

There is considerable difficulty over comparison of the accounts of Jesus' instructions over provisions in Mark, Matthew and Luke. Normally Mark's reads as the earliest, least polished and therefore often the most difficult of the gospels (see Mk. 6:5 and Mt. 13:58 as an example). This may of course be the case here, too, since a total prohibition of the items mentioned in verses 8–9 is simpler than the reflective one Mark provides. On the other hand allowing a staff and sandals is a softening of the regime. The truth is that we do not know why there is this difference, unless for once Mark, seeing how applicable these instructions would be for travelling preachers of his day, also recognized that they could not go without sandals and staff. But that is guesswork, and it would be out of keeping with his usual passionate holding to what he received, however difficult it was.

Above all we must avoid being so taken up with the detail that we miss the point. They are not to make provision for a long journey for this is a comparatively short and urgent task. Preaching the kingdom left no time for fuss about personal well-being. It took priority over such concerns and yet, in a strange way, contained assurance that such concerns would be taken care of (see Mt. 6:25–34, especially 33: 'But [instead of a variety of worldly cares listed] seek first his kingdom and his righteousness, and all these things will be given to you as well'). Kingdom preachers were expected to live by the kingdom message they proclaimed.

The same urgency attached to the preachers' accommodation (6:10–11). They were to stay where they were first received, pre-

---

[22] See Acts 3:1–10; 8:14–25; 11:30; 12:25; 14:21–28; 15:40 – 17:14.

sumably meaning that they must neither seek better treatment, nor move to more comfortable surroundings if they were offered. Neither were they to stay in a place where their message was not welcomed. There was no time for that. The injunction to shake the dust off their feet relates to the Jewish custom of doing so whenever they left a heathen area. To do this in relation to other Jews was therefore a dramatic way of spelling out the seriousness of this rejection and of the judgment which they were courting, perhaps with the hope that they might even then change their minds. The tone throughout is one of urgency.

Mark says little about the content of the preaching (6:12–13), but the idea of the disciples being an extension of Jesus' mission means that we need only one indicator of the substance of the message. The reference to repentance reminds us at once of Jesus' preaching, recorded in 1:15. They preached what their master preached.

Reference to anointing with oil occurs in the New Testament only here and in James 5:14 in association with miraculous healing. (In Lk. 10:34 the Good Samaritan uses it as part of the medical treatment of the man attacked by robbers.) The oil evidently symbolizes the gracious and powerful word of healing which accompanied it and which healed people. The change of tense in the verb for anointing may suggest that the healings were the occasional events which took place in the context of the major task of preaching the word of the kingdom. This certainly would be in harmony with Mark's emphasis throughout.

Overall, the impression created by verses 12–13, and verse 30, is that the disciples succeeded in what they were sent to do. One more stage in their training was completed.

The time to risk oneself, do something, and grow

It is difficult to exaggerate the risk Jesus took in sending his disciples out to teach and heal. The impression of them created by Mark so far falls well short of complimentary! They do not understand his teaching (4:10). They do not trust his will or power to protect them (4:28). They are not sensitive to his extraordinary perception (5:31). Yet they are sent out, albeit in pairs, to teach, heal and exorcize.

The implication of this act of Jesus, as of Mark's teaching as a whole so far, is that no amount of hearing, teaching or observing miracles or even being with Jesus, is enough. They must risk themselves in dependence on the gospel and the power that accompanies it. There is, of course, enormous satisfaction and challenge in

125

hearing the word and seeing the mighty deed. But the real test, and the true moment of growth, arrives when I myself am able to speak a word of witness, or do some gospel deed, in which my reputation, my being depends on there being a power there to sustain me.

This truth applies at different levels. In individual experience too many Christians have few, if any, non-Christian friends. We spend our days, whenever the choice is ours, with believers. As a result we rarely put the gospel to the test as the disciples were having to do. We go for safety in the faith, while trying to follow a Lord who risked himself in incarnation and all that followed it. We build up our security while serving the Lord who went by death to resurrection! The result is a narrowing of the power of the gospel, and of our perception of its possibilities. Our plea that we need more training is met by the simple observation that the disciples needed more training – much more training; yet they were sent out, and were effective.

There is a corporate parallel in churches where our lives are so often centred upon ourselves, albeit including the attempt to 'bring people in'. This passage is about 'being sent out'. Churches may be mistaken who provide for every part of the cultural life of their members. They need to be exposed more to life outside the church, where they will prove the power of the gospel rather than the safety of the church.

It is also true at the level of apologetics and Christian participation in society as a whole. The advance of learning, the development of culture, the facing of huge national and international problems, the outright opposition to spiritual values are often viewed by Christians as threats to be avoided, or issues to be involved with as little as possible. Our real interests are spiritual! Yet if we transpose the setting of Jesus to our international, multi-cultural, media-linked global society, then great new developments are the contexts for proclaiming the message, offering healing and casting out demons. Our failure to address the biggest modern issues, from a proper gospel basis, may well be one major reason for our not being as effective as we ought. A safe church is rarely an influential one.

Mark 6:14 – 8:26
4. Missionary outreach beyond Galilee in spite of the disciples' limitations

1. The death of John the Baptist (6:14–29)

King Herod heard about this, for Jesus' name had become well known. Some were saying, 'John the Baptist has been raised from the dead, and that is why miraculous powers are at work in him.'

15Others said, 'He is Elijah.'

And still others claimed, 'He is a prophet, like one of the prophets of long ago.'

16But when Herod heard this, he said, 'John, the man I beheaded, has been raised from the dead!'

17For Herod himself had given orders to have John arrested, and he had him bound and put in prison. He did this because of Herodias, his brother Philip's wife, whom he had married. 18For John had been saying to Herod, 'It is not lawful for you to have your brother's wife.' 19So Herodias nursed a grudge against John and wanted to kill him. But she was not able to, 20because Herod feared John and protected him, knowing him to be a righteous and holy man. When Herod heard John, he was greatly puzzled; yet he liked to listen to him.

21Finally the opportune time came. On his birthday Herod gave a banquet for his high officials and military commanders and the leading men of Galilee. 22When the daughter of Herodias came in and danced, she pleased Herod and his dinner guests.

The king said to the girl, 'Ask me for anything you want, and I'll give it to you.' 23And he promised her with an oath, 'Whatever you ask I will give you, up to half my kingdom.'

24She went out and said to her mother, 'What shall I ask for?'

'The head of John the Baptist,' she answered.

25At once the girl hurried in to the king with the request: 'I want you to give me right now the head of John the Baptist on a platter.'

26The king was greatly distressed, but because of his oaths and his dinner guests, he did not want to refuse her. ²⁷*So he immediately sent an executioner with orders to bring John's head. The man went, beheaded John in the prison,* ²⁸*and brought back his head on a platter. He presented it to the girl, and she gave it to her mother.* ²⁹*On hearing of this, John's disciples came and took his body and laid it in a tomb.*

Lest the missionary outreach of the disciples should give the impression that opposition to the kingdom message was now abating, Mark introduces here a reminder of how the great forerunner of Jesus, John the Baptist, met his end. This interlude will make clear that gospel effectiveness does not, as we at times imagine, produce widespread warm response. It can sharpen the opposition's attack in a most bitter and callous way. In this one story in his gospel which does not focus on Jesus, Mark both hints at what is coming for Jesus, and shows that it is the way of true discipleship to Jesus also.

The story has details which prepare us for the trial, condemnation and execution of Jesus. The involvement of Herodias is also reminiscent of the Old Testament accounts of Jezebel and Esther (1 Ki. 16:29–34; 19:1–3). This does not necessarily mean that such considerations 'shaped' the story, however.

It is not surprising that Herod received reports of what was happening about Jesus (6:14). This is Herod Antipas, ruler of Galilee and Perea from 4 BC to AD 39. Mark gives him the honorary title of *king* (a gesture from Rome or simply popular usage?) while Matthew and Luke designate him with more formal correctness as 'tetrarch' (Mt. 14:1; Lk. 9:7).

The text does not say what Herod heard, whether about the disciples' mission in particular, or rather the ministry of Jesus in general. The context, following 6:12–13, implies the former: the reference to Jesus' name (6:14) suggests the latter. There is no strong reason to reject the possibility that it was both. Most important is the comment of Anderson that 'The *name* (cf. also 9:37–39, 41; 13:6, 13) is synonymous with the total person as expressed in his word and deed.'[1]

Although some commentators prefer 'Some people were saying . . .' in verse 14, it seems wise to follow the majority of manuscripts in translating 'Herod was saying . . .'. It does not fit so well with verse 15 ('Others . . . others . . . .'), but it does focus attention on the troubled conscience of Herod, and he is the central figure in the explanation of John's death. John did not perform miracles, as far as we know, but it would not be surprising for

---

[1] Anderson, p. 167.

people to attribute miracles to a John the Baptist who had returned from the dead. Herod knew he had done wrong in ordering John the Baptist's death. The news of Jesus' preaching and miracles brought it back to the surface again. The crowds, or their spokesmen, saw Jesus as Elijah or one of the prophets (Mal. 3:1; 4:5; Dt. 18:15).

Herod's statement, *'John . . . has been raised from the dead!'* (16) introduces us to the story of how John the Baptist died. Verses 17–20 tell of Herod's relationship to John the Baptist, with the ominous insertion in verse 19 of Herodias' vindictive attitude to John.

There is a complication about the plot behind this part of the story. Josephus (*Antiquities* xviii 136) records that Herodias was married to Herod, the son of Herod the Great and Mariamne II. Mark says she was married to Philip. The best known member of the family by that name is Philip the Tetrarch, who in fact married Salome, Herodias' daughter, who by her dancing and request played so crucial a part in Mark's record. The name Philip is omitted by some ancient manuscripts. R. P. Martin assumes that the Herod to whom Herodias was married was also called Philip.[2] We should not lightly assume that Mark has 'got it wrong'.

John the Baptist had consistently (*had been saying*, 18) told Herod that he had broken holy law by taking his brother's wife (Lv. 18:16; 20:21). Herod had rejected his first wife, the daughter of Aretas, King of Arabia and, according to Jospehus had suffered military defeat as a result. Herodias had deserted or divorced her husband in order to be with Herod. John had not let them forget this, or the wrongness of it, yet they reacted differently.

Herod imprisoned John, partly to keep him safe (17, 20) and also because he did not wish such public criticism by a renowned prophet and preacher. Yet he did not wish to put him to death, as Herodias did (19). Rather he listened to him often with a mixture of fear, enjoyment and inner disturbance (the best reading, though not in the majority of manuscripts). Matthew's addition of fear of the crowd as a motive (Mt. 14:5) also fits in here. The mixture is convincing in relation to Herod's character, as we shall see. The link with Agrippa in Acts 26:3 points in the same direction. But to listen to and provide protection for this *righteous and holy man* (20) was not enough when the battle became fiercest. Sides had to be taken for or against; and Herod's middle way of indecision proved wholly inadequate.

The scene portrayed in verses 19, 21–29 is reminiscent of the

[2] Martin, *Action*, p. 47.

Esther story, but with a villainous rather than a noble queen determining the way forward. A conflict between Tiberias (the assumed setting since Herod's main residence was there), and Machaerus where Josephus says that John the Baptist died, is not necessary. Certainly the speed with which John is despatched requires the feast and his prison to be adjacent. But there is no indomitable reason against Herod giving this banquet in Machaerus. The same is true about the bizarre sight of a princess dancing before such a gathering. One has only to examine 'normal' behaviour in the Herod family, and to link it with the scheming character of Herodias, whose opportunity it was (21), to accept the likelihood of this scenario. Martin quotes words of T. W. Manson about Herodias, that 'the only place where her marriage certificate could safely be written was on the back of the death warrant of John'.[3]

Herod's foolish or doubtless semi-intoxicated promise to the girl recalls Old Testament passages like Esther 5:3, 6; 7:2; and 1 Kings 13:8. This does not cast doubt on the accuracy of Mark's account, but it does raise questions about the reliability of the rulers involved. Herod could not have given his kingdom away like this, of course, but it would be wrong to take the promise literally anyway.

What it did do was to provide Herodias with the chance, through an obedient daughter who seems to have added the macabre detail of the head being brought in *on a platter* (25). She was a worthy daughter of her mother! John's life was swiftly brought to an end, and the disciples of John claimed and buried the body. Matthew (14:12) records that they went and told Jesus what they had done. In Palestine they would be less and less a significant separate group.

a. *The price a disciple may have to pay*

Mark's portrayal of discipleship has now reached its deepest point, not surpassed until the account of Jesus' own death. The one who 'prepared the way' has not only not been set free by Jesus, he has met his death because of his faithfulness. We may begin to see now why Jesus does not encourage discipleship purely on the basis of hearing his teaching, observing his miracles, following with the crowd. The demands are too great for that. To be a disciple, as the second half of the gospel will make clear, means following Jesus all the way to the cross and beyond. As R. P. Martin[4] has argued

---

[3] Martin, *Action*, p. 48, quoting T. W. Manson, *The Servant Messiah* (Cambridge University Press, 1953), p. 40.

[4] Martin, *Mark*.

cogently, John the Baptist is not just the forerunner of Jesus. As Mark presents him, he is the prototype too.

b. True faith is for dark days also

Mark may well have been sending this message to readers of his own time. There has always been a tendency in Christianity to lay too much stress on the miraculous, the exciting, the triumphal nature of Christian experience. The difficulty in practice is that while such a presentation is initially attractive and effective, especially for young people, it often proves inadequate to cope with the wide spectrum of life's experiences and of human personality. The result is either that the particular body of Christians narrows down the life and expectations of its members, or that it loses them as their experiences broaden out, but replaces them with a steady supply of new members in at the other end. Successes are publicized: failures are not.

Mark's picture is meant to correct such a one-sided view. John the Baptist's discipleship was not like that. Nor, much more significantly, was the pattern of Jesus' obedient sonship. With all his evident power and perception he goes steadfastly to Jerusalem and to death, because the realities of evil and goodness, hate and love, required it. John the Baptist's death shows that no shallow triumphalism will do. Nor will faithful witness always bring praise. There is a price to pay; for John the Baptist it was the ultimate price.

What does discipleship of Jesus offer, then? It offers a sense that one is living according to the truth, is walking with Jesus, is giving oneself in love to the service of God in the world. The reward is not success, or triumphalist patterns, but the knowledge that one is faithfully serving God's purposes in the world.

2. Jesus feeds the five thousand (6:30–44)

The apostles gathered round Jesus and reported to him all they had done and taught. ³¹Then, because so many people were coming and going that they did not even have a chance to eat, he said to them, 'Come with me by yourselves to a quiet place and get some rest.'

³²So they went away by themselves in a boat to a solitary place.

The introductory section, verses 30–32, is full of words typical of Mark. *Apostles* (30) is a notable exception, occurring only here in Mark, since in 3:14 it probably ought not to be present. There are two sides to Mark's references to their work in pairs, on which they now report (with excitement) to Jesus.

131

On the one side the title 'apostle' – and it seems better to take it as a title, rather than a more general equivalent of missionary – draws attention to their special role. Paul's later defence of being appointed by Jesus as an apostle,[5] shows how highly regarded such a description was. In Mark the Twelve are now so described. They are honoured.

Yet, on the other side, the origin of the word, as well as Mark's brief account of their work, shows another aspect of the story. Assuming the background to be the Hebrew *saliah* (Aramaic *sᵉlîha*), then the 'sent one' is not so much the military force or colonizing party as the authorized representative of an individual, corporation or community. As such they have a particular commission after which their authorization lapses. They are dependent on the commission from the commissioning person. It is his status which counts, not theirs. As far as they are concerned it is the function, the role that is important, not the status. That his position and commission are crucial is shown by their coming back to him to report (30), and by his subsequent decision to take them away for some rest.

One has to add to this how little Mark makes of this first excursion into ministry by the apostles. It is almost as though more important than what they had done is their coming back to him to report it. Can Mark be saying that even preaching, teaching, healing and casting out demons do not, of themselves, make those who do them disciples of Jesus? The clue is in their being sent by him, doing what they were instructed to do by him, returning to him and then staying with him until sent out again. All these other things they have been doing may be fruits of true discipleship but they are not its root. The root is attachment to Jesus himself, from whom the disciples' life comes.

Jesus now continues their training (31) with the decision that they must get away from the crowds flocking after them. Maybe the disciples would have liked nothing better than to stay. Maybe, on the other hand, they were weary and needed a break. Certainly there is a sharpness in their treatment of Jesus over how to cope with the crowds (36–37). Whatever his motives, to protect them from over-exposure and excitement at their new-found power, or to save them from exhaustion, he tries to get them away.

a. Function matters more than status

The meaning of 'apostle' has considerable significance for today. It

[5] 1 Cor. 15:8–12; 2 Cor. 12:12; Gal. 1:1.

is generally agreed that all ministry and mission by Christians is an extension of Jesus' own ministry and mission. Christians share, that is, in the apostolic mission given to the whole church, which has been sent into the world (Jn. 17:18; 20:21). It is also clear from the study above that even the element of 'being sent' focuses attention on the status of the sender, not of the sent one. The stress as far as the apostle is concerned is on function, not status. Indeed the commission relates to the task itself. The Twelve had a particular function, as companions, eye-witnesses and authorities on his ministry. Yet in most of our denominations we seem more committed to 'status' definitions than to 'function' definitions, to 'structures' rather than to 'tasks', and to 'self-preservation' rather than to 'ministry' and 'mission' to others. It is not that status is somehow wrong, or that structures are evil. It is simply that they play too large a part in our thinking and activity, while function and service play too little.

b. The humanity and fallibility of the disciples

Before moving to the next stage of Mark's story we do well to notice how Jesus reminded the disciples of their frailty and humanity. They had been used. They were excited. They were also probably tired. Jesus helped them to face their humanity without being ashamed of it. He seemed to have resources hidden from them, as the feeding of the crowd and the walking on the water were to show. They were not to imagine that they could keep going endlessly. They needed quiet, and re-creation, and more opportunities to learn. So do we.

³³*But many who saw them leaving recognized them and ran on foot from all the towns and got there ahead of them.* ³⁴*When Jesus landed and saw a large crowd, he had compassion on them, because they were like sheep without a shepherd. So he began teaching them many things.*

³⁵*By this time it was late in the day, so his disciples came to him. 'This is a remote place,' they said, 'and it's already very late.* ³⁶*Send the people away so that they can go to the surrounding countryside and villages and buy themselves something to eat.'*

³⁷*But he answered, 'You give them something to eat.'*

They said to him, 'That would take eight months of a man's wages! Are we to go and spend that much on bread and give it to them to eat?'

³⁸*'How many loaves do you have?' he asked. 'Go and see.'*

When they found out, they said, 'Five – and two fish.'

133

[39]Then Jesus directed them to have all the people sit down in groups on the green grass. [40]So they sat down in groups of hundreds and fifties. [41]Taking the five loaves and the two fish and looking up to heaven, he gave thanks and broke the loaves. Then he gave them to his disciples to set before the people. He also divided the two fish among them all. [42]They all ate and were satisfied, [43]and the disciples picked up twelve basketfuls of broken pieces of bread and fish. [44]The number of the men who had eaten was five thousand.

In verses 33–34 the keenness of the crowds emerges. Galilee is so small, and the boats used so minute that a crowd by land could often reach their destination more quickly than the sailors. Quite where Mark thought this happened is not clear. Luke says Bethsaida (Lk. 9:10), but the favoured text of Mark 6:45 has Bethsaida as their destination, after performing the miracle of the feeding, and going 'to the other side' (RSV) of the lake to get there. Some manuscripts omit 'to the other side' and that would solve the problem. In any case Mark, as we have seen, is not very interested in exact geographical locations. The action is what matters to him.

The action is that the crowds are greatly attracted to Jesus (a feature of Mark's gospel) and that Jesus does not turn them away, even if he seeks at times to protect his disciples from them (31). The word to describe his attitude to them, translated *had compassion* (34) or 'was filled with pity', means to be inwardly moved so as to have to do something about it. It is the word used in the story of the Good Samaritan (Lk. 10:33), and is in effect the hinge on which the whole parable turns. It is interesting to note that this verb is used only to describe Jesus himself (Mk. 8:2; Mt. 9:36; 14:14; 15:32), or to explain the actions of people in his parables who resemble him (Mt. 18:27; Lk. 10:33; 15:2). Are the gospel writers suggesting that this kind of compassion has its source in Jesus alone, or at very least that he is the supreme example of it? Certainly, however much his disciples needed rest and training, Jesus would not, could not turn this crowd away because *they were like sheep without a shepherd* (34). The warmth of that compassion is deeply moving.[6] The need of others is a genuine motive for Christian service.

By contrast (35), and maybe with some impatience, the disciples notice how late it is getting, how many people there are, and how far they are from adequate sources of food. The crowds seem not to be noticing. Jesus seems not to be caring. The disciples, however, were maybe wanting their private time with Jesus, or even just a

[6] For the background of the imagery see Nu. 27:17; 1 Ki. 22:17; 2 Ch. 18:16; Ezk. 34:5.

quiet rest. They advise Jesus to send the crowds away (36).

They could hardly have been ready for his response. They have preached, healed, exorcized. Now he invites them to copy his power still further. *'You give them something to eat'* (37). Their reaction shows how little, even now, they are willing to trust him to do the unusual thing. They enquire, incredulously and impossibly, whether they are meant to go and spend the huge amount of money required to buy so much food (37). The scene is thus simply and sharply set for the miracle of feeding (38–44).

Many different interpretations of the feeding are offered, both about what happened and about what it means. As to the former, apart from the acceptance of miracle, the explanations range from people being inspired by an act of Jesus to share their food with one another, to the idea that it was a sacramental meal with each one receiving only a morsel.

The difficulty facing such explanations is that so much in Mark's account points to his intention to describe a miracle. The sharpness of the disciples' question in verse 37 would surely have been soft-ened if a miraculous element was being inserted at a later date into a story of the kind outlined above. There are other elements which could be typical of, and suggest, an eye-witness account, especially the details of the organization and the place. There is also the way the need of the people is set out by the disciples. They were without food to meet appetites. If they had food to share there was no problem. If they had no food then sacramental fare would not do. Mark says Jesus fed them from five loaves and two fish (38). Whether or not he could do this is not so much a question about the text as about the presuppositions we bring to it about what Jesus could do or did.

The second question, about the meaning of the miraculous feed-ing, is more complicated. The link with the manna in the wilderness (Ex. 16) must have struck many Jewish readers. So is the parallel with the last supper in Mark 14:22–26. This does not necessarily mean, however, that Mark wrote such a story because of the other two, or that details are included from one or other as additions to what actually happened. If God's grace is revealed in the feeding of his people then one would expect both consistency and likenesses in the various occurrences. On the other hand, this does not exclude the possibility of describing what actually happened in terms related to the manna and the last supper. But these distinctions are impor-tant for a proper understanding of what Mark says actually took place. Ideas of the people in rows (39–40) as students of a rabbi, or as soldiers in a revolution (partly dependent on Jn. 6:14–15) are possible insights into the seating arrangements, but they do not spring naturally from Mark's account, where the crowds have come because they like to hear Jesus, and where the seating by rows simply enables the feeding to happen tidily and in order.

The description of Jesus taking bread, blessing God with eyes heavenward and the distributing, fits the normal pattern of a father at a Jewish meal (41). The record that they had enough (42) reinforces the view that it was a proper meal. The twelve baskets full, as a leftover more than they began with, can be both physically true and therefore reflective of God's gracious ways with the kingdom. That the baskets here are described by a word for a particularly Jewish kind, while in 8:8 and 20 the word is peculiarly about what Gentiles used will be relevant then. For the moment Jesus has provided enough for their bodily needs, not a messianic banquet but sufficient for the continuing of the journey through the wilderness to the last supper and beyond. Provision has been made, but the ministry has a long way to go yet. So has the understanding of the disciples, as is clear from the next event.

c. *The flexibility of grace*

It is worth noting that things did not turn out as even Jesus planned. The idea of withdrawing from the crowds was good and necessary. But he had not allowed for their keenness to hear or, if John's account covers Mark's also, their determination to give him political authority. In this gospel the turn of events underlines the hidden momentum evident throughout. God is establishing his kingdom. Even Jesus has to adjust according to new developments. The result is a major miracle of divine provision, reminding the perceptive of the manna in the wilderness, preparing the committed for the journey ahead by way of the last supper. And all because of an unscheduled event!

Strategies, plans, time charts and objectives are all necessary in the on-going life of the church, but they must all be made as possible rather than essential developments. Some of the most effective moments come when events do not work out as planned, and we are completely wrong-footed but trust God in the unusual circumstance. In 1746, when the Methodist Revival in England was at its most uncertain, John Wesley testified at the Methodist Conference, 'We desire barely to follow Providence, as it gradually opens'. His continuing in that spirit is one of the secrets of Methodism's establishment and growth. There is about Christianity at its strongest a clear sense of our not being able to control what happens around and to us.

d. Love, not ideology, should determine all our actions

We should not miss the fact that Jesus' compassion for the crowd, an inner perturbation which led to action, caused him both to teach them spiritually and mentally, and to feed them physically. The determining factor in this was not his plan for the occasion, since it was not part of the expected itinerary. The reason for his action along these two lines of teaching and feeding, was his perception of their need. Doctrinaire positions about what the gospel allows or does not allow, and whether Christians ought to be involved in this or that form of service in the world, should be subordinated to the needs of people around us, as seen through the eyes of Christ. From that perspective most of our distinctions fall to the ground. We are to respond to people in their need for Christ's sake, Christ who meets all needs.

3. Jesus walks on the water (6:45–52)

Immediately Jesus made his disciples get into the boat and go on ahead of him to Bethsaida, while he dismissed the crowd. ⁴⁶After leaving them, he went up on a mountainside to pray.

⁴⁷When evening came, the boat was in the middle of the lake, and he was alone on land. ⁴⁸He saw the disciples straining at the oars, because the wind was against them. About the fourth watch of the night he went out to them, walking on the lake. He was about to pass by them, ⁴⁹but when they saw him walking on the lake, they thought he was a ghost. They cried out, ⁵⁰because they all saw him and were terrified.

Immediately he spoke to them and said, 'Take courage! It is I. Don't be afraid.' ⁵¹Then he climbed into the boat with them, and the wind died down. They were completely amazed, ⁵²for they had not understood about the loaves; their hearts were hardened.

One remarkable miracle is followed by an even more outstanding one. As with the feeding of the crowd, judgment about whether or not it happened depends on our larger perception of who Jesus was, and how his power was exercised. We need to remember, however, that our judgment of that broader issue is meant to be influenced by what Mark and the other gospel writers claim to have happened on whichever occasion it is we are studying. They are, after all, the prime witnesses. They were neither fools nor charlatans. The main problem with the approach to demythologizing is the inadequacy of most of the re-mythologizing which replaces first-century myths with twentieth-century myths. What

137

results does not adequately explain why Jesus died nor why he would be worth dying for today. Taking the stories at the face value Mark gives them does at least account for both.

The likelihood of a reminiscence from Peter is strong here. The link with the previous story (*immediately*, 45) reinforces this view. So does the frank account of the disciples' responses. Typical, too, of a primitive account is the difficult sentence in verse 48, *He was about to pass by them*, meaning literally that he 'wished' to do so. It all has about it the marks of an only too familiar picture of the natural power of Jesus and the awful struggle of the disciples to comprehend. This double emphasis certainly seems to be Mark's purpose in telling the story at all.

Making *his disciples . . . go on ahead* (45) shows Jesus' determination to provide the rest for his disciples which he intended. The timing difficulty with *late in the day . . . already very late* (35) and *When evening came* (47) is not insoluble if with Taylor we take the verse 35 reference as meaning 'late afternoon'. The meaning of verse 47, together with the details of verse 48, is that it was very much later than the time when it would have been sensible, in normal circumstances, to send a crowd away to find food.

Mark refers again to a strand in Jesus' ministry that he, Mark, wishes us to note (46). Not only the disciples needed quiet; Jesus also needed the communion of prayer with his heavenly Father.

After this he sees the disciples struggling on the lake (48), and sets out towards them, *walking on the lake*. The next sentence is as bewildering as the previous one! *He was about to pass by them.* Sometimes we simply have to admit our puzzlement, and make the best guess we can. The idea that he wished to reach the other side before them seems contrived, since no reason is given and no purpose would be served. The association with Luke 24:28 and John 20:15, where Jesus adopts a pose to help others to burst through into newer perceptions or greater maturity is more convincing, though why Mark does not say so is a little uncertain unless he was yet again remaining totally faithful to what he had received. Matthew does not have this sentence. A third possibility is that he was truly passing them in order to test their capacity to have learned from the stilling of the storm. They were on their own in the boat, as they had felt themselves to be when Jesus slept in the prow. He was again with them now, and again not doing anything directly to help them. Could they grasp this time that they were safe when he was near?

The answer is that they could not! Not only are they not assured by his presence, they do not even recognize it (49–50). The form of his presence which was meant to comfort them in fact frightened them. Whether it comforted or frightened them depended on what they perceived in the light of what they had already experienced. They failed the test again, they *cried out* and *were terrified* (49). When he made himself known by more normal means, the word of comfort, the command not to fear, the physical presence in the boat, they calmed down, as did the storm (50–51). But they were still amazed (51).

Mark's explanation of their failure is also somewhat surprising (52). We might have expected a reference to the stilling of the storm (4:35–41). His choice not to do so forces us to ask what the feeding of the five thousand had particularly in common with the walking on the water.

The clue may rest in the Old Testament background. God is there described as feeding his people, not only with the manna (Ex. 16) but also in other ways and places (1 Ki. 17:8–16; 2 Ki. 4:1–7, 42–44). He was therefore known as a God who feeds his people (Ne. 9:15; Ps. 78:24–25). In sharing in the feeding of the crowd they had first hand experience of this God feeding his people miraculously yet again, through Jesus. This is the link they ought to have seen, for the Old Testament also speaks of God walking on or through the waves (Jb. 9:8; 38:16; Ps. 77:19; Is. 43:16). This does not necessarily imply that they should have recalled those passages to mind. It is rather that the experience of any one of these miracles ought by now to be for them an avenue for perceiving that the one with whom they are dealing, Jesus their teacher, is endowed with the kind of power they normally expect only of the God revealed in their Scriptures. For them, it seems, 'the penny has not yet dropped'. They still treat each miraculous event as self-contained. In so far as they ascribe it to Jesus they have not yet learned to look within and behind him to discern the source, a perception which will at once open their eyes to who Jesus is.

This may account for the manner of Jesus' address to them on the water. The *It is I* is reminiscent of the divine self-revelation in the Old Testament (Ex. 3:14; Is. 41:4; 43:10; 52:6). How much clearer can he make it without removing the one thing for which he looks, which he seeks to stimulate but cannot and will not impose, trusting faith in himself?

We have much in common with the first disciples

It is easy to be over critical of the first disciples, or even to disbelieve Mark's account of their apparent inability to see what is so obvious to us. Three things may help us here. One is to remember that most of us were not raised on a strong monotheistic faith like that of the Jews. We have our own difficulties about the deity of Christ, but nothing like the problem of Jews having to believe what they were expected to believe about a person presencing himself among them as Jesus did.

In the second place, we read the story from the vantage point of its conclusion and beyond. We are not plagued by the uncertainty of 'whether he can keep this up' or 'how long it will last' or 'what will happen when the opposition really gets going'. They had to live with that every day. Nor could they possibly have imagined how things could become as bad as they would *and* be at the same time as good as they turned out to be. We have the enormous advantage of knowing about the cross and the resurrection.

Thirdly, we are often no better. We may be fine when God comes to us in Christ along the recognizable avenues, even if they are miraculous, so long as they are good and affirming. How awesomely splendid to have distributed bread to a crowd, knowing how little Jesus began with and yet seeing that there was more than enough for everyone. Many of us have our own version of that experience. But how different it was in the middle of the night, when the wind was high, and rowing hard, and safety threatened, to see a ghostly figure dimly passing you by on the waters!

Most Christians have our own version of that, too. It happens when events conspire to disappoint us, or trusted friends hurt us, or illness and loneliness overtake us, or spiritual dryness oppresses us. The bread-providing Master at the centre of the crowd is often then more like the ghostly figure on the stormy sea 'wishing to pass us by'. It is much easier then to take fright and cry out. But such experiences are meant to have the opposite effect. They are intended to strengthen our faith, to assure us that we are growing, to signal that Jesus can trust us to go through such storms not needing to have our hands held all the time but knowing that the God and Father of our Lord Jesus Christ, who feeds his people and stills the storms and walks on the waters will never leave us or forsake us. It is in that sense that the darkest days we go through can produce the greatest degree of inner illumination.

4. The crowds flock to Jesus (6:53–56)

When they had crossed over, they landed at Gennesaret and anchored there. [54]As soon as they got out of the boat, people recognised Jesus. [55]They ran throughout that whole region and carried the sick on mats to wherever they heard he was. [56]And wherever he went – into villages, towns or countryside – they placed the sick in the market-places. They begged him to let them touch even the edge of his cloak, and all who touched him were healed.

Mark now underlines once more Jesus' popularity with the crowds, but not with any suggestion that they are becoming true disciples. On the contrary, no teaching or preaching is mentioned. The people seem to be coming for 'what they can get', healing by even simply touching the fringes of Jesus' clothing. People needed to be healed, and they achieved that. They needed very much more but there is no indication that they pressed for that as fully as they did for physical health.

Gennesaret (53) is probably the fertile plain south of Capernaum. They were aiming for Bethsaida, and are generally viewed as having been blown off course. The crowds, however, were not! (54–56). With great energy the people brought the sick on their mats (55). Jesus, like every Jewish man, was required to wear fringes or tassels on his garment (Nu. 15:37 ff; Dt. 22:12). The idea of concentration of divine power in the person of Jesus is so strong that touching his garments is taken to be a source of healing (5:28). That much they knew and responded to. The rest they evidently missed. This summary account reinforces Mark's picture so far.

5. Religious opposition to Jesus intensifies (7:1–23)

The Pharisees and some of the teachers of the law who had come from Jerusalem gathered round Jesus and ²saw some of his disciples eating food with hands that were 'unclean', that is, unwashed. ³(The Pharisees and all the Jews do not eat unless they give their hands a ceremonial washing, holding to the tradition of the elders. ⁴When they come from the market-place they do not eat unless they wash. And they observe many other traditions, such as the washing of cups, pitchers and kettles.)

⁵So the Pharisees and teachers of the law asked Jesus, 'Why don't your disciples live according to the tradition of the elders instead of eating their food with "unclean" hands?'

⁶He replied, 'Isaiah was right when he prophesied about you hypocrites: as it is written:

' "These people honour me with their lips,
but their hearts are far from me.
⁷They worship me in vain;
their teachings are but rules taught by men."

⁸You have let go of the commands of God and are holding on to the traditions of men.'

⁹And he said to them: 'You have a fine way of setting aside the commands of God in order to observe your own traditions! ¹⁰*For Moses said, "Honour your father and your mother," and, "Anyone who curses his father or mother must be put to death." ¹¹But you say that if a man says to his father or mother: "Whatever help you might otherwise have received from me is Corban" (that is, a gift devoted to God), ¹²then you no longer let him do anything for his father or mother. ¹³Thus you nullify the word of God by your tradition that you have handed down. And you do many things like that.'*

¹⁴*Again Jesus called the crowd to him and said, 'Listen to me, everyone, and understand this. ¹⁵Nothing outside a man can make him "unclean" by going into him. Rather, it is what comes out of a man that makes him "unclean".'*

¹⁷*After he had left the crowd and entered the house, his disciples asked him about this parable. ¹⁸'Are you so dull?' he asked. 'Don't you see that nothing that enters a man from the outside can make him "unclean"? ¹⁹For it doesn't go into his heart but into his stomach, and then out of his body.' (In saying this, Jesus declared all foods 'clean'.)*

²⁰*He went on: 'What comes out of a man is what makes him "unclean". ²¹For from within, out of men's hearts, come evil thoughts, sexual immorality, theft, murder, adultery, ²²greed, malice, deceit, lewdness, envy, slander, arrogance and folly. ²³All these evils come from inside and make a man "unclean".'*

This section also carries on an already established theme, but shows considerable development of what has gone before. Opposition from the Jewish religious authorities becomes more intense. In the way the story of the gospel moves forward this section identifies some of the major areas of disagreement. There is also strong evidence here that Mark is writing for Gentile readers since he pauses to explain what most Jews already know (7:3–4, 11). One senses that the case against Jesus from the Jewish leadership is now being prepared in detail.

Jerusalem in Mark's gospel (7:1) is clearly represented as the focal point of opposition to Jesus. The coming from Jerusalem of Pharisees and teachers of the law therefore carries additional threat.

The first issue (2–4) concerns ceremonial impurity. Evidently Jesus' disciples were not adhering to the rules laid down in connection with eating (2), and Mark explains the nature of those rules (3–4). The text behind this passage is not easy. Attached to the words *give their hands a ceremonial washing* is a Greek word meaning 'with the fist'. Some manuscripts offer an alternative or simply miss it out, but this seems to be the appropriate reading. It may mean rubbing the fist in the palm of the hand, but more likely involves washing the hands up to the wrist, or even using a fistful of water rather than a larger amount. Cranfield[7] offers a fuller discussion of the issues raised, together with a contrast between the amounts of water used here and in the actions described in verse 4.

It is not certain that all the Jews (3) followed such rules. Mark is telling his readers that it was a widespread custom, particularly on returning from the market (a better rendering than 'anything that comes from the market') since there they might be defiled by touching Gentiles in the crowd and so become ritually unclean. The shadow of a Gentile falling across a dish or plate made it unclean.

The tradition of the elders (3) lies at the heart of the dispute. This refers to the Jewish oral tradition, added to the law as commentary to spell out the details, implications and applications of the law itself. This issue is raised by Jesus' opponents in verse 5, *according* to the teaching handed down by their ancestors. It is clear that this body of teaching, meant to safeguard the proper understanding and keeping of the law, was under threat by what appeared to be the ritual carelessness of Jesus' disciples. The Pharisees and Scribes were bringing an accusation which would have interested the crowd, since so much of their lives was dominated by such considerations.[8]

Jesus responds by going on to the offensive (6–8). He quotes from the Septuagint, the Greek version of the Old Testament, as Mark records his words. But neither the Masoretic text (the Hebrew version) or the Septuagint provide a basis for the criticism Jesus here brings. It is that by raising the human commentary to a level of importance equal to the divinely given law, they have actually negated the real purpose and spirit of the law itself. Thus they can go through the ritual of word and deed, dependent on the rules given in 'the tradition', without being committed in their hearts to the spiritual intentions of the law (6–7). The final step, never originally intended, nor perhaps any part of the evolution of the tradition, is that God's law is actually set aside in favour of human teaching based on it (8).

Jesus now takes a particular case to illustrate his point (9–13), the issue of Corban (11). The Aramaic word in the text transliterates a Hebrew equivalent, frequently used in Leviticus, Numbers and

[7] Cranfield, p. 233.
[8] That it continued to be an issue as the Christian church grew is clear from Acts 15:19–21; 1 Cor. 8:4–13; 10:23–33; Gal. 2:11–17; Rom. 14:14–23; Col. 2:20–22 and Heb. 13:9–10.

Ezekiel to mean 'an offering to God'. The root of the Hebrew word has to do with 'bringing near', and he implies that the gift, brought near to God, is holy and not available for any other purpose. Something therefore that was designated as Corban, even if it remained in the possession of the owner, was simply not available for ordinary use.

In the case Jesus quotes (was it a real case or a hypothetical one?), a man declares as Corban that which would have been valuable in support of his parents (11), thus contravening, in Jesus' opinion, the law's requirement of filial obligation (10). But the tradition excuses him from it (12).

It is not clear that all Jewish religious teachers would have supported that judgment in the time of Jesus, though there is evidence of Corban being used to keep possessions from ordinary use. It seems most likely that Jesus is not issuing a blanket condemnation of the tradition, or of all uses of it, but rather saying that their attitude to his disciples' behaviour demonstrates how easily (as Isaiah declared) they slip from honouring the law (and so the God who gave it), to elevating the tradition (and so human ingenuity which produced it). They keep the heart and spirit from God in applying the rules from men. So he declares, '*And you do many things like that*' (13).

As further evidence of this Jesus now moves to the much wider principle of what really defiles human beings (14–23).

In verses 14 to 15 there is a negative principle then a positive one. The negative concerns the effect on purity of food entering the body. It does not affect who or what the person is. But that which comes out of a person *is* expressive of who or what that person is. What these statements mean is clarified in the explanation offered, along with a rebuke, to his disciples in 17–19.[9]

Full marks to the disciples for having the courage to ask for help even though they perhaps sensed that they should not, by now, be needing it in this way. Jesus seems to agree with them if that was their judgment of themselves (18)! The clue to understanding verses 14–15 is how you define the essence of a person. The *that enters* is largely a reference to food (*into his stomach*, 19). *What comes out* relates to all the ways in which a person reveals his or her character, outlook, and perspective on life (that is, relating to *the heart*, 19). The harmlessness of food itself, in the spiritual sense, is clear from what happens to it (19).

The implication of this section is now drawn out by Mark in his

[9] Some manuscripts also have the challenge to 'hear carefully', in verse 16, which would actually fit very well at this point, as the story moves from statement to explanation.

own comment, *In saying this, Jesus declared all foods 'clean'* (19). This goes beyond the boundaries of the specific cases being discussed, though it does emerge directly from Jesus' words in verses 18–19. The effect of Mark's summary is the abrogation of the rules on food and diet contained in law, as well as the 'tradition' linked to them. By implication all the ritual regulations and their social implications go with them. Does Jesus abrogate the whole of the Mosaic law? This hardly coheres with his words in 7:10, or in 2:44, still less those recorded by Matthew in Matthew 5:17–20. Yet here, and in the Matthew passage, there is enough to suggest that a new vantage point is being offered from which to view the Mosaic law. Here in Mark Jesus reminds his hearers of the spiritual purpose of the laws. In Matthew they are exhorted to exceed the scribes and Pharisees in doing God's will. The vantage point, from which a new perspective is offered, is Jesus himself. They are to look at it all again in the light of his teaching and (though they did not realize it yet) all that was yet to be in his overall ministry, including death and resurrection. Ceremonial laws will be brought to an end, for Jesus' death will provide the secret of forgiveness, cleansing, and purity. The social regulations will no longer apply because God's people will be newly constituted, not according to physical birth but by new birth through the Spirit's action in response to faith in Christ. The moral laws will receive new depth as Jesus reveals their original intention in terms more of inner attitude than outward standards. This much seems clear from Matthew's record of the Sermon on the Mount.

This line of approach in Mark is hinted at but never expressed openly. The disciples' inability to grasp this spiritual perspective shows both how limited they were as those still holding to the old way *and* how correct was their hunch in coming to Jesus for help. They will find it nowhere else! He simply wishes that they had perceived more already. It cannot become clear to all till the whole drama is lived out. After his death and resurrection the social regulations will no longer apply to those people of God constituted by faith; the ritual prescriptions will have been totally consummated and surpassed; and the moral injunctions will be perceived in a new and deeper light altogether. For the present the disciples are examples to us of those who are feeling for understanding but have some way to go. Sadly the Jewish authorities represent those who are not able to see because their vision is hindered by the wall they have built to protect the very law of God which Jesus has come to interpret and fulfil. That which they have built (the tradition) does not so much safeguard the law as imprison them so that they are not free to perceive its deeper meaning and embrace it.

145

The catalogue of evils not dealt with by a legalistic approach is then set out in devastating fashion (20–23). Of the twelve in the list, the first six are plural nouns, describing acts which are committed. The second six are singular, dealing with different kinds of evil. Jesus' point is that whatever stimulus there may be from outside, it certainly does not come from the ritual connected with eating food. The origin of these deeds and vices is within, in 'the heart' not 'the stomach' – see verse 19. To concentrate on issues of ritual cleanliness for eating, while neglecting the source of evil in human life, is truly to be imprisoned. That the religious leaders could criticize Jesus' followers for neglecting external ritual when so many people were being challenged and liberated at the inner level, showed that the critics had fallen precisely into the error which Jesus described.

a. What is good tradition?

All Christians are challenged by this passage, for all of us are in danger of substituting the tradition for the spiritual content, and not least those who criticize others for being too tied to tradition! Human life depends heavily upon tradition, from family upbringing to national and international custom. It joins different periods of our history; varied areas of life; individuals and groups who otherwise would be disconnected. It is often responsible for coherence, order and continuity when these would be under threat. It is learned by observation and practice and is sometimes unspoken or untaught but simply assumed and assimilated. It is largely related to 'the same thing', and this is its strength and its danger. In Christian terms it stretches from monastic rules and formal traditions associated with Catholic practice (which often seem to Protestants to be a threat to scriptural authority, which some of them are), to the local rules and regulations of Protestant congregations, many of them unwritten (which often appear to Catholics to be nervous, cheap and nasty, which some of them are). The point is not whether or not we have tradition. Human life seems not to be able to last long without it. One simply looks at the number of groups which start up 'without any tradition' to see how quickly they develop them. The question is whether traditions are kept in proper perspective, which in Jesus' teaching here means being tested by God's word in Scripture (which the traditions claim to explain) and by the highest demand of the kingdom, which is inner purity. Given these, the tradition is likely to change constantly in the light of new circumstances. For evidence of this we need only to look back in history to what our forefathers considered good tradition, or to look around us in the world to see what other groups of Christians in different contexts from ours consider to be good tradition. The test is not whether all conform to the same pattern but whether each, in its own setting, is true to the Scripture it claims to interpret and to the requirement of inner purity. We do well, in the interests of these, to hold lightly to our traditions. It was this that Jesus' hearers found so hard to accept.

b. Getting priorities right

Much the saddest part of this story relates to the way Jesus' critics used the failure to follow certain patterns of ritual as a reason for not accepting the spiritual and physical liberation being made available to the needy by the very people the religious leaders criticized. The sick were being cured, evil spirits cast out, sins forgiven, but the critics fastened on failure to wash hands before eating. The signs of the kingdom were neglected in the interests of ritual ablutions.

It is important to distinguish between adherence to tradition and obedience to God, in other people's lives too, particularly those whom we are inclined to criticize. Denominational and theological rivalries have been fuelled by concentration on the traditions and practices of others – in worship or organization or life style – to the neglect of the deeper question of whether they follow God's word or whether they are marked by spiritual integrity. Of course the distinction is not always easy to make, but this passage enjoins us to attempt it.

6. The faith of a Gentile woman (7:24–30)

Jesus left that place and went to the vicinity of Tyre. He entered a house and did not want anyone to know it; yet he could not keep his presence secret. [25] In fact, as soon as she heard about him, a woman whose little daughter was possessed by an evil spirit came and fell at his feet. [26] The woman was a Greek, born in Syrian Phoenicia. She begged Jesus to drive the demon out of her daughter.

[27] 'First let the children eat all they want,' he told her, 'for it is not right to take the children's bread and toss it to their dogs.'

[28] 'Yes, Lord,' she replied, 'but even the dogs under the table eat the children's crumbs.'

[29] Then he told her, 'For such a reply, you may go; the demon has left your daughter.'

[30] She went home and found her child lying on the bed, and the demon gone.

147

Mark now tells a story which both illustrates the point made above about ritual and even daringly suggests that perhaps Jesus learned an unexpected application of the point in the course of an unlikely conversation.

The story itself contains a number of distinguishing features. Jesus moves into a new area (24). Mark's geography and topography are no more precise here than anywhere else. But reference to Tyre certainly takes him out of wholly Jewish territory. And Tyre was a city of importance, associated with an empire and a former enemy of Israel.

Jesus stays in this new area (24) and there is no mention of the disciples being with him (Matthew does include them, Mt. 15:23.) Mark does not, like Matthew (Mt. 15:22) so describe the woman as to leave open the possibility that Jesus did not himself go into the city. Mark's blunt statements again suggest the awkward truths.

We do not know why Jesus was there. The best guess, if he was alone, is that he wanted to be alone and left alone. But Mark says that this was not possible (24). That Jewish crowds sought and followed him is perhaps not too surprising (6:33). What now transpires does however take the reader by surprise, and there is some evidence that it took Jesus by surprise, too.

A Greek woman, Syrophoenician by birth (25–26), finds him out, and asks healing for her daughter. The description as *Greek* must be understood religiously not nationally. She is a pagan, not a Jew, is the point. In relation to Jewish traditional practices she is breaking all the rules, hence one link with the previous story. But what is Jesus to do? Opposed by his own religious leaders, doubted by his family, followed often for the wrong reasons by the crowd, accompanied by disciples who only partially understand, yet recognized by evil spirits and trusted implicitly by the desperate, Jesus unexpectedly faces a totally new possibility. The outcome has implications for all that is to follow, not least in the attitude of fellow-Jews to his claims. Matthew's reference to the disciples at this point serves to sharpen the choice (Mt. 15:23).

The response of Jesus (27) is a balanced one. On the one side he states his commitment and calling to the Jews. *'First let the children eat all they want.'* On the other side the introduction of the word 'first' does not entirely extinguish hope. He refers to her and those like her as *dogs*, which is not complimentary; yet the use of the diminutive does at least suggest the household pets, not the scavenging, dangerous street dogs. Overall, then, his reply is not encouraging for the present, but not dismissive in the long run.[10]

The woman might well have felt some satisfaction at a generous, if for the moment negative, response. But she was not going to leave matters there. Woman and Gentile she might be (and she seems willing even to accept the derogatory nature of Jesus' reference to her and her ilk), but she is the mother of a needy child. Balanced theological responses which do not change the situation are not enough for her! She accepts as true everything Jesus says (28), but presumes to add one further touch to the homely picture Jesus had painted of the children being fed. The little dogs get the crumbs! It does not have to be one or the other. Nor need he be deflected from his main mission to the Jews in order to do something for her daughter. She will accept the humiliating position assigned to her in his response. Will he accept her gloss on his interpretation? His response will indicate what ultimately will be the scope of his earthly ministry.

That response (29) signals the opening up, eventually, of the kingdom to the Gentiles. Whatever her background she had cast herself wholly upon him in her need. She had wrestled with him in her believing. She went home to find her daughter healed (30).

Mark has in this account confirmed much of his story to date, and has added one significant new element. To his list of factors which do not necessarily induce faith in Jesus – hearing the parables, seeing the miracles, witnessing the exorcisms, even travelling with Jesus, knowing the law – Mark now notes one factor that does not prevent faith in Jesus, being a Gentile. It is true that in the words of Jesus to this woman (27) there is here more a promise of what is to come than of what will now be. But a breakthrough has been made. Her daughter is healed. Gentiles are included in the kingdom of God being established in Jesus.

a. Crossing boundaries and breaking down barriers

This important story operates at two levels of insight for us. The first is related to the ministry of Jesus himself. Just as many could not yet see who he was because so much was yet to be done – particularly in his death and resurrection – and yet the evidence was there for those who could see, so in relation to the Gentiles there is a hope set out which at that point in his ministry lay out in the future but would one day be fulfilled. The difficulty Jesus' own early disciples had with this idea becomes clear in the Acts of the Apostles, and particularly in Acts 15 where the entire mission

[10] See Is. 2:2–4; 42:1 ff.; 50:1 ff.; for Old Testament support for his position.

to the Gentiles was in question. Truth prevailed when it was seen that God's offer of salvation through Jesus was for all irrespective of national or natural origin.

The other level concerns the crossing of national and religious boundaries to help those in need. The difference between the perspectives of Jesus and this woman is very clear in Mark's blunt account. For him there is the question of adequately reflecting the purposes of God in a balanced (theological) way. For her there is a sick child whom she believes he can heal. In response to that Jesus crosses the many barriers in the way – nationality, religion, sex, tradition – and grants healing in response to faith. Like the Samaritan in his own story (Lk. 10:30–35) he risked in order to save.

b. Today's barriers

The historical and contemporary implications of this make sad reading for Christians. Too often reasons have been given of an allegedly Christian kind to justify the building of barriers between groups and nations, and even the fighting of wars and wholesale killings. Not so long ago we read in the news of 'Christian militiamen' fighting Moslem troops in Lebanon. Too much of the 'Irish problem' has been prolonged by religion even though its causes are not religious. More personal, localized and group attacks on minorities often stem from similar sources. Against this the Christian church must see itself as committed to breaking down barriers which prolong human need or prevent the needy from being helped. One does not necessarily agree with another person's theology, nationhood, life style, nor outlook by meeting their need. One simply shows the love of God to another human being. The world needs to see Christians following their Master more clearly at this point.

7. The deaf hear and the mute speak (7:31–37)

Then Jesus left the vicinity of Tyre and went through Sidon, down to the Sea of Galilee and into the region of the Decapolis. [32]*There some people brought to him a man who was deaf and could hardly talk, and they begged him to place his hand on the man.*

[33]*After he took him aside, away from the crowd, Jesus put his fingers into the man's ears. Then he spat and touched the man's tongue.* [34]*He looked up to heaven and with a deep sigh said to him, 'Ephphatha!' (which means, 'Be opened!').* [35]*At this, the man's ears were opened, his tongue was loosened and he began to speak plainly.*

³⁶*Jesus commanded them not to tell anyone. But the more he did so, the more they kept talking about it.* ³⁷*People were overwhelmed with amazement. 'He has done everything well,' they said. 'He even makes the deaf hear and the mute speak.'*

The healing of a deaf and mute man provides another example of Jesus crossing boundaries to set people free. This time the boundaries are those of acute physical disability. A man *who was deaf and could hardly talk* (32) is brought by others with the request for healing.

Mark describes an unusual route for Jesus – from Tyre north to Sidon and then back by a south-easterly journey to the Decapolis – but as usual he offers no explanation or timing. It is the activity of Jesus that matters, and what it means. Timing and topography matter less to Mark.

What does matter is the light shed by this miracle on who Jesus is. The word to describe the man's difficulty with speech occurs only twice in the Greek version of the whole Bible, here and in Isaiah 35:6. It is surely significant that the words of the crowd, expressing amazement at the miracle (*'He even makes the deaf hear and the mute speak'*, 37) are also reminiscent of Isaiah 35:5–6. Since that passage in Isaiah is one of those in which the prophet speaks of the coming Messiah, the link is all the more important. As so often in this gospel, Mark sends signals to his readers, signals which enable them to understand the meaning of Jesus' activity. Those involved in the story being unfolded seem not to have understood. Why they did not understand is, of course, a theme at the centre of Mark's purposes. Their words, as Mark records them, contain the clue to who Jesus is – Messiah, God's anointed one (*'He has done everything well'*, 37). Yet they seem incapable of making the connection themselves. The story has not yet reached its conclusion, when whole-hearted response will be possible.

Jesus seems to co-operate with the process of their not grasping the meaning of all that he is doing. In verse 33 he takes the man on one side to heal him. In verse 36 he instructs them not to tell anyone about what they have seen. The healings are the signs of the kingdom, not the kingdom itself. Running through this story, as through most of the gospel, there is a sense of there being a great deal which is not yet revealed, but which lies out in the future.

The method of the healing is not unique. Such practices were used by other healers. The uniqueness lay in the person performing the healing, and therefore in what the healing signified – the coming of God's kingdom.

It is wholly in keeping with this that Jesus sighs deeply – an indication of the spiritual battle taking place. Paul uses this word of the Christian's inner struggle, in Romans 8:22–27 and 2 Corinthians 5:2, 4. The battle against evil is joined in this man's healing.

The notion of struggle is borne out by the use of the Aramaic word *Ephphatha*, which means 'Be opened'. It is not limited to the opening of ears and the loosening of a tongue. It is the whole person who is opened up, set free, in relation to God's kingly rule.

The people are amazed and speak in highest terms of Jesus' achievements. Yet they are not truly disciples of Jesus. Two recurring emphases of Mark are present. In the first place, they have not yet witnessed the entire gospel story. Trial, crucifixion and resurrection still lie out in the future. In the second place, genuine faith commitment to Christ, as Mark understands it, is a miracle anyway. Only the '*Ephphatha*' of Jesus can set us free to believe.

A lesson for evangelism

All Christians are called to be witnesses, but some have a God-given gift of leading others to faith by making the story known publicly and helping those who listen to commit themselves. This is especially true of evangelistic preachers. The expectations of Christians who invite and support such evangelists can place heavy burdens on the evangelists' shoulders. They may be judged by their 'success', that is, by how many they can bring to response.

This passage provides a helpful corrective to that kind of pressure. Crowds being impressed by the things Jesus did, even if they tell others excitedly about them, do not necessarily become disciples. There is need for a perception of the meaning behind the things Jesus did and said. Without this, true faith is likely to be lacking. The process by which such perception is reached is part of a spiritual struggle between good and evil in the world. It does not happen easily. What is more, as Mark is hinting in this passage, there is an element of the miraculous about it. The bringing of people to faith is God's work by the Holy Spirit, however we understand the necessary human response.

8. The feeding of the four thousand (8:1–21)

During those days another large crowd gathered. Since they had nothing to eat, Jesus called his disciples to him and said, ²'I have compassion for these people; they have already been with me three days and have nothing to eat. ³If I send them home hungry, they will collapse on the way, because some of them have come a long distance.'

152

⁴His disciples answered, 'But where in this remote place can anyone get enough bread to feed them?'

⁵'How many loaves do you have?' Jesus asked.

'Seven,' they replied.

⁶He told the crowd to sit down on the ground. When he had taken the seven loaves and given thanks, he broke them and gave them to the disciples to set before the people, and they did so. ⁷They had a few small fish as well; he gave thanks for them also and told the disciples to distribute them. ⁸The people ate and were satisfied. Afterwards the disciples picked up seven basketfuls of broken pieces that were left over. ⁹About four thousand men were present. And having sent them away, ¹⁰he got into the boat with his disciples and went to the region of Dalmanutha.

¹¹The Pharisees came and began to question Jesus. To test him, they asked him for a sign from heaven. ¹²He sighed deeply and said, 'Why does this generation ask for a miraculous sign? I tell you the truth, no sign will be given to it.' ¹³Then he left them, got back into the boat and crossed to the other side.

¹⁴The disciples had forgotten to bring bread, except for one loaf they had with them in the boat. ¹⁵'Be careful,' Jesus warned them. 'Watch out for the yeast of the Pharisees and that of Herod.'

¹⁶They discussed this with one another and said, 'It is because we have no bread.'

¹⁷Aware of their discussion, Jesus asked them: 'Why are you talking about having no bread? Do you still not see or understand? Are your hearts hardened? ¹⁸Do you have eyes but fail to see, and ears but fail to hear? And don't you remember? ¹⁹When I broke the five loaves for the five thousand, how many basketfuls of pieces did you pick up?'

'Twelve,' they replied.

²⁰'And when I broke the seven loaves for the four thousand, how many basketfuls of pieces did you pick up?'

They answered, 'Seven.'

²¹He said to them, 'Do you still not understand?'

Verses 1–10 raise immediately questions about a doublet of 6:30–44, the feeding of the five thousand. A crossing and a landing prepare the way for both. Jesus' attitude of compassion for the crowd is noted in both. The disciples are surprised in both stories by Jesus' instruction to them to feed the crowds. Both involve bread and fish (perhaps not so surprising). In both there is a remarkable residue. On the other hand there are significantly different details, in the numbers, for example. In one he suggests their need for food: in the other it is the disciples. There is much more detail about arrangements in the first than in the second. There is even the possibility, based on location and different words used for the baskets (6:43, 8:19), that the former was Jewish and the latter Gentile. As to the surprise of the disciples the second time (8:4), Mark himself draws attention to their slowness later in the same chapter (8:17–21). We could be critical of them except that we so often are equally dull and blind. So although at least the internal evidence in the two stories is inconclusive either way, if we began with what Mark evidently believed we have two such occasions. He uses the word 'again' in 8:1 (as RSV), translated by the New English Bible as 'on another occasion'. Since on one side the gospel writers had to select their material carefully because of shortage of space, and on the other there must have been many similar situations not recorded, we may take it as it stands and learn what it teaches. In this case the lessons seem to relate to what follows in 11–13 and 14–21. The setting is a different one, but the link with the feeding of the crowd is implicitly strong in the debate with the Pharisees about signs (11–13) and explicitly in the discussion with the disciples about the *yeast of the Pharisees* (14–21). Mark appears to intend us to hold these three sections (1–10, 11–13 and 14–21) together.

He is in effect raising two separate questions. The first (in 11–13) is, 'When the Pharisees ask for a sign, why doesn't a man who has miraculously fed 5,000 and 4,000 show them one?' One answer to that question would to be that Jesus performed such signs only when, in the normal course of events, the needs of people confronted him and he responded with compassion (6:34, 8:2). Although it would not have been difficult for Jesus to find needy people every time, he refused to contrive a situation in order to prove a point about himself. His ministry was not primarily about proving his claims about himself; it was primarily about embodying God's love for all he has made and gathering it into the kingdom. Anything that distracted attention from the natural outflowing of divine love – like a 'signs competition' – would be abhorrent.

The second answer would be that they came with the wrong attitude anyway. Mark says they came *to test him* (8:11). The miracles, like the teaching, of Jesus were not offered as signs to convince spectators; they were done as acts of love to people in need. They only *became* signs for those with the humility and openness to perceive and receive the meaning. This the Pharisees clearly did not possess, as their attitude towards him shows.

But, to take the second question (raised by 14–21), 'Why can't the disciples perceive the signs when they see them before their eyes?' The answer here seems to lie in his warning about *the yeast of the Pharisees and that of Herod* (15). Because they had forgotten to bring bread (14, a sign of their general confusion?), they thought he was warning them about being careful from whom they received bread. We have all been in the classroom situation where we were so puzzled that we turned the simplest thing into complex issues and so misunderstood them totally!

Yeast is usually employed in the Bible as an image of something evil (Lv. 2:11; 1 Cor. 5:6–8; Gal. 5:9). The yeast caused the bread to rise. It can therefore represent something spectacular or diverting. Matthew 16:12 identifies it as their teaching. Luke 12:1 sees it as hypocrisy. Jesus, in Mark's account here, is warning the disciples against falling into the Pharisees' mistake of needing incontrovertible proof about who he was (8:11), or of Herod in refusing to follow the light he had and authorizing the death of John the Baptist (6:14–29). All they can think about is bread for their next meal! If the Pharisees are demanding a special display of divine pyrotechnics in the heavens to convince them, the disciples have not yet got their eyes off ground level! The one group is demanding far too much: the other expecting far too little.

a. Faithfulness and relevance

Jesus' firm stand against doing signs to prove his authenticity, put alongside the slowness of the disciples to understand what he was about, raises serious questions about the role of the Christian church in any culture. We today in the West are under enormous pressure to demonstrate our relevance. The message of our world to us so often seems to be, 'If you were more obviously useful we would have more time for you.'

Our response is often to fall into the trap. We quote John Wimber, with his signs and wonders approach to power evangelism. When people see dramatic healings and exorcisms, and when they hear words of prophecy and knowledge, we think, they will surely believe. Or we quote Jim Wallis, deeply committed to changing the structures of society so that there will be a better deal for the poor, the blacks, the women. When people see the extent of our social commitment, we say, they will surely believe. For good measure we quote the now time-honoured examples of Mother Teresa of Calcutta, Martin Luther King Jr, and Archbishop Desmond Tutu.

The point is not, let it be made abundantly clear, that such people themselves do these things in order to impress. But the church is under enormous pressure both to cite their example and to copy it in order to prove our authenticity or demonstrate our work in society. Two things result. One is that we, and others who take notice, confuse the sign with the reality. The reality is God's love for his world supremely revealed in Jesus. All the work referred to above is done because of that love; it is done to show that love, not to be a sign to impress society with our relevance. When the love is served and embodied, then signs are there for those who can perceive them. If we emphasize the signs the love which lies at their centre is often missed.

The other error which results from the wrong emphasis is the concentration on spectacular or outstanding expressions of gospel love by human beings. But our regular attendance at worship is a sign; our concern for our neighbours in Christ's name is a sign; the holy lifestyle of believers is a sign; daily work well done in service of Christ is a sign. We, and more seriously those outside the faith, miss all these signs by our concentration on the large-scale and the spectacular. Each Christian is privileged to concentrate on living out God's love in our lives. God will take care of the signs.

b. Not too high: not too low

Following on from the above is the related point arising from the mistakes of the Pharisees and of the disciples in Mark 8:14–21. The Pharisees expected too much: the disciples saw too little. The Christian testimony is that serving Christ is neither an endless succession of exciting experiences nor a dull round of taking life at its face value. Between those two is the point where ordinary elements in life are invested with divine purpose and significance. This is the reason why Jesus' parables of the kingdom of God are all focused on details from everyday life in his time. Seen through his eyes all of nature provides doors and windows on to spiritual realities. This is why the apologetic task, answering the objections to Christian faith and demonstrating its relationship to and encompassing of all forms of knowledge, is so vital. It is not in order to demonstrate our relevance: it is to show how God's love is present in all forms of truth, if we could but see it. Too often, as in our story here (8:17–21), it is to his own disciples that Jesus has to say, *'Do you still not see or understand?'*

9. The blind man at Bethsaida (8:22–26)

They came to Bethsaida, and some people brought a blind man and begged Jesus to touch him. ²³He took the blind man by the hand

and led him outside the village. When he had spat on the man's eyes and put his hands on him, Jesus asked, 'Do you see anything?'

²⁴He looked up and said, 'I see people; they look like trees walking around.'

²⁵Once more Jesus put his hands on the man's eyes. Then his eyes were opened, his sight was restored, and he saw everything clearly. ²⁶Jesus sent him home, saying, 'Don't go into the village.'

This story of the blind man at Bethsaida is probably intended by Mark to be a comment on what had gone before, dealing with a man who regained his sight by (two) stages. The Twelve should not lose heart! It may point forward also, to Peter's imperfect faith in relation to Jesus' nature and work (27–33) and to the full revelation given to the three disciples at the Transfiguration (9:2–7). Yet it has a ring of authenticity about it, too, not least in the implication that even the touch of Jesus did not always heal altogether. Exactly what is involved Mark does not tell us, but it certainly bears a message for the unrealistic utopianism to which we Christians easily succumb. 'If God is with me why doesn't . . . ?' The God of history seems to take his own time with us, for his own reasons but always, we must remind ourselves, in love for us.

Mark 8:27 – 10:52
5. Going to Jerusalem

With all the outer parts of the puzzle now set out Mark moves the story inexorably towards Jerusalem for the centre pieces to be put in place. He begins in Caesarea Philippi (8:27) and then portrays the series of incidents which mark the journey. As this movement takes place it is characterized by an increased openness on Jesus' part about how it will all end, and consequent pressure on all around him, and all whom he meets, to make up their minds about where they stand in relation to him. The incidents at Caesarea Philippi are a good introduction to this new phase.

1. Peter's confession about Christ (8:27 – 9:1)

Jesus and his disciples went on to the villages around Caesarea Philippi. On the way he asked them, 'Who do people say I am?'

28They replied, 'Some say John the Baptist; others say Elijah; and still others, one of the prophets.'

29'But what about you?' he asked. 'Who do you say I am?'

Peter answered, 'You are the Christ.'

30Jesus warned them not to tell anyone about him.

31He then began to teach them that the Son of Man must suffer many things and be rejected by the elders, chief priests and teachers of the law, and that he must be killed and after three days rise again. 32He spoke plainly about this, and Peter took him aside and began to rebuke him.

33But when Jesus turned and looked at his disciples, he rebuked Peter. 'Get behind me, Satan!' he said. 'You do not have in mind the things of God, but the things of men.'

34Then he called the crowd to him along with his disciples and said: 'If anyone would come after me, he must deny himself and take up his cross and follow me. 35For whoever wants to save his life will lose it, but whoever loses his life for me and for the gospel

158

*will save it. *[36]*What good is it for a man to gain the whole world,
yet forfeit his soul? *[37]*Or what can a man give in exchange for his
soul? *[38]*If anyone is ashamed of me and my words in this adulterous
and sinful generation, the Son of Man will be ashamed of him when
he comes in his Father's glory with the holy angels.'*

*[9:1]And he said to them, 'I tell you the truth, some who are
standing here will not taste death before they see the kingdom of
God come with power.'*

Peter's confession about Christ is a high-point in the story so
far. It has parallels in Matthew 16:13–16 and Luke 9:22–27. The
acceptance of the likelihood that the gospel writers arranged some
of their material in order to make a particular point, rather than
chronologically, does not preclude the possibility that Caesarea
Philippi was a turning point in Jesus' ministry, a case widely
accepted when Mark's gospel was viewed as a chronological presentation. It makes good sense and remains highly likely that, after
the break-through of perception by Peter, and his verbalizing what
perhaps others had thought but hesitated to say about Jesus, the
Master would from now on concentrate increasingly on the preparation of the disciples for what lay ahead. After this, if they are
present, the crowds listen in on the training of the Twelve. This
was probably encouraged, and necessitated, by the two parts of the
Caesarea Philippi experience (27–30, 31–33), the promising and the
disappointing.

The promising part relates to the question Jesus asks them – the
preliminary examination before the course begins, so to speak.
What are people saying about him? Some thought he was John the
Baptist back to life. (Certainly Herod did, 6:14.) Others thought
Elijah had returned, much as some had thought about John the
Baptist, according to John 1:21. Malachi 4:5 contained the promise,
'See, I will send you the prophet Elijah before that great and
dreadful day of the Lord comes.' Now for the sixty-four thousand
dollar question: *'Who do you say I am?'* (29). Peter, ever ready to
rush into a vacuum of silence with a comment, probably took
everyone's breath away, *'You are the Christ'* (29).

'The Christ' in Greek and 'Messiah' in Hebrew and Aramaic
mean 'the Anointed One'. It carries the sense of consecration by
God for a particular task, and was used, for example, of kings and
priests in the Old Testament (Ex. 29:7, 21; 1 Sa. 10:1). Not only
is there divine choice; there is also divine empowering for the task
(1 Sa. 10:1, 6; 16:13; Is. 61:1). More recently the title had increasingly been used of the one who would set the Jews free of their
oppressors, and here the concept of the Son of David was widely

159

used. (Hence Jesus' correction of the teachers of the law about the relationship of this person to David, 12:35–37.) To call Jesus Messiah was thus a momentous step for Peter to take. (In Matthew he is recorded as adding 'the Son of the living God'. Also in Matthew Jesus encourages Peter, who may have taken his own breath away by his confession! 'Blessed are you, Simon, son of Jonah, for this was not revealed to you by man, but by my Father in heaven.' He then goes on to the saying about Peter as the rock, Mt. 16:15–19.)

Three things are noteworthy in what follows. First, Jesus makes no attempt, even in Mark's (typically) much briefer account, to deny what Peter has said. He accepts this confession as accurate. He *is* God's anointed one to bring in God's kingdom. Secondly, however, he instructs them not to spread this news abroad (30). We may guess that his reason is twofold: (i) that his contemporaries had a fixed and political view of how the Messiah would set them free, and (ii) because he wished to shape the Messiahship according to his Father's will in ways which they could not yet properly understand.

The confirmation of this intention is the third noteworthy element. Although not denying the status of Messiah, he goes on to speak of (presumably) his future in terms not of Messiah but of Son of Man, and of the sufferings of this Son of Man (31–33).

The expression Son of Man can be interpreted simply to mean 'a person', 'a man', 'a fellow', and in the Old Testament it is so used. In Daniel 7:13, however, it refers to an exalted figure, representing 'the saints of the Most High' (Dn. 7:18) and most closely associated with them. He receives 'authority, glory and sovereign power'. Then 'all peoples, nations and men of every language worshipped him. His dominion is an everlasting dominion that will not pass away, and his kingdom is one that will never be destroyed.'

If this is, as the majority of scholars believe, the source of the expression, then to use it of himself is not out of keeping with the acceptance of the confession of Messiahship by Peter. But it does remove it from the dangers of a well-formed popular definition which Messiah had in his time. And it allows him to fill Son of Man with fresh meaning, perhaps along the lines of Isaiah 53 and the suffering servant, as he now proceeds to do. Contrary to all the images conjured up by Peter's ascription of Messiahship, Jesus says the Son of Man *must suffer . . . must be killed*. The sense of purposefulness is strong (31). (We can hardly be surprised, if Jesus did speak also of resurrection, if the disciples present neither remembered it nor understood it. The shock of the death announcement must have had a devastating effect on them.)

Into the vacuum of silence comes Peter again! *Peter took him aside and began to rebuke him* (32). Having (according to Mt. 16:17–19) been praised by Jesus for his previous contribution, Peter now finds himself scolded in the stronger terms '*Get behind me, Satan!*' '*You do not have in mind the things of God, but the things of men*' (33). The first rebuke is reminiscent of Jesus' rebuttal of the devil in the desert (Mt. 4:1–11; Lk. 4:1–13). The second virtually says that in this opinion Peter is no different from all his fellow Jews in looking for an earthly, military deliverer. That, Jesus is making clear, is not the part chosen by God for his Messiah. Somehow, God's offer of liberation will be made via death and resurrection, not via armies and military victories.

Lest this should not be enough shock for one day, Jesus now adds another, this time for the crowd as well as the disciples (8:34 – 9:1). Not only must he go this way of death; so too must anyone who would be a disciple of his. As C. F. D. Moule points out,[1] Jesus is not using cross-bearing to describe the human experience of carrying some burden through life. It is much more comprehensive than that. 'People carrying crosses were people going to execution.' Cross-bearing as a follower of Jesus means nothing less than giving one's whole life over to following him. And here comes another surprise. This is the way of total freedom. If you clutch your life wholly to yourself, protecting it against all others, asserting all your rights, needs and privileges, you lose it because it isn't life any longer. If, however, you acknowledge that life is not yours by right, that all is privilege, and that it is to be lived in the love that the gospel story reveals, self-giving love, then you possess it wholly. There is now nothing to lose and everything to gain (35). Supposing you gain all the world's riches, and lose the inner freedom of loving and being loved by God – what then? (36). What will you give in exchange for that divinely given inwardness, which is the centre of all that is spiritual, the aspect of everything you are, where God wishes to dwell? These are the choices now being offered by Jesus, Messiah, Son of Man. The apparently gloomy news of the cross is actually the way to total freedom and fulfilment.

But if this makes any of his hearers ashamed of him, then they should know that another day is coming, a day of glory (is Daniel 7:13 again the main image?), and the Son of Man will be ashamed of them on that day.

Lest this should all seem somewhat idealized and theoretical, or even far-fetched, Jesus says that some present there will see God's

[1] Moule, p. 67. This point is also made by H. B. Swete in his 1898 comentary.

kingdom come with power (9:1). Since the next verse (9:2) refers to something *six days* later Jesus may be referring to the Transfiguration as a power demonstration of the kingdom. Or he may mean that the coming events in his own ministry (in particular his death and resurrection) will constitute the kingdom coming with power. In this context this makes far more sense, and is more appropriate, than the idea that Jesus mistakenly thought the consummation of the kingdom would come in the lifetime of some standing there.

Making up one's mind

In one sense Mark's gospel is a succession of challenges to make up one's mind, from the ministry of John the Baptist onwards. The story Mark tells is not meant to be of academic, historical or antiquarian interest. Its purpose is to help people to be clear about the kind of discipleship to which Jesus calls them, and to enable them to respond positively to the call. So far, in this gospel, few have done so.

Peter's response at Caesarea Philippi marks a turning point. He, and maybe some others amongst the Twelve, is making progress (8:29), though how faltering the progress is becomes painfully clear at once (8:32–33). But on the evidence so far Peter had reached a conclusion – Jesus is the Christ.

The method is important, both for those who stand on the brink of Christian discipleship and for those who seek to help others in that position. It involves making the story of Jesus known in a way which helps others to test its implications for their own lives. Does the teaching ring true in relation to life as I know it? When I protect my life from others does it lose much of its meaning? When I live openly to others is life enriched? Is life satisfying when taken at its face value, or do I discern signs of hidden reality which suggest there may be much more? Do healings and the exorcisms say something about my own needs, crises and inner struggle? Is the totally self-giving love of Jesus a sea into which I could commit myself by faith? Of course, at chapter 9, the story is by no means complete, but the central feature is the person of Jesus and his challenge for commitment to all with whom he comes into contact. Humanly speaking, it is still the case today.

2. The transfiguration of Jesus (9:2–13)

After six days Jesus took Peter, James and John with him and led them up a high mountain, where they were all alone. There he was transfigured before them. [3]His clothes became dazzling white, whiter than anyone in the world could bleach them. [4]And there appeared before them Elijah and Moses, who were talking with Jesus.

[5]Peter said to Jesus, 'Rabbi, it is good for us to be here. Let us put up three shelters – one for you, one for Moses and one for Elijah.' [6](He did not know what to say, they were so frightened.)

[7]Then a cloud appeared and enveloped them, and a voice came from the cloud: 'This is my Son, whom I love. Listen to him!'

[8]Suddenly, when they looked round, they no longer saw anyone with them except Jesus.

[9]As they were coming down the mountain, Jesus gave them orders not to tell anyone what they had seen until the Son of Man had risen from the dead. [10]They kept the matter to themselves, discussing what 'rising from the dead' meant.

[11]And they asked him, 'Why do the teachers of the law say that Elijah must come first?'

[12]Jesus replied, 'To be sure, Elijah does come first, and restores all things. Why then is it written that the Son of Man must suffer much and be rejected? [13]But I tell you, Elijah has come and they have done to him everything they wished, just as it is written about him.'

The transfiguration (9:2–8) is one of the best-known stories about Jesus, not least because of its combination of the extraordinary event (2–4), and the wholly ordinary and predictable response of Peter (5–6).

The first question to ask about the transfiguration is not the most important question, but it is not easy to move forward without asking 'What happened?' Moule[2] reminds us that Peter, James and John would probably have had difficulty in answering! Yet although the meaning matters more than the occasion, we must ask what the occasion was.

In opposition to the suggestion that this is really a resurrection narrative read back into the life of Jesus, Cranfield[3] convincingly points out that in resurrection appearances Jesus is usually first absent (!); that he speaks and the sayings are a central part of resurrection appearances; that Moses and Elijah are a curious couple to be in a resurrection story; that Peter's response (9:5) would hardly be in place; and that Jesus would have had something different to say to Peter anyway (Jn. 21).

Similarly, over against this being a symbolic narrative there is the reference to *after six days* (unusually precise for Mark), Peter's

[2] Moule, p. 69.   [3] Cranfield, p. 293.

address to Jesus as rabbi, not something common in the early church which would be responsible for a symbolic narrative; Peter's suggestion of a building project by way of commemoration, and perhaps also the analogy of the bleached garments (9:3). Mark intends us to know that something did actually happen. But what?

Mark, with the other synoptists (Lk. 9:28–36; Mt. 17:1–13), is saying that something took place which transcended normal experience. The mountain, in the Bible, is the place of divine revelation (Moriah and the sacrifice of Isaac averted, Gn. 22; Sinai and the giving of the law, Ex. 19; Horeb and reassurance for Elijah, 1 Ki. 19). The cloud stands for the divine presence (Ex. 13:21; 19:9; 33:9; Nu. 9:15). The brightness of Jesus' garments is reminiscent of the Shekinah, the divine presence in a pillar of fire. All these images were part of the three disciples' heritage. Here were all the signs of an experience of the numinous.

As to the detail, Luke's account helps. He says Jesus was praying (Lk. 9:28), and that 'As he was praying, the appearance of his face changed, and his clothes became as bright as a flash of lightning'. Communion with his heavenly Father changed his appearance, as it had done for Moses (Ex. 34:29). On a natural reading of these accounts one concludes that the writers are saying that this actually happened. Luke also says the disciples awoke from sleep (Lk. 9:32). Was the rest of the story some visionary and auditory perception, given by God and shared by all three, sparked off by the real change in Jesus' appearance on the one hand and leading to Peter's understandable but inappropriate down-to-earth suggestion on the other? The truth is that we cannot know what happened apart from these accounts, but the above reconstruction attempts to do justice to all the factors involved.

The more important question is, 'What did it mean?' Moses and Elijah are usually taken to represent the law and the prophets. Of course no prophetic writing is ascribed to Elijah, but he was perhaps the most forceful of the prophets. Even more significant is the fact that both Moses and Elijah made an unusual departure from this life (Dt. 34:5–5; 2 Ki. 2:11). This is all the more meaningful in the light of another piece of evidence from Luke, namely that they were talking to Jesus 'about his departure (lit. exodus), which he was about to bring to fulfilment at Jerusalem' (Lk. 9:31). Maybe, too, these men represented God's bringing in of his kingdom. Moses as the one who led God's people to the Promised Land; Elijah as the one expected as a sign of that kingdom (Mal. 3:1; 4:5; Mk. 9:11). On all these grounds Moses and Elijah could appropriately minister to Jesus, representing all the painstaking care of divine preparation, about the next and final steps in his ministry.

As so often, we can sympathize with Peter's outburst (5). *He did not know what to say, they were so frightened* (6). It would not, evidently, have occurred to Peter not to say anything! Yet the nature of his response should not be neglected. The human passion to capture a unique moment forever was not limited to the first century.

The cloud (7), heavy with the sense of divine presence, enveloped them and the disciples became forcibly aware that Peter's suggestion was ill-advised. The repetition from heaven of the words from Jesus' baptism by John (Mk. 1:11; Mt. 3:17) is striking. Jesus is God's Son as no-one else is. In such an atmosphere the only thing to do is to listen. Then (8) it was all over. They saw only Jesus now.

There is danger that our concern with the transfiguration will cause us to miss a vital clue to Mark's purpose in writing his gospel (9:9–13). They are instructed by Jesus *not to tell anyone what they had seen until the Son of Man had risen from the dead*. We are familiar in this gospel with the instruction not to tell anyone (1:34, 44; 3:12; 5:43; 7:36; 8:26, 30). Now, however, for the first time, that ban is not absolute. When the Son of Man has risen from the dead they will be free to tell. The implication seems to be that these people will be in a position to understand what it all means. Mark is signalling why Jesus has not thus far been open about who he is, and what will be the proper basis on which people *will believe and understand what discipleship truly means*. 'There is no way rightly to understand who Jesus is until one has seen him suffer, die and rise again.'[4]

Luke does not record this section. Matthew does (Mt. 17:9), but spares the disciples some embarrassment. Mark, blunt and faithful to his sources as ever, does not. *They kept the matter to themselves*, he records, *discussing what 'rising from the dead' meant* (10). They did not yet understand, but neither did they ask him. This sounds like a very honest note of personal reminiscence.

What they did ask him about (11) was the expectation that Elijah would come before the Messiah (Mal. 3:1; 4:5). Jesus replies (12) that the teaching is right. '*Elijah does come first, and restores all things.*' But what was the nature of that restoration? It must have something to do with what John was preparing for. What he was preparing for was the coming Son of Man, but he must suffer, as it is written. The language here suggests Isaiah 53 as the writing referred to. But how would 'Elijah' restore all things for a Messiah like that? One answer might be, 'By setting the pattern'. This, says

---

[4] Williamson, p. 160.

165

Jesus, is precisely what has happened. John the Baptist is the Elijah of the prophecy, and look what happened to him.

3. A deaf, mute boy is healed (9:14–29)

When they came to the other disciples, they saw a large crowd around them and the teachers of the law arguing with them. [15]As soon as all the people saw Jesus, they were overwhelmed with wonder and ran to greet him.

[16]*'What are you arguing with them about?' he asked.*

[17]*A man in the crowd answered, 'Teacher, I brought you my son, who is possessed by a spirit that has robbed him of speech. [18]Whenever it seizes him, it throws him to the ground. He foams at the mouth, gnashes his teeth and becomes rigid. I asked your disciples to drive out the spirit, but they could not.'*

[19]*'O unbelieving generation,' Jesus replied, 'How long shall I stay with you? How long shall I put up with you? Bring the boy to me.'*

[20]*So they brought him. When the spirit saw Jesus, it immediately threw the boy into a convulsion. He fell to the ground and rolled around, foaming at the mouth.*

[21]*Jesus asked the boy's father, 'How long has he been like this?'*

'From childhood,' he answered. [22]'It has often thrown him into fire or water to kill him. But if you can do anything, take pity on us and help us.'

[23]*"If you can"?' said Jesus. 'Everything is possible for him who believes.'*

[24]*Immediately the boy's father exclaimed, 'I do believe; help me overcome my unbelief!'*

[25]*When Jesus saw that a crowd was running to the scene, he rebuked the evil spirit. 'You deaf and mute spirit,' he said, 'I command you, come out of him and never enter him again.'*

[26]*The spirit shrieked, convulsed him violently and came out. The boy looked so much like a corpse that many said, 'He's dead.' [27]But Jesus took him by the hand and lifted him to his feet, and he stood up.*

[28]*After Jesus had gone indoors, his disciples asked him privately, 'Why couldn't we drive it out?'*

[29]*He replied, 'This kind can come out only by prayer.'*

The healing of the deaf, mute boy is a chilling reminder of how far the Twelve have yet to go. (You can put it the other way round by reading Acts 3:1–10 and marvelling at what God was going to do with them. When Mark wrote his gospel, that side of their experience was also known.)

The central part of the story is introduced by the father's words to Jesus, '*I asked your disciples to drive out the spirit, but they could not*' (18). The detail of the account is by now predictable. An incurable person is brought to Jesus, who cures him. (For the relationship of demons to disease see pp. 55–56.) The crowd still cannot believe in Jesus' power: *The boy looked so much like a corpse that many said 'He's dead'* (26). But the boy recovers totally, raising for the disciples – or at least for the nine who had been at the original incident, the question, '*Why couldn't we drive it out?*' (28). The answer is given, not only in verse 29, '*This kind can come out only by prayer*', but also in two other sayings by Jesus, interspersed throughout the story. In verse 19 he is saddened by such an atmosphere of unbelief, '*O unbelieving generation, how long shall I stay with you? How long shall I put up with you?*'; and in verse 23, in response to the father's tentative (now doubting?) enquiry, '"*If you can?*" *Everything is possible for him who believes.*' The father, the only other person to come well out of this story, has pleading and honesty in his reply, '*I do believe; help me overcome my unbelief!*' (24). Jesus heals the boy. The whole story has a strong feeling of personal reminiscence about it.

a. The pressure of the culture

Bishop Lesslie Newbigin and others have drawn attention to the power of 'plausibility structures'. They are the publicly accepted criteria for knowledge in any given society, making it easier or harder for those who belong to that society to ascribe trust or falsehood to particular statements or claims. In our culture, for example, claims with a scientific explanation attached are likely to be accepted. Whether or not the general public understands the scientific explanation itself, these will be taken to be matters of public knowledge. Faith claims, however, will not be widely accepted, since these in our culture are seen as matters of private opinion. In such a setting it is both harder to believe and harder to lead others to faith. In the light of such a situation at least two responses are necessary. One is that Christians should recognize how important this factor is, and not blame themselves by contrast with Christian eras when no such factors operated. The other is that Christian scholars, thinkers and preachers must work patiently to explore and explain why we need a wider and deeper view of knowledge than that which can be scientifically proven, and how that wider and deeper view must be based on the exercise of faith if we are to be truly human, let alone Christian. This is a vital part of our apologetic task.

b. Belief, unbelief and partial belief

The word of Jesus and the father's response (23–24) raise an important point. Does Jesus' *'Everything is possible for him who believes'* mean, 'I, Jesus, can do everything because of the amount or quality of my faith', or 'Everything is possible to you if only you had that amount or quality of faith', or 'Everything is possible if you have faith in what I can do for you', placing the emphasis not upon the degree of faith but upon the relationship of trust between the man and Jesus? If it was the first then the man clearly misunderstands what Jesus means, and goes uncorrected, which would be unusual in Mark's gospel. If it meant the second then the man seems to be disqualifying himself. The third fits best, since it allows for the battering the man's faith has taken in the failure of the disciples (*'I brought you my son . . . I asked your disciples . . . they could not'*, 17–18).

The main point of this third way is that the miracle does not depend on the degree, quality or amount of the man's faith, but only on his having faith to link him effectively with the ministry of Jesus. It is the 'faith as small as a mustard seed' principle at work (Mt. 17:20; Lk. 17:6). The emphasis then is not on the quality of our faith but on the power of the Master with whom we are joined by faith. What is more, within that relationship there is room for our faith to grow. *'I do believe; help me overcome my unbelief!'* (24). We are not left on our own.

4. Teaching the Twelve (9:30–50)

They left that place and passed through Galilee. Jesus did not want anyone to know where they were, ³¹because he was teaching his disciples. He said to them, 'The Son of Man is going to be betrayed into the hands of men. They will kill him, and after three days he will rise.' ³²But they did not understand what he meant and were afraid to ask him about it.

³³They came to Capernaum. When he was in the house, he asked them, 'What were you arguing about on the road?' ³⁴But they kept quiet because on the way they had argued about who was the greatest.

³⁵Sitting down, Jesus called the Twelve and said, 'If anyone wants to be first, he must be the very last, and the servant of all.'

³⁶He took a little child and had him stand among them. Taking him in his arms he said to them, ³⁷'Whoever welcomes one of these children in my name welcomes me; and whoever welcomes me does not welcome me but the one who sent me.'

[38]'*Teacher,*' *said John,* '*we saw a man driving out demons in your name and we told him to stop, because he was not one of us.*'

[39]'*Do not stop him,*' *Jesus said.* '*No-one who does a miracle in my name can in the next moment say anything bad about me,* [40] *for whoever is not against us is for us.* [41]*I tell you the truth, anyone who gives you a cup of water in my name because you belong to Christ will certainly not lose his reward.*

[42]'*And if anyone causes one of these little ones who believe in me to sin, it would be better for him to be thrown into the sea with a large millstone tied around his neck.* [43]*If your hand causes you to sin, cut if off. It is better for you enter life maimed than with two hands to go into hell, where the fire never goes out.* [45]*And if your foot causes you to sin, cut if off. It is better for you to enter life crippled than to have two feet and be thrown into hell.* [47]*And if your eye causes you to sin, pluck it out. It is better for you to enter the kingdom of God with one eye than to have two eyes and be thrown into hell,* [48]*where*

> ' "*their worm does not die,*
> *and the fire is not quenched.*"

[49]*Everyone will be salted with fire.*

[50]'*Salt is good, but if it loses its saltiness, how can you make it salty again? Have salt in yourselves, and be at peace with each other.*'

The prophecy of the death and resurrection of the Son of Man (9:30–32) is now becoming a refrain (see 8:31 and 10:33–34). Mark makes it clear both that this is part of Jesus' policy to concentrate on training the Twelve and that he will have difficulty getting them to understand. It is no part of their credibility structure that the Messiah should be betrayed and killed, whatever Jesus says about rising from the dead. But they kept their ignorance and doubts a secret, a dangerous thing to so, as time would reveal.

Now follow various reflections on discipleship.

Who was the greatest among them they were eager to discuss (9:33–37). They kept quiet after Jesus' question because of the contrast between his self-giving (31) and their self-aggrandizement (34). How could they follow the one by the other?

Mark stresses the importance of the next saying by the threefold emphasis, *Sitting down . . . called the Twelve . . . said* (35). What followed must simply have thrown the disciples into even greater confusion. Jesus stands worldly human values on their heads in saying that true primacy is the primacy which comes from putting everyone before oneself, and in being outstanding in the role of servant! (35). Then, with a child (the age isn't clear) in his arms (or in his embrace), he tells them that a welcome to a child in his name both welcomes him and *'the one who sent me'* (37). The child held a very lowly place in the Graeco-Roman world. Jesus is saying, 'If you want to know the mood in which to welcome my ministry, remember how you feel when you welcome a child.' Implicit is something so much deeper and for the disciples unacceptable, 'I and God come that way, along the lowly road of being last, being servant, being child.' How could *'the Christ'* (8:29) say that?

The question of 'who was on his side' now becomes the dominant theme (38–41). The Twelve, not surprisingly, were adopting a proprietorial attitude to Jesus. Hadn't he called them, and no-one else, to be permanently with him? Wasn't he now, quite deliberately, giving most of his time to teaching them? That they were twelve in number, as there were twelve tribes of Israel, gave a completeness to their establishment which neither needed nor allowed anyone else. For once they felt confident about having done something right in forbidding outsiders who cast out demons in the name of Jesus (38). This could safely, therefore, be reported to him. Who better to tell him than John, the beloved disciple? But they were in for one further shock and disappointment.

They should not have stopped such activity. If people truly perform miracles in the name of Jesus they are not likely to begin speaking badly of that name. Had the disciples thought that the use of his name was like some powerful and magical formula? Jesus makes the point that people can only do miracles in his name if they are in a proper relationship to that name (person).[5] So those who do miracles in the name will not oppose the person whose name it is. Even *a cup of water in* his *name*, hardly a miracle, is not without worth (41).

Causing others to sin really is something they should be concerned about (42–49). The *these little ones* of verse 42 may be a reference to *these little children* of verse 37, referring to our particular responsibility not to lead the young astray. Or it might be a reference to 'little ones' in the faith, to new believers, even to those in verses 39–40 whom the disciples had prohibited from performing miracles. It is not at all unusual for new believers to have the ability to witness powerfully for Christ, nor for those in leadership positions to be extremely nervous about such activity. Whether causing someone to sin has a particular meaning in this context is not clear. It could be by hindering their proper place in the Christian community or hindering their witness, as in verses 36–41, or it

[5] The name was taken truly to represent the person. See Acts 4:10–12.

could be interpreted in the light of the warnings about sin which follow. Since these are introduced by the same expression *causes . . . to sin* (42, 43) then the latter seems most likely. The *large millstone* is a reference to that usually pulled by a donkey as opposed to a lighter one operated by humans. The whole section about being *'thrown into the sea'* refers to a Roman punishment (42). The cutting off of a hand or foot, or the plucking out of an eye, cannot be literal. You would still have one left, and they are not the source of the sin in any case. Jesus is deliberately using the most severe language to stress that sin is to be opposed at all costs. To be 'complete', in the world's judgment, but to go to Hell (Gehenna was the place where offal and rubbish was permanently on fire) is infinitely worse than to be limited, in worldly terms, in what you do, but to enjoy eternal life.[6]

Everyone will be salted with fire (49), is plainly a bridge verse between the 'fire' statements which precede (43–48), and the 'salt' statements which follow in verse 50. There is no ground for any doctrine of purgatory, for the fire in verses 43–48 is punitive and destructive. The first purifies, which is the link with salt, which combats decay. One alternative form of this verse in some New Testament manuscripts, though almost certainly not the original text, may provide an indication of how Jesus' hearers would understand it. This version, probably dependent on Leviticus 2:13, relates it to sacrifices which had salt added to them (Lv. 2:13, Ezk. 43:24). If this does offer the most likely clue, then the self-denial in the interests of holiness referred to in verses 43–48 is now linked to the sacrifice to be offered by the Son of Man in 9:31 and 8:31. Once more, as for the Master, so for the disciple.

Two further salt sayings are added (50). One is the uselessness of unsalty salt. How can you possibly re-salt salt? This must be a warning against turning back from the path of discipleship, particularly in the light of verses 35–37 and 43–47. The second concerns the inner state of wholesomeness within the community of disciples, characterized by peace, perhaps particularly relevant at this point if, while Jesus is on his way to suffering and death they are establishing a league of greatness among themselves.

The disciples' way

The starkness and blatancy of the mistakes of the Twelve must not be allowed to mask our own equivalents. Not many modern

---

[6] Which must be the sense of 'life' here – verses 43 and 46, confirmed by the equivalent in verse 47, 'the kingdom of God'.

disciples would engage in public disputation about who is greatest, but our ecclesiastical and societal hierarchies provide us with a structure to disguise equivalent tendencies. Perhaps most subtle of all is the choice between obedience to Christ and preserving one's reputation.

In a similar way our denominational structures, and our cross-denominational theological and sacramental groupings, provide every opportunity we need for the equivalent of the disciples' 'We told him to stop, because he was not one of us' (38). Defending the truth, feeling the best ways of living by it, and searching for purity in all things are laudable aims. But Jesus' test is the simpler one of pedigree. Were the others living and acting in the power of his name?

The sharpness of his strictures concerning sin must not be minimized. We have constantly to be making judgments about right and wrong, since the world's standards are so different from ours (35–37). Some of the self-denial involved will not be easy. The fundamental question is which life and which location we prefer (43–49).

For those who have had some insight into God's kingdom the prospect, individually or corporately (50), of being unsalty salt should help us to see the right way forward. All that this involved for the first disciples, in following Jesus, they would shortly discover.

5. The issue of divorce and marriage (10:1–12)

Jesus then left that place and went into the region of Judea and across the Jordan. Again crowds of people came to him, and as was his custom, he taught them.

²Some Pharisees came and tested him by asking, 'Is it lawful for a man to divorce his wife?'

³'What did Moses command you?' he replied.

⁴They said, 'Moses permitted a man to write a certificate of divorce and send her away.'

⁵'It was because your hearts were hard that Moses wrote you this law,' Jesus replied. ⁶'But at the beginning of creation God "made them male and female". ⁷'For this reason a man will leave his father and mother and be united to his wife, ⁸and the two will become one flesh." So they are no longer two, but one. ⁹Therefore what God has joined together, let man not separate.'

¹⁰When they were in the house again, the disciples asked Jesus about this. ¹¹He answered, 'Anyone who divorces his wife and marries another woman commits adultery against her. ¹²And if she divorces her husband and marries another man, she commits adultery.'

A question on marriage and divorce now intensifies the struggle between Jesus and his opposition, represented this time by the Pharisees (2), though a number of reliable manuscripts omit their presence. The setting now is *the region of Judea and across the Jordan* (1). There is a curious break in the concentration on training the Twelve, since the crowd, and in it some Pharisees, are again the setting. Yet at the end of the section (10–12), it is the disciples who are the focus of attention once more (see similar instances in 4:10, 7:17 and 9:28). The best interpretation of the geographical reference in verse 1, with the unexpected 'and' between Judea and across the Jordan is that he is moving towards Jerusalem.

It has been suggested that in view of Deuteronomy 24:1–4, to which the conversation is directed in verse 4, it is inconceivable that Jews, and particularly Pharisees, would ask such a question. If anything, at that time the mood was becoming even harder and there would come a time when a man was forced to divorce his wife in the circumstances alluded to in Deuteronomy 24:1, though there remained both a stricter and a more lenient view of which circumstances precisely provided grounds for the divorce. Here, however, the point is probably a simpler one. If a general crowd is the audience, then what is more natural than to try out this new teacher on a thorny topic like marriage and divorce? If there were Pharisees present, then such a question might provide more evidence in the dossier against him, since the words *tested him* (2) mean 'to try out the defences' or 'to catch unguarded'. The aim is to get him to say something clearly contrary to the accepted norms of the time.

As so often, Jesus cuts through the discussion of details or the points of legal declarations, and points to the heart of the matter, God's will and purpose (compare Mt. 5:21–48). The point is not the interpretation of 'becomes displeasing' and 'something indecent', nor the provision for a 'certificate of divorce'; nor what should happen and not happen if she remarries and subsequently is divorced once more (Dt. 24:1–4). The real question is the positive one, namely, 'What did God intend by giving marriage in the first place?' For the answer to that he goes to Genesis 1:27 and 2:24. God's original purpose was lifelong faithfulness of a man and a woman in marriage. We should note at this point, in relation the sharp words of verse 11, that Jesus here introduces the concept of a man committing adultery against a woman, not a normal line of thought or expression at that time.

In private with his disciples, Jesus reaffirms the ideal (10–12). God's purpose for marriage, and the meaning of breaking it, is set out with stunning clarity.

173

The crucial question is what we are to make of verses 3–5. Jesus invites their rehearsal of the situation (3). Nor did he say that Moses did wrong in what he provided (5). What is wrong is neither God's original purpose nor Moses' provision. What is wrong is the sinfulness of the human heart which goes contrary to God's purposes and those ideals associated with them, and wreaks havoc in human life. Faced with that divine ideal and human failure to live up to it, Moses did the best he could to preserve the ideal (presumably under God's guidance) yet face the human situation before him. The fact that Matthew (in Mt. 19:9) records Jesus as allowing one exception to the adultery rule, is very significant. The exception suggests that a marriage can be broken by what is called 'marital unfaithfulness', the breaking of the 'one fleshness' of Genesis 1:24, Matthew 19:5, and Mark 10:7. Jesus refuses to be a law-giver or legislator. He states the two realities – the divine intention and the human failure. He does not condemn Moses' solution, though making clear that it is less than the best. In Matthew 19:9 he allows the awful reality of marriage failure. As so often, he turns the question back to the questioner, and to us. What, in the light of God's purpose for marriage and human failure to sustain it, is the legal provision which does the most to hold up the ideal while sadly facing the reality of human failure?

Provision for marriage and divorce

Few issues should cause such concern as the breakdown of marriages in our Western culture, not only because of the turmoil and pain to the partners involved but also because of the untold and unpredictable damage to children and others, well into the future. There is also the disintegration of a fundamental part of the structure of society. Above all there is a breaking of a purpose of God for his creatures.

Yet any who have experience of pastoral care for married people will know that, sadly and tragically, people do choose badly, make mistakes, change dramatically, fall out of love. To one happily married, or to one not married at all, these may seem to be inconceivable developments. The 'Why don't they . . .' syndrome operates strongly. Yet the fact is that marriages do lose their inner core of meaning. People do feel trapped. Deteriorating relationships do destroy the participants. Society's pressures, increasing mobility, non-Christian standards and life styles all militate against stable marriage.

In such a situation the Christian church must find a way to hold up, teach, prepare people for, and sustain couples in, the original divine purpose of one man, one woman for life. Yet at the same time it has to find ways of showing the deep compassionate sympathy and understanding of Jesus towards those for whom life has not turned out according to the highest ideals.

6. Trust and possession (10:13–31)

People were bringing little children to Jesus to have him touch them, but the disciples rebuked them. [14]*When Jesus saw this, he was indignant. He said to them, 'Let the little children come to me, and do not hinder them, for the kingdom of God belongs to such as these.* [15]*I tell you the truth, anyone who will not receive the kingdom of God like a little child will never enter it.'* [16]*And he took the children in his arms, put his hands on them and blessed them.*

[17]*As Jesus started on his way, a man ran up to him and fell on his knees before him. 'Good teacher,' he asked, 'what must I do to inherit eternal life?'*

[18]*'Why do you call me good?' Jesus answered. 'No-one is good – except God alone.* [19]*You know the commandments: "Do not murder, do not commit adultery, do not steal, do not give false testimony, do not defraud, honour your father and mother."'*

[20]*'Teacher,' he declared, 'all these I have kept since I was a boy.*

[21]*Jesus looked at him and loved him. 'One thing you lack,' he said. 'Go, sell everything you have and give to the poor, and you will have treasure in heaven. Then come, follow me.'*

[22]*At this the man's face fell. He went away sad, because he had great wealth.*

[23]*Jesus looked around and said to his disciples, 'How hard it is for the rich to enter the kingdom of God!'*

[24]*The disciples were amazed at his words. But Jesus said again, 'Children, how hard it is to enter the kingdom of God!* [25]*It is easier for a camel to go through the eye of a needle than for a rich man to enter the kingdom of God.'*

[26]*The disciples were even more amazed, and said to each other, 'Who then can be saved?'*

[27]*Jesus looked at them and said, 'With man this is impossible, but not with God: all things are possible with God.'*

[28]*Peter said to him, 'We have left everything to follow you!'*

[29]*'I tell you the truth,' Jesus replied, 'no-one who has left home or brothers or sisters or mother or father or children or fields for me and the gospel* [30]*will fail to receive a hundred times as much in this present age (homes, brothers, sisters, mothers, children and fields – and with them, persecutions) and in the age to come, eternal life.* [31]*But many who are first will be last, and the last first.'*

Welcoming the children here ties in with 9:33–37. Whether or not, in the context in which Mark wrote his gospel, there was serious discussion of infant baptism, which is at least possible, a much deeper point is being made here. Indeed it is yet another way to sound the fundamental note of the gospel. Children are not to be excluded, because they characterize the required attitude of the true disciple. The *'kingdom of God belongs to such as these'*(14). The child is entirely dependent upon the parent in the very nature of things. Total trust is the centre of a child's existence. So it must be for the disciple. As Mark refers it to disciples, they cannot earn it or deserve it or make it, but only accept it thankfully as God's gift.[7] This is why group after group have so far in the story failed to enter in. They have all brought their own agenda – religious leaders, family, crowd. Only those helplessly needing to be healed, and occasionally the disciples, have burst through into the world of self-abandoning trust, like that of a small child. It is they who receive the blessing (16). At this point in the gospel of course, as we must remind ourselves constantly, people have not seen the main reason for total commitment. Hints are being given (8:31; 9:31; 10:33–34), but at present such hints are more likely to frighten people away than to bring them in! For the moment, however, the concentration on teaching the disciples has continued. They have been offered two new lessons, namely, 'Don't exclude the children!' and become 'childlike' (not 'childish') if you wish to know the secret of faith.

The problem with possessions, as a hindrance to total trust, is now spelt out (10:17–31). The first section (17–27) focuses on financial wealth. After that it extends (28–31) to everything that enriches life, with loving relationships as a particular emphasis (29). There is a plausible unity to this section, though the three passages 17–22, 23–27 and 28–31 could exist independently, and verse 31 occurs in other settings too.

The story of the man who came to Jesus (17–22) is described in all three synoptic gospels. Mark says he was *a man* (17) with *great wealth* (22). Luke says he was a 'ruler' (Lk. 18:18) and 'a man of great wealth' (Lk. 18:23). Matthew adds that he was a 'young man' (Mt. 19:22). Putting all three together we get the popular traditional designation of him as 'the rich young ruler', and see the value of having more than one gospel account of Jesus' ministry. As is usually the case, Mark's account is more vivid and succinct, with brisk and pointed questions and answers.

The man shows a keenness and vigour of search which surpasses

[7] Moule, p. 79.

anything so far in the gospel. He runs (few people ran under the hot sun) and kneels (17). For his reference to Jesus as teacher, see the exposition of 1:21–22. He wants eternal life. This way of describing the spiritual goal is more typical of John's gospel than of the synoptics. Here it probably means 'the life of the coming kingdom of God'. Evidently he had kept the law scrupulously, but did not feel that he had yet found the quality of spiritual life that satisfied (19–20). Is it significant that a rich man's (22) construction of the search is to ask what *he can do* to get it? (17).

Verse 18 has puzzled commentators to this day! Matthew obviously had difficulty with it, too, and offers the softest form available, 'Why do you ask me about what is good?' (Mt. 19:17). Mark's account is sharper.'*Why do you call me good? No-one is good – except God alone*' (18). He might be correcting the man for being too obsequious. Or he may be saying something much deeper. 'Do you realize the meaning of ascribing to me what belongs to God only? Do you understand how near the truth you are?' Jesus knows. Mark knows. By raising the question of the rich man's knowledge Mark is also asking his reader to decide.

That this is not a game of words becomes plain in what follows. Mark says that *Jesus looked at him and loved him* (21). There is something attractive about his earnestness in keeping the law, and his humble determination to find a conclusion to his search. But the way is not to be his usual success story – 'What can I do to cross this barrier?' Jesus invites him to do something contrary to the previous direction of his whole life. '*Go, sell everything you have and give to the poor, and you will have treasure in heaven. Then come, follow me*' (21). If he is to find the childlike way of discipleship set out in verses 13–16, then he must first loosen the grip of that in which he trusted now, namely his wealth. Without that step, he was not even keeping the Ten Commandments (Ex. 20:3–4). For this man it had to be a straight choice – riches or the kingdom. His reaction showed how accurately Jesus had understood him. He wouldn't give up his wealth, so instead of following Jesus, he went away (22).

Jesus' reflection on this incident is provided in verses 23–27. How difficult it is to hold on to riches and enter the kingdom, like trying to get a huge camel through a needle's eye! (23–25). In a society like theirs the disciples find the idea of the kingdom excluding the rich inconceivable, forgetting how often in Israel's history it was 'the poor in the land' who had remained faithful (see Ps. 37 as an example). But if those who know how to succeed in life cannot make it, then who can? (26). The answer is crushingly simple; only God can save (27). That is why the childlike are saved, since they put their trust wholly in him. And it is why the rich often are not, since they are possessed by their possessions, as this young man was (22). But the last word is not gloomy. There is an optimism of grace. God can do what humans cannot.

This particular challenge of grace is applied to the disciples again in verses 28–31. Peter, as ever, offers an explosive, if somewhat boastful contribution (28). To some readers of Mark's gospel were the costs of discipleship seeming too great? Or were some teaching that discipleship was a triumphalist road? Either way, Peter's words and Jesus' reply put the matter in perspective then and now.

Jesus makes no attempt to disguise any of the cost (29). He even reinforces it with a sobering reminder during the optimistic part of his statement – 'and with them, persecutions' (30). But whatever it costs to be a disciple in terms of the self-denial of verse 29 is far outweighed by the gain of belonging to the family of God's kingdom and all that it involves (30), with the experience of eternal life (for which the rich young man had asked, 17) now and forever.

In that setting, life will be full of surprises (31). One might have seen it as obvious that children could not be part of the kingdom vision. But they are (13–14). It would be clear that a devout law-keeping rich young man who so much wanted to enter the kingdom of God would do so. But he did not (22). It would seem self-evident that the powerful rich, as a group, would be needed. But they are not (23–25). Anyone can see that disciples of Jesus, giving up everything, possess nothing. But they are immensely rich in every area of life (29–30). Truly, the meek do inherit the earth! (Mt. 5:5). By the same token, of course, the Twelve must not begin to elevate themselves as superior disciples through having literally left all behind. 'Many who are first will be last, and the last first' (31).

a. Child-like trust and giving everything up

This whole passage allows for considerable misunderstanding. For example, the commending of the little children (13–17) makes only the single point of childlike trust as the dominant factor in their lives. It does not commend simplistic attitudes like rejection of learning, prohibition of planning, neglect of natural and God-given abilities and high profile activity. It certainly warns against trusting any of these, but not against using them.

The rich young man approaches the same issue from the other end. He could not let go of his wealth, as Jesus guessed and the story makes clear (22). Yet Jesus did not always call rich people to give everything away. (See Lk. 14:25–33, where 'giving up everything' is used in the same context as 'hating' father, mother, wife, *etc.*) The emphasis is upon commitment to Christ being the prior commitment, before all else. It begins with the discovery that we find salvation (eternal life, a place in the kingdom of God) only by trusting God and not anything we have or can do.

b.   Commitment cannot be forced

There is a curious juxtaposition of ideas in verses 21 and 22. Jesus loved the young man, yet made no attempt to dissuade him from walking sadly away when he could not or would not take up Jesus' challenge. Jesus makes no further attempt to persuade him. The conditions had been set: the young man must make up his mind. Our evangelism does well to copy this pattern from our Lord. He neither hectors nor pesters people into the kingdom, nor lowers the levels of commitment required.

c.   Poor and rich

This passage does not support the contention that the poor are somehow naturally spiritual or people of faith. Nor does it say that the rich are automatically materialistic or sinful. It says that in the matter of salvation those with wealth, and presumably the power that goes with it, are more inclined to trust those things than to give themselves primarily in faith to God. Yet there are many rich saints who are not controlled by their money and who serve their Lord outstandingly. The poor do not automatically believe, and are under many pressures to be more materialistic and greedy than the rich. Yet it cannot be a coincidence that in many places today it is amongst the poor that revival is breaking out and deep new insights into the Christian faith are being discovered. To speak of God's 'bias to the poor' as some do, is properly to recognize that it is not God's will in his world for the minority to have most and the majority to have least. For that situation rich Christians, which includes most of us in the West, will be called to account, and we should be doing more about it now than we do.

7.   What discipleship is about (10:32–45)

They were on their way up to Jerusalem, with Jesus leading the way, and the disciples were astonished, while those who followed were afraid. Again he took the Twelve aside and told them what was going to happen to him. [33]'We are going up to Jerusalem,' he said, 'and the Son of Man will be betrayed to the chief priests and

179

teachers of the law. They will condemn him to death and will hand him over to the Gentiles, ³⁴who will mock him and spit on him, flog him and kill him. Three days later he will rise.'

³⁵*Then James and John, the sons of Zebedee, came to him. 'Teacher,' they said, 'we want you to do for us whatever we ask.'*

³⁶*'What do you want me to do for you?' he asked.*

³⁷*They replied, 'Let one of us sit at your right and the other at your left in your glory.'*

³⁸*'You don't know what you are asking,' Jesus said. 'Can you drink the cup I drink or be baptised with the baptism I am baptised with?'*

³⁹*'We can,' they answered.*

Jesus said to them, 'You will drink the cup I drink and be baptised with the baptism I am baptised with, ⁴⁰but to sit at my right or left is not for me to grant. These places belong to those for whom they have been prepared.'

⁴¹*When the ten heard about this, they became indignant with James and John. ⁴²Jesus called them together and said, 'You know that those who are regarded as rulers of the Gentiles lord it over them, and their high officials exercise authority over them. ⁴³Not so with you. Instead, whoever wants to become great among you must be your servant, ⁴⁴and whoever wants to be first must be slave of all. ⁴⁵For even the Son of Man did not come to be served, but to serve, and to give his life as a ransom for many.'*

The prediction of death and resurrection is repeated once more (32–34). Mark does seem to speak figuratively as well as literally now, when he reports that Jesus was *leading the way* (32). The combination of his commitment to fulfil his Father's calling, and the growing perplexity of the Twelve, which was communicated to the others who followed him, creates a strong atmosphere of tension. He led, the disciples were astonished (a frequent word in Mark), and the rest were afraid (32).

Yet the teaching must go on. The disciples are again taken on one side and the now familiar lesson is repeated. For the first time in such sayings Jerusalem is specifically mentioned, as is the fact that *'the chief priests and teachers of the law . . . will hand him over to the Gentiles, who will mock him and spit on him, flog him and kill him'* (33–34). The detail is impressive, though each part is not unusual once one had decided that death in Jerusalem was the outcome of the journey. The backcloth for the coming drama is now being painted in more detail, and extended significantly. This is not going to be simply a Jewish ending. Gentiles who could do such things to the Son of Man can only be the Romans. Whatever happens to the Son of Man will be on the world stage.

The contrasting perceptions of the future are graphically portrayed next (35–45). James and John ask for seats on Jesus' right and left in his *glory* (37). Mark frankly puts the request down to them, Matthew says their mother did the asking! (Mt. 20:20). Even there, however, they are standing (or 'kneeling') with her, since Jesus' response is a question to them. Luke omits the whole embarrassing story. What is clear is that the greater the pressure upon them from the fateful journey they are now taking, the more the Twelve settle into discussion of their own greatness and status (compare 8:31–32, followed by 33–35).

Mark's *'in your glory'* is probably interpreted by Matthew as 'in your kingdom' (Mt. 20:21), meaning the Messiah's kingdom which the Jews believed would precede the kingdom of God. By contrast, Jesus' reply is not in their terms of courts and thrones, but in terms of a cup and a baptism (38). The cup, in a number of Old Testament passages, is about suffering and punishment, usually at God's hand.[8] This suggests that what lies ahead for the Son of Man is to be full of woe. That the Jewish authorities and Romans will somehow be meting out the cup for God would be light years away from James' and John's perception at that time, though they would remember and realize much later, not least in the light of their Old Testament scriptures like Isaiah 53:10, 'Yet it was the Lord's will to crush him and cause him to suffer, and though the Lord makes his life a guilt offering, he will see his offspring and prolong his days, and the will of the Lord will prosper in his hand.' If one asks how God could ever bring this suffering servant figure to drink such a cup, then verse 6 of Isaiah 53 provides an answer, 'We all, like sheep, have gone astray, each of us has turned to his own way; and the Lord has laid on him the iniquity of us all.' This suffering servant, whose image comes to mind again and again in the words of Jesus about the Son of Man, is bearing for sinners what they cannot bear for themselves, the result of their sins in the wrath of God. This is the cup of the Son of Man.

Baptism is another violent image connected with sorrow and grief. It has about it the sense of being forcibly plunged beneath the waters, cast into the depths.[9]

Martin points out that the disciples may have associated 'the cup' with celebration and the baptism with the current idea among many of their fellow Jews that baptism was 'a token of God's renewal of

---

[8] Ps. 75:8; Is. 51:17–23; Je. 49:12; La. 4:21; Ezk. 23:31–34.
[9] Pss. 42:7; 69:2, 15; 124:4, 5; Is. 43:2, the latter again referring to the suffering servant.

His people as a prelude to the coming of the Kingdom'.[10] They answer confidently that they can share his cup and baptism. Jesus confirms their answer, though not their meaning by it (39). They had hardly begun to experience the 'death and resurrection' nature of discipleship. But in any case, the right and left places in glory were not for Jesus to grant (40).

By contrast, the other ten disciples might have come out of this incident well, but when they learned what had happened they showed their anger with James and John, perhaps at being upstaged by them! This leads Jesus to collect them together for a rebuke (42). They are still behaving like those outside the kingdom, even outside the Jewish faith. In the kingdom greatness is characterized by the degree of service to others (42–43). As supreme example they should note carefully what he has been teaching them about the Son of Man. He came not *'to be served, but to serve, and to give his life as a ransom for many'* (45).

This is a further enlargement of the meaning of his prediction of death and resurrection in 8:31, 9:31, and 10:33–34. If the Twelve did not see the point of such a process Jesus is now trying to help them to do so. The 'ransom' was a familiar image in Jewish, Roman and Greek cultures. It was the price paid to liberate a slave, a prisoner of war, or a condemned person. The paying of the price cleaned the slate. To set a person free like this was known as 'redemption'. Jesus Christ's action in setting us free is described as 'redeeming' us in Luke 1:68; 2:38, Titus 2:14; Hebrews 9:12 and 1 Peter 1:18. Again the suffering servant of Isaiah 53 hovers in the background of every discussion of what this means. There is no benefit in asking to whom the ransom price was paid: this is not the point of the image. Its single purpose is to make clear that Jesus Christ, Son of God and Son of Man *was himself* the price paid to set us free. At the source of all Christian service in the world is the crucified and risen Lord who died to liberate us into such service.

Forgetting the point

It may amaze us that the disciples could be so slow to grasp 'what it was all about'. We need not spend too long on that line. Jesus' teaching in these verses shows discipleship as a self-denying, self-risking, self-giving part of lowly service for the redemption of the world. Yet so much of Christian life as one can now observe it is about gaining a secure position in society, inviting others to join

[10] Martin, *Action*, p. 91.

us where we are, doing little to change the structures of our political and social life, thus lending our support to structures which oppress the poor and needy at home and abroad, and largely leaving it to preachers and full-time evangelists to spread the good news about Jesus. We are not (mostly!) as crass as the disciples in jockeying for seats of power in the kingdom, but by much more subtle behaviour we show how little we grasp what it means to be disciples of a crucified Lord who gave *his life as a ransom for many* (45).

8. The healing of blind Bartimaeus (10:46–52)

Then they came to Jericho. As Jesus and his disciples, together with a large crowd, were leaving the city, a blind man, Bartimaeus (that is, the Son of Timaeus), was sitting by the roadside begging. ⁴⁷When he heard that it was Jesus of Nazareth, he began to shout, 'Jesus, Son of David, have mercy on me!'

⁴⁸Many rebuked him and told him to be quiet, but he shouted all the more, 'Son of David, have mercy on me!'

⁴⁹Jesus stopped and said, 'Call him.'

So they called to the blind man, 'Cheer up! On your feet! He's calling you.' ⁵⁰Throwing his cloak aside, he jumped to his feet and came to Jesus.

⁵¹'What do you want me to do for you?' Jesus asked him.

The blind man said, 'Rabbi, I want to see.'

⁵²'Go,' said Jesus, 'your faith has healed you.' Immediately he received his sight and followed Jesus along the road.

The healing of blind Bartimaeus provides a more encouraging note on which to end this section of the gospel. He hears who is coming and calls to *'Jesus, Son of David'* – the kind of description Jesus has tried to avoid from the crowd because of its association with the great military deliverer (47). But this man knows what he wants, and no rebukes from the crowd will keep him silent (48). Jesus hears and summons the man, who throws off his robe and runs forward, in enormous contrast to the gait and manner of the disciples making their way behind Jesus to Jerusalem (32). Jesus asks the man an obvious question, but it enables the man to exercise his choice (51). He is not told that he is healed, but to *'Go, your faith has healed you'* (52). The man has not earned his cure, but in Mark's gospel it is the response of faith commitment which provides the arena within which the drama of salvation takes place. As he goes, *Immediately he received his sight and followed Jesus along the road* (52). How tired the disciples' steps must have looked by contrast.

183

Mark 11:1 – 13:37
6. Jesus enters Jerusalem

1. The lowly entry (11:1–11)

*As they approached Jerusalem and came to Bethphage and Bethany
at the Mount of Olives, Jesus sent two of his disciples, ²saying to
them, 'Go to the village ahead of you, and just as you enter it, you
will find a colt tied there, which no-one has ever ridden. Untie it
and bring it here. ³If anyone asks you, "Why are you doing this?"
tell him, "The Lord needs it and will send it back here shortly." '*

*⁴They went and found a colt outside in the street, tied at a
doorway. As they untied it, ⁵some people standing there asked,
'What are you doing, untying that colt?' ⁶They answered as Jesus
had told them to, and the people let them go. ⁷When they brought
the colt to Jesus and threw their cloaks over it, he sat on it. ⁸Many
people spread their cloaks on the road, while others spread branches
they had cut in the fields. ⁹Those who went ahead and those who
followed shouted,*

> *'Hosanna!'*
> *'Blessed is he who comes in the name of the Lord!'*
> *¹⁰'Blessed is the coming kingdom of our father David!'*
> *'Hosanna in the highest!'*

*¹¹Jesus entered Jerusalem and went to the temple. He looked
around at everything, but since it was already late, he went out to
Bethany with the Twelve.*

The different intentions of all four gospel writers come out clearly
in their account of the entry into Jerusalem. Matthew draws attention to the fulfilment of Old Testament prophecy (Mt. 21:4–5),
and to the exciting questioning which this event provoked
(21:10–11). Luke highlights the self-evident nature of what was
happening. If the disciples did not cry out, the stones would! (Lk.
19:39–40). For John it is the fact that the disciples understood much

184

later the full meaning of what happened on that day, as they reflected in the light of other events which took place later (Jn. 12:16).

Mark simply tells the story without comment, yet the way he tells it provides another perspective. His words are heavy with Old Testament implication, as we shall see below, but he does not point that out. As with the parables, his story invites the perception of something deeper but does nothing to enforce or ensure it. He plays down the size of the crowd (*many people* [11:8], by contrast with Matthew, 'a very large crowd' [Mt. 21:8–9], Luke 'the whole crowd' [Lk. 19:37], and John [12:12–13]). Those present did and shouted all the right things (8–10), but there is no indication that they grasped the real significance of what was happening. For Mark it is the lowliness and humility of the entry into Jerusalem which matters, not its triumphal nature. It is a kingship of hidden majesty, of humble power to save. Perhaps this is why he does not take the account of the entry straight on into the cleansing of the temple, as Luke does (Lk. 19:44–45), nor simply make a temporal distinction between the two as Matthew does (Mt. 21:18, 'Early in the morning, as he was on his way back to the city'). Mark records that there was a deliberate choice by Jesus to view the temple from inside and *only then*, because it was evening, to go back to Bethany.

Though it is by no means the most important issue at stake, the four gospel accounts need not be seen as contradicting one another, so long as we remember that the writers are not offering tight historical accounts on a minute by minute sequential basis. Each tells his story in order to bring out certain significant items. Descriptions of crowd sizes are relative. Even Matthew's reference to all Jerusalem being agitated with questions need mean no more than that it was a common talking point. Since neither the Jewish authorities nor the Romans took action, nor was it brought against Jesus in his trial, the entry was plainly not in the category of 'unlawful disturbance'. In Luke's account the meaning might be self-evident to Jesus, but that does not necessarily imply that the crowds grasped it, as the gospel stories make clear again and again. (See, as a striking example, Peter's perception and then lack of perception about Jesus in the incident at Caesarea Philippi, Mk. 8:27–33, Mt. 16:13–23.) The disciples and the crowds were, like us, sometimes able to see what was meant by what was happening, and sometimes not able, and variously so across a bewildering spectrum. Different gospel accounts help us to see parts of that variety.

In Mark the now familiar emphases are here. Jesus is the messianic figure, coming on the untried colt of Zechariah's prophecy

185

(Mk. 11:2, 7; Zc. 9:9). The way the colt is obtained has hints of Jesus' unusual knowledge and power (2–6). Attempts to explain *the Lord* (3) as meaning God, or meaning the owner of the colt who must therefore have been with Jesus, or as the content of a pre-arranged deal, show ingenuity, but all seem to miss Mark's point. The man who rides the donkey is more than an ordinary man, though the crowds do not yet know this. Only the disciples are privileged to see it (if even they can).

The disciples' and the crowd's spreading of cloaks (7–8) is reminiscent of a customary way of treating a king (see 2 Ki. 9:12–13). The waving of palm branches (though only John's gospel identifies them as palm) and the shouts of *Hosanna!* (9), are usually taken to relate to Psalm 118. The word here is a transliteration of the Aramaic form of the Hebrew used in Psalm 118:25, meaning 'save now'. Since this psalm was used on the Feast of Tabernacles and at Passover, the cry from the crowd may simply have picked up the celebratory spirit of those other occasions. Cranfield points out the appropriateness of this in relation to Tabernacles, since bundles of palm, myrtle and willow were waved during the festival whenever Hosanna occurred in the liturgy.[1]

'*Blessed is he who comes in the name of the Lord!*' (11:9b) is quoted from Psalm 118:26. It refers to the pilgrims who pray to be 'blessed in the name of the Lord'. Did anyone perceive the possibility of linking *in the name of the Lord* with *he who comes* rather than with *blessed*?

'*Blessed is the coming kingdom of our father David!*' '*Hosanna in the highest!*' (10) are not quotations, but shouts which Jews of Jesus' day could raise with deep feeling for freedom. Their messianic implications are clear. How the coming kingdom might be interpreted is not. The messianic link would be stronger if the crowd had the Passover in mind.

Whatever they thought, the account which Mark offers ends on a low key, yet with meaning for the whole story (11). A quiet survey of the inside of the temple is hardly a fitting climax to a rowdy uprising, but as Mark tells it, there is promise of something to come.

Mark's strong story lines are discernible from start (1–6) to end (11). Jesus is in control of the situation, initiating activity whose meaning is clear to us now, and would become clear to the disciples after his resurrection and ascension (Jn. 12:16). Whether or not he intended that meaning is not self-evident from the account, but there is good reason for believing that he did.

[1] Cranfield, p. 351.

Certainly it fits Mark's portrayal throughout.

The second Markan feature is the sense of momentum towards a conclusion, a momentum not due to the initiative of the disciples or the crowd. Events are moving forward, with Jesus as both instigator and focal point. All the others play their part with varying degrees of insight about what is happening.

The disciples may have grasped some of it, especially if the arrangement about the donkey was not made in advance. The crowd shouted all the right things – especially 'Save now' – but seem more to have been in the celebratory mood of traditional festivals than to be entering into deeper understanding of this important event. Mark's reticence about explaining the meaning of things, and his low-key ending, are in line with his general approach of hiddenness. The climax is drawing nearer, yet only those who perceive what is hidden, and follow through to the end, will be saved. The crowds shout, 'Save now', but must continue if they are to see their cry answered. They repeat 'Blessed is he who comes in the name of the Lord' and 'Blessed is the coming kingdom' (9–10), but it will take more than participation in one happy procession to achieve that. What will achieve it still lies ahead, and discipleship means following 'the man on the donkey' all the way. It still does!

About enthusiasm and perception, groups and individuals

Mark helps us here about the distinction between enthusiasm and truth, and between group spirit and individual perception. Group spirit and movement can hold us in the initial period of belief, and can sustain us during difficult times. But it is no substitute for individual understanding and commitment. As such, group spirit can prevent us from making our own discoveries, and can hinder the truth from reaching the deepest areas of our personality. The more exciting the group experience, whether in its free expression, sacramental mystery or corporate oneness, the more carefully do we need to ensure that our understanding is keeping track of our public activity, and our spiritual growth matching the group life. We need the experience of both social faith and personal growth. It is often the latter which is neglected. Mark's focus on Jesus as the only one who both enters the activities and perceives their significance is a reminder about the true nature of discipleship.

2. The fig tree and the temple (11:12–25)

The next day as they were leaving Bethany, Jesus was hungry.

187

[13]*Seeing in the distance a fig-tree in leaf, he went to find out if it had any fruit. When he reached it, he found nothing but leaves, because it was not the season for figs.* [14]*Then he said to the tree, 'May no-one ever eat fruit from you again.' And his disciples heard him say it.*

[15]*On reaching Jerusalem, Jesus entered the temple area and began driving out those who were buying and selling there. He overturned the tables of the money changers and the benches of those selling doves,* [16]*and would not allow anyone to carry merchandise through the temple courts.* [17]*And as he taught them, he said, 'Is it not written:*

> *' "My house will be called
> a house of prayer for all nations"?*

But you have made it "a den of robbers".'

[18]*The chief priests and the teachers of the law heard this and began looking for a way to kill him, for they feared him, because the whole crowd was amazed at his teaching.*

[19]*When evening came, they went out of the city.*

[20]*In the morning, as they went along, they saw the fig-tree withered from the roots.* [21]*Peter remembered and said to Jesus, 'Rabbi, look! The fig-tree you cursed has withered!'*

[22]*'Have faith in God,' Jesus answered.* [23]*'I tell you the truth, if anyone says to this mountain, "Go, throw yourself into the sea," and does not doubt in his heart but believes that what he says will happen, it will be done for him.* [24]*Therefore I tell you, whatever you ask for in prayer, believe that you have received it, and it will be yours.* [25]*And when you stand praying, if you hold anything against anyone, forgive him, so that your Father in heaven may forgive you your sins.'*

Mark again folds one story inside two parts of another, telling the beginning (12–14) and end (20–25) of the incident of the cursing of the fig tree around the cleansing of the temple in Jerusalem (15–19).

The cursing of the fig tree (12–14, 20–25) is one of the most difficult stories in the gospels. It represents a destructive use of supernatural power. It suggests that Jesus expected figs at a time which was not the season for figs, and yet blamed the tree nevertheless. Then the verses which offer Jesus' comment on the incident (22–25) are about faith, and prayer, and forgiveness; though if the curse of the fig tree was possibly about faith, it was less obviously about prayer, and certainly not about forgiveness.

Not surprisingly, a variety of explanations have been offered.

One suggests a withered fig tree along the road giving rise to a legend. Another thinks it was a parable Jesus told that was turned into story. Still another offers the possibility that the event happened at a different time of the year when there might just have been fruit (say in autumn when although the season was over there might have been some residual fruit) and that Jesus' words meant that before the next fruit-bearing season the kingdom of God would have come, but the disciples misheard and so misunderstood his words.

Yet there are difficulties with these alternatives, also. There are elements suggesting personal reminiscences, like verse 21. *It was not the season for figs* (13) would hardly fit into a legend. Both verses 20 and 21 fit uneasily into any of the options offered.

But suppose we are dealing with an acted parable. The fig tree was a well-known representation of Israel.[2] Shortly Jesus would enter the temple and find much to disappoint him, as he had with the fig tree. As Cole points out, in Luke 19:41–44 a nearly parallel passage has him prophesying doom for Jerusalem on the way in. Luke 13:6–9 records a parable which points in the same direction. And the Greek does suggest that he was greatly surprised by the lack of figs; perhaps the leaves suggested some pre-main crop earlier. Of course none of this is conclusive, but since Mark's custom is faithfully to report what he received and to tell stories as they happened (with a regular link of personal reminiscences in his source), and when no alternative is as satisfactory, we are justified in taking the story as it stands, and in seeing in its starkness and destructiveness a solemn warning of what was in fact to happen in the destruction of Jerusalem in AD 70. The words of Jesus, originally in Aramaic, could especially have been simply a statement of fact, rather than a curse, 'No-one will . . .'.

The offered interpretation of this event (22–25) undoubtedly moves steadily away from the incident itself. The commendation of faith ('*Have faith in God*', 22) is of course wholly apt, especially in view of the time elapsing between his curse of the tree and the discovery of its withered condition. The promise of moving mountains into the sea is plainly a form of exaggeration to make the point. Imagine the state of things if it were to be taken literally! The point, which Mark draws us to again and again throughout the gospel, is the need for the risky commitment of faith, which most people we meet in the gospel story do not make.

It isn't unusual that this should lead on to reflection on prayer, since the faith section has pointed in that direction, and since prayer

---

[2] Ho. 9:10, 16; Mic. 7:1–6; Je. 8:13; 29:17.

is the 'wishing and believing' which verse 23 describes. Nothing will be achieved without prayer, as Mark signals at the beginning (1:35), the middle (6:46), and the end of the gospel (14:32–40). Prayer is the highest sign of faith commitment, since the time is most completely wasted if there is nothing in it. The other side of the coin is that for this very reason it is crucial to true discipleship.

Yet although 'prayer changes things', it is not an exercise in magic. It, like everything else in the disciple's experience, has its proper environment. The 'culture' for prayer is the forgiving spirit. Since God's forgiveness of us is the essential ground over which we approach him in prayer, a lack of a forgiving spirit on our part destroys the atmosphere in which prayer is offered and answered. So the line from the fig tree story, through faith and prayer to forgiveness is clearly recognizable.

The cleansing of the temple (11:15–19) is part of the development of Mark's story towards its climax, and is full of threat for both Jesus and those who are now clearly his opponents. The temple, together with the worship offered in it, represented Jewish life and religion. Following the acted parable of the fig tree there is now the acted parable of God's judgment on Israel itself.

He *began driving out those who were buying and selling there* . . . (15–16). The activity of these verses refers to the support system for the sacrificial rituals. The sacrificial creatures – animals and birds – could be bought in the outer court, and foreign Jews could change their money there in order to have local coinage for the temple tax. The point of Jesus' complaint, however, seems to be that it all took place in the Court of the Gentiles. Hence (17) quoting Isaiah 56:7, the bone of contention is that the place intended for Gentiles (*'all nations'*) to pray, was being misused by the Jews for trade (and profit). *'Den of robbers'* (17) is very strong language, and may have its origin in Jeremiah 7:11. The anger of Jesus is clear.

So is the reaction of the chief priests and teachers of the law (18). Earlier hints not only of unbelief but of opposition are now openly hardened into finding a way to put him to death. It will not be easy, however, because (another feature of Mark's story) *the whole crowd was amazed at his teaching* (18). There is also the curious element that the religious leaders themselves feared him – feared, but did not submit. The battle lines are now quite clearly drawn, and Jesus and the Twelve leave the city for the night (19).

The reality of judgment

We come now to parts of the gospel story which we find less

palatable. Most of us by nature prefer the brighter side of the gospel story. After all, it is Good News! Yet it is only good news because it saves us from bad news. This double story by Mark reminds us that we can put ourselves on the wrong side of God's grace, the side which rejects it and faces the consequences. We see it in the world around us. In a moral universe, to play fast and loose with the truth brings danger, then destruction. The evidence is on every side of us. What we see in the Bible is the spelling out of the eternal consequences of that truth – we can project ourselves into eternity choosing to be on the wrong side of grace. In Mark's gospel, at this point, there was still opportunity for the religious leaders to turn back from their course of implacable opposition to Jesus. But from now on it became increasingly difficult to do so.

3. A challenge to Jesus' authority (11:27–33)

They arrived again in Jerusalem, and while Jesus was walking in the temple courts, the chief priests, the teachers of the law and the elders came to him. ²⁸'*By what authority are you doing these things?*' *they asked. 'And who gave you authority to do this?*'

²⁹*Jesus replied, 'I will ask you one question. Answer me, and I will tell you by what authority I am doing these things.* ³⁰*John's baptism – was it from heaven, or from men? Tell me!*'

³¹*They discussed it among themselves and said, 'If we say, "From heaven", he will ask, "Then why didn't you believe him?"* ³²*But if we say, "From men"....' (They feared the people, for everyone held that John really was a prophet.)*

³³*So they answered Jesus, 'We don't know.'*

Jesus said, 'Neither will I tell you by what authority I am doing these things.'

We omit verse 26 as a later addition to the text. The scene is Jerusalem again, and now the point at issue is one of authority. The importance of the occasion, for the authorities and for the development of Mark's story, is that all three groups comprising the seventy-one strong membership of the Sanhedrin or Council, the highest legal body in Judaism, are mentioned – *the chief priests, the teachers of the law and the elders* (27). It is a very significant test case.

For Mark's presentation of the Good News the occasion is crucial because it focuses on precisely the two issues of who Jesus is, and whether or not people will truly believe in him. Here the Sanhedrin faces that challenge on authority, but it runs on into the

191

five following incidents or stories (1–12 the vineyard, 13–17 taxes to Caesar, 18–27 marriage and resurrection, 28–34 the greatest commandment and 35–40 on whose son is the Christ). The battle is truly joined!

The questions *'By what authority are you doing these things?'* (these things probably limited to his recent actions in cleansing the temple), and *'Who gave you this authority?'* (28) are not directly answered, and yet they are. Jesus' return question (29), with its commanding *'Tell me!'* (30) and its conclusion, both asserts his authority in practice and tests whether they are able to discern true authority anyway. The question about John the Baptist's baptism was a point at which the Sanhedrin's judgment flew in the face of that of the ordinary people (31–32). If either they could not or would not answer that question (concerning, in Mark's eyes, Jesus' prototype in John the Baptist), then they had no qualifications for hearing an answer to their own question either.

And yet they did receive an answer. After all, John the Baptist proclaimed the Coming One (1:1–4). At the baptism of Jesus the heavenly voice answered their question about authority ('You are my Son, whom I love; with you I am well pleased', 1:11). What further answer was needed?

A problem for leaders

The story at this point underlines how hard it is to be a leader. Everyone accepts that 'it's the job of leaders to lead'. Moreover, when the majority disagree with the leadership, there is the cynic's question, 'When was the majority last right about anything?' Yet history provides many examples inside the church and outside it, of leaders becoming out of touch, not only with their people but with reality. The political developments in Eastern Europe in the recent past provide a good example.

The solution is not that, 'the people are always right', but that leaders need to be sure they keep near to the people and that they remain open to new truth and new ways forward. The solidifying effect of 'holding office' and the pressure to 'preserve the past' are greater than most of us realize.

4. The parable of the vineyard tenants (12:1–12)

He then began to speak to them in parables: 'A man planted a vineyard. He put a wall around it, dug a pit for the winepress and built a watchtower. Then he rented the vineyard to some farmers and went away on a journey. ²At harvest time he sent a servant to

the tenants to collect from them some of the fruit of the vineyard.
³But they seized him, beat him and sent him away empty-handed.
⁴Then he sent another servant to them: they struck this man on the
head and treated him shamefully. ⁵He sent still another, and that
one they killed. He sent many others; some of them they beat,
others they killed.

⁶'He had one left to send, a son, whom he loved. He sent him
last of all, saying, "They will respect my son."

⁷'But the tenants said to one another, "This is the heir. Come,
let's kill him, and the inheritance will be ours." ⁸So they took him
and killed him, and threw him out of the vineyard.

⁹'What then will the owner of the vineyard do? He will come
and kill those tenants and give the vineyard to others. ¹⁰Haven't
you read this scripture:

> *' "The stone the builders rejected*
> *has become the capstone;*
> *¹¹the Lord has done this,*
> *and it is marvellous in our eyes"?'*

¹²Then they looked for a way to arrest him because they knew
he had spoken the parable against them. But they were afraid of
the crowd; so they left him and went away.

The parable of the tenants of the vineyard clearly depends on Isaiah
5:1–7 (many of the Greek words here occur in the Septuagint
version of Isaiah 5), for its basis, but not for its development. The
parable seems to be told chiefly to the chief priests, teachers of the
law and elders, whose reaction is recorded in verse 12. The vineyard
was a common picture of Israel (see Ps. 80:8 ff. and Je. 2:21 as
other examples).

The flexibility of the method of teaching by parable is illustrated
here. The difference between a parable and an allegory is that the
parable has a single meaning and is taken as a whole, whereas an
allegory depends on a 'one for one' significance of each part of the
story, as listeners or readers identify what each item means or
resembles. Yet the detailed significance of each part of this parable
can hardly have been lost on the hearers, not least because of the
Isaiah 5 basis where these points of the story are directly related
to their contemporary setting (see Is. 5:7). On the other hand,
although the parable is pushed to the boundaries of allegory by
these factors, Jesus makes no attempt to identify contemporary or
historical groups as equivalent to people in the story. What is more,
the restraint here contrasts very strongly with the indulgence of
early Christian commentators who saw the wall as the law, the

tower as the temple, and the winepress as the altar! By contrast we're dealing here with a parable so told that the main allegorical possibilities were not lost on the hearers. The central meaning of the parable is that the son of the owner has come to claim what the owner rightly expected from his vineyard. The parable's conclusion sets out the all-too-possible scenario which might develop. As such it reinforces the plea of Jesus that the religious authorities should heed the evidence about them, not least the crowd's response (12), and themselves render to God what is his due. Sadly they understand all too well, but reject the offer (12).

Grace and judgment

At the heart of this story, in its place in Mark's gospel, is the possibility that even now the leaders could have heard, understood and responded to Jesus. We can only guess at the outcome in history had they done so. There is a very deep issue here of God's overall purpose and sovereignty on the one hand, and human choice and freedom to participate on the other. For this story, and many other parts of Scripture, to be taken with absolute seriousness we have to avoid a doctrine of God so controlling things that it always works out in detail as he plans. God's sovereignty is neither wholly pro-active nor wholly reactive: it is interactive, and it is a privilege of our humanity that we can be part of that process of interactivity. The chief priests, teachers of the law and elders could still have turned back from their plot to kill Jesus, but they wouldn't. Another chance was refused.

5. Paying taxes to Caesar (12:13–17)

Láter they sent some of the Pharisees and Herodians to Jesus to catch him in his words. [14]They came to him and said, 'Teacher, we know you are a man of integrity. You aren't swayed by men, because you pay no attention to who they are; but you teach the way of God in accordance with the truth. Is it right to pay taxes to Caesar or not? [15]Should we pay or shouldn't we?'

But Jesus knew their hypocrisy. 'Why are you trying to trap me?' he asked. 'Bring me a denarius and let me look at it.' [16]They brought the coin, and he asked them, 'Whose portrait is this? And whose inscription?'

'Caesar's,' they replied.

[17]Then Jesus said to them, 'Give to Caesar what is Caesar's and to God what is God's.'

And they were amazed at him.

194

Paying taxes to Caesar becomes the next point of controversy. The situation itself is a tricky one because of the presence of Pharisees ('separated ones') who stood for strict obedience of the law, in its written and oral forms. They opposed strongly the Roman rule though they were not revolutionaries. By contrast the Herodians, attached somehow to the Herod family, whose position depended upon Rome, were therefore supportive of Roman authority. That a question about taxes to Caesar should be put by representatives of these groups is in itself a recipe for disaster for Jesus. However he answers he will not please one group or the other. Even worse is the fact that in the background was the view of the Zealots, that the tax should not be paid. With that view many (most?) of the crowd probably agreed. No wonder the verb used, *to catch him* (13), is taken from the world of the hunter with his net or trap.

Jesus perceived their trickery (15). The word *hypocrisy* has behind it the idea of acting a part or wearing a mask. He also asserts his authority with the demand for a coin, and the question about the inscription (15–16). In his answer he changes the word used to describe the tax (a distinction which is confused by the NIV translation). They used a word meaning 'give', suggesting a choice openly faced. Jesus uses a word which stresses 'payment', carrying the idea of an obligation for services received. The image of Caesar on the coin represented all the benefit received from the Roman Empire, and their use of the coins signalled implicit acceptance of these. 'Pay up for what you gain!' is his point.

Lest, however, he be seen to have taken sides he now delivers the real blow. *'Give . . . to God what is God's'* (17). Had reference to an image on a coin conjured up memories of God's image in humanity (Gn. 1:26–27)? If so, what would that signify about their overall debt to God? Jesus doesn't pose tax to Caesar over against what is due to God. He seems to include the former in the latter. They must judge whether paying for services gained from Roman rule harmonized with their service to God (the implication being that if it didn't, why were they using the coins and taking the benefits?). Like the crowd, his opponents were also now amazed at him! (17)

Making political decisions

There isn't enough here on which to base a theology of church and state, nor of the citizen's involvement in social, economic and political activity. But there is an affirmation and a warning. The response of Jesus does commit his hearers to playing their part in the situation in which they find themselves. The warning is the ease with which we may become caught up in details and lose our hold on the broader perspective, which is our major contribution. We know ourselves to be made in the image of God, and that our commitment to him is the only absolute commitment that can be expected of human beings. Everything else must be worked out in the light of that one, total duty. Once we lose that broad perspective we rapidly become little different from any other groups in our involvement. Governments need consistently the reminder which Christians can give, that only God ultimately reigns, and that all policies should be worked out in relation to that. In particular one wonders whether the growing power and claims of nationalism around the world do not need sharp examination by this criterion from Jesus.

6. Marriage and the hereafter (12:18–27)

Then the Sadducees, who say there is no resurrection, came to him with a question. [19]*'Teacher,' they said, 'Moses wrote for us that if a man's brother dies and leaves a wife but no children, the man must marry the widow and have children for his brother.* [20]*Now there were seven brothers. The first one married and died without leaving any children.* [21]*The second one married the widow, but he also died, leaving no child. It was the same with the third.* [22]*In fact, none of the seven left any children. Last of all, the woman died too.* [23]*At the resurrection whose wife will she be, since the seven were married to her?'*

[24]*Jesus replied, 'Are you not in error because you do not know the Scriptures or the power of God?* [25]*When the dead rise, they will neither marry nor be given in marriage; they will be like the angels in heaven.* [26]*Now about the dead rising – have you not read in the book of Moses, in the account of the bush, how God said to him, "I am the God of Abraham, the God of Isaac, and the God of Jacob"?* [27]*He is not the God of the dead, but of the living. You are badly mistaken!'*

The testing now moves on to marriage and the after-life. This time the question comes from another interested party, the Sadducees. Cranfield's description of them is helpful:

> The Sadducees were the aristocratic party, made up of the high priestly and leading lay families of Jerusalem. They were wealthy and worldly. Their arrogance and harshness in the administration of justice were notorious. Conservative in doctrine, they rejected what they regarded as Pharisaic innovations; but their main con-

cern was for the maintenance of their privileges not for doctrinal purity. The origin of the name is uncertain.[3]

We may add, for a proper understanding of this story in Mark, that only the written law in the five books ascribed to Moses was authoritative for them. They rejected the oral law. On this basis they also refused the idea of resurrection (Acts 23:8). The aim of their question is therefore to show what trouble you get into by believing in an after-life. Since they were responsible for the trading in the temple which Jesus had interrupted and criticized (11:17), their question is all the sharper. *'At the resurrection whose wife will she* (a woman widowed seven times!) *be, since the seven were married to her?'* (23)

There is enormous skill in Jesus' answer. First, the Scripture he quotes to them comes from the bit of the Old Testament they did accept. Their basis was probably Deuteronomy 25:5 (the so-called Levirite law, from Latin, *levir*, brother-in-law). Jesus replies in terms of Exodus 3:6, arguing that the meaning of that verse is that Abraham, Isaac and Jacob are still alive in God at the time of Moses. How can there not, therefore, be resurrection? The case depends on the continuation of scriptural teaching and the power of God, the latter, as Nineham suggests,[4] including the idea that the God they have known reveals such goodness that he will surely be caring for them now. As C. F. D. Moule puts it 'death cannot break a relationship thus begun'.

Secondly, Jesus touches them on a raw spot. Their knowledge of Scripture at deep levels was not their strongest characteristic. Jesus told them so! Even more, they plainly knew little of the power of God (because they did not believe in resurrection?) (24).

Thirdly, they had missed the point that resurrection life is not simply the projection of this life on to a timeless scale. It is of a different quality altogether (*'like the angels in heaven'*, 25). What a lot they were missing by rejecting this idea. How limited a vision!

Scripture and the power of God

The interlocking of these two provides an interesting commentary on our interpretation of Scripture. The two need to be held in proper balance – perhaps even tension. A concentration on Scripture alone so easily locks us into discussion of texts and provenances, likelihoods or unlikelihoods, and becomes increasingly academic. It needs consideration of the power of God to save it from 'lowest common denominator' conclusions. On the other

[3] Cranfield, p. 373.   [4] Nineham, p. 322.

197

hand, a spirituality dominated by 'the power of God' concept soon becomes less and less related to proper guidelines, to sound knowledge and to healthy doctrine. It ends up wild and unrelated to the truth of everyday life. We need both, in healthy interaction.

7. The greatest commandment (12:28–34)

One of the teachers of the law came and heard them debating. Noticing that Jesus had given them a good answer, he asked him, 'Of all the commandments, which is the most important?'

[29]'The most important one,' answered Jesus, 'is this: "Hear, O Israel, the Lord our God, the Lord is one. [30]Love the Lord your God with all your heart and with all your soul and with all your mind and with all your strength." [31]The second is this: "Love your neighbour as yourself." There is no commandment greater than these.'

[32]'Well said, teacher,' the man replied. 'You are right in saying that God is one and there is no other but him. [33]To love him with all your heart, with all your understanding and with all your strength, and to love your neighbour as yourself is more important than all burnt offerings and sacrifices.'

[34]When Jesus saw that he had answered wisely, he said to him, 'You are not far from the kingdom of God.' And from then on no-one dared ask him any more questions.

An individual teacher of the law now asks about the 'greatest' commandment. This does not appear to be an adverse question. Nor was it novel. There is considerable evidence of rabbis being asked to choose the most fundamental commandment. There was also some discussion about whether what was needed was a commandment which reinforced the need to keep all the others, or one which, if kept, meant that the others were less important. This question Jesus seems also to have answered.

Jesus responds to the request for one commandment by giving two, though both are dominated by the one requirement to love. (In Lk. 10:27 it is a lawyer who puts these two together, but the circumstances and conclusions are so different as to provide ground for following T. W. Manson's view that this was a different incident altogether.) It is by no means clear that Jesus was the first to put these two sayings together. What is clear is the significance of his doing so, both in the setting of his ministry in Jerusalem where a unique fulfilment of this double injunction was soon to be witnessed, and in his designating these two as the heart and fulfilment of that law, not simply as a reinforcement of the rest.

This becomes clearer in the teacher's response. He (properly) applies the love requirement to the whole of the disciple ('*heart . . . understanding . . . strength*') and places it as primary over against '*burnt offerings and sacrifices*' (33). Since Mark sets all these questions in the temple courts (11:27; 12:35; 12:41 and 13:1) this statement is all the more significant. The one who has already pronounced judgment on the temple, who has enunciated the double law of love which surpasses all other laws, and who now receives with approval the relegation of sacrifice and burnt offerings, will himself shortly act out the whole scenario as the basis of salvation for all who will respond.

As though to make this forward momentum clear, Jesus tells the teacher of the law that his answer shows that he is not far from the kingdom of God.

Sharpening the point about salvation

The puzzle of belief or unbelief in relation to Jesus and the kingdom has become a little clearer because of this episode, and preceding ones. It is about love, love of God and love of neighbours, about a love which involves soul, mind and strength, and it focuses even more clearly on Jesus as various alternative approaches are seen to be inadequate – Israel (11:12–14, 22–25); the temple (11:15–18); the Sanhedrin (11:27, 12:12), the Pharisees and Herodians (12:13–17), the Sadducees (12:18–27), legal regulations, burnt offerings and sacrifices (12:28–34). The stage is being cleared for the final act.

8. The teachers of the law (12:35–40)

While Jesus was teaching in the temple courts, he asked, 'How is it that the teachers of the law say that the Christ is the son of David? [36]*David himself, speaking by the Holy Spirit, declared:*

> ' "*The Lord said to my Lord:*
> '*Sit at my right hand*
> *until I put your enemies*
> *under your feet.*' "

[37]*David himself calls him "Lord". How then can he be his son?'*
The large crowd listened to him with delight.
[38]*As he taught, Jesus said, 'Watch out for the teachers of the law. They like to walk around in flowing robes and be greeted in the market-places,* [39]*and have the most important seats in the synagogues and the places of honour at banquets.* [40]*They devour widows'*

houses and for a show make lengthy prayers. Such men will be punished most severely.'

The next discussion takes up the previous point exactly, by focusing on the Christ (12:35–37). Jesus himself introduces the topic, having evidently dealt with all the questions raised, in Mark's presentation of events. Jesus now puts a question-mark against the doctrine of the teachers of the law. If they wanted a debate . . . !

Many years ago Ezra Gould[5] pointed out that it was the narrowness of the teachers that Jesus was criticizing. They stressed that the Christ was the Son of David, and a great deal followed from that, not least in their setting of occupation by a foreign nation. The Son of David would surely be, like his 'father', able to rid the Jews of oppression, presumably as David had done. But Jesus presents a conundrum. Both sides accepted David as author of Psalm 110. If David was superior to the Messiah who was to come, how, asks Jesus, could he speak of that Messiah as, *'my Lord'* (Ps. 110:1, Mk. 12:37). It is not the Davidic (human) line that matters more: it is this anointed (divine) line that is superior. It is not necessary in following this story to see it either as Jesus openly proclaiming his messiahship, or trying to argue that the Messiah was not David's son at all. The most natural interpretation is that offered above. In one sense this was 'theological knock-about' to teach the teachers a lesson. They had chosen to engage him in disputation. Jesus returned more than they served. The crowd loved it!

It was not a joke, however. He now warns them most severely against the teachers of the law (12:38–40). He must surely be speaking of common tendencies among them, or of specific cases. They *'walk around'* in their robes. (The teachers had particularly identifiable robes to be worn during their work. It must be the walking about in them, more generally, which Jesus criticized, because of the respect and deference it gained them.) Then they liked the important seats in synagogue and banquet. And they made financial profit out of widows for their religion, though their lengthy prayers were a pretence, not genuine spirituality.

Two contexts, or three?

It seems at least likely (some would say obvious) that Mark's selection and presentation of his material was influenced by the experiences of the early church at the time of writing, as well as by what actually happened during the ministry of Jesus. That would

[5] Gould, p. 235.

not be surprising. We are all greatly influenced in our judgments and choices by our contexts, perhaps most of all in those times when we think we aren't. If this is to be accepted, however, two other points must be made with at least equal strength. In his choices and arrangement Mark shows extraordinary determination to record what he received even, as we have seen, in places where some alteration would have made his task easier. He means us to have what Jesus said and did. Secondly, we must not neglect the work of God's Spirit in inspiring those who put these writings together. The foundation documents of our faith are intended to bring us God's word.

Yet God's Spirit uses circumstances of everyday experience to teach us God's way, as Christian disciples in every age would testify. In Mark's day no doubt there was the larger general question of why more people did not believe, and the quite specific issues which the Christian of Mark's day had to face not least in opposition from fellow Jews who did not believe in Jesus. In the section from 11:12 to 12:40 many such issues are raised. Mark may well be providing, quite specifically, both the affirmation of the testimony and the material for response, in such situations.

But there is a third context – ours. We should be no less ready to apply ourselves to a keen appreciation of what our testimony is today to Jesus the Christ: how total is our commitment of soul and mind and strength, how we respond to objections and opposition, and whether we are in danger of any of the condemnations by Jesus of religious leaders of his day.

9. The widow's offering (12:41–44)

Jesus sat down opposite the place where the offerings were put and watched the crowd putting their money into the temple treasury. Many rich people threw in large amounts. [42] *But a poor widow came and put in two very small copper coins, worth only a fraction of a penny.*

[43] *Calling his disciples to him, Jesus said, 'I tell you the truth, this poor widow has put more into the treasury than all the others.* [44] *They all gave out of their wealth: but she, out of her poverty, put in everything – all she had to live on.'*

The delightful story of the widow's offering brings a warmer, though not uncritical, mood to the end of this chapter. Different receptacles for the gifts have been suggested. What is clear is that from where Jesus was sitting he could see what people were putting in. Some gave much, much more than this widow, but from her appearance it was clear that she had given all, where others had not.

This may seem to be a somewhat idyllic way to end a stormy chapter, but we should not be misled. The issue, with Jesus at the centre, is still about giving all, total trust, utter commitment.

10.   The 'little apocalypse' (13:1–37)

As he was leaving the temple, one of his disciples said to him, 'Look, Teacher! What massive stones! What magnificent buildings!'

²'Do you see all these great buildings?' replied Jesus. 'Not one stone here will be left on another; every one will be thrown down.'

³As Jesus was sitting on the Mount of Olives opposite the temple, Peter, James, John and Andrew asked him privately, ⁴"Tell us, when will these things happen? And what will be the sign that they are all about to be fulfilled?'

⁵Jesus said to them: 'Watch out that no-one deceives you. ⁶Many will come in my name, claiming, "I am he," and will deceive many. ⁷When you hear of wars and rumours of wars, do not be alarmed. Such things must happen, but the end is still to come. ⁸Nation will rise against nation, and kingdom against kingdom. There will be earthquakes in various places, and famines. These are the beginning of birth-pains.

⁹'You must be on your guard. You will be handed over to the local councils and flogged in the synagogues. On account of me you will stand before governors and kings as witnesses to them. ¹⁰And the gospel must first be preached to all nations. ¹¹Whenever you are arrested and brought to trial, do not worry beforehand about what to say. Just say whatever is given you at the time, for it is not you speaking, but the Holy Spirit.

¹²'Brother will betray brother to death, and a father his child. Children will rebel against their parents and have them put to death. ¹³All men will hate you because of me, but he who stands firm to the end will be saved.

¹⁴'When you see "the abomination that causes desolation" standing where it does not belong – let the reader understand – then let those who are in Judea flee to the mountains. ¹⁵Let no-one on the roof of his house go down or enter the house to take anything out. ¹⁶Let no-one in the field go back to get his cloak. ¹⁷How dreadful it will be in those days for pregnant women and nursing mothers! ¹⁸Pray that this will not take place in winter, ¹⁹because those will be days of distress unequalled from the beginning, when God created the world, until now – and never to be equalled again. ²⁰If the Lord had not cut short those days, no-one would survive. But for the sake of the elect, whom he has chosen, he has shortened them. ²¹At that time if anyone says to you, "Look, here is the Christ," or, "Look, there he is!" do not believe it. ²²For false Christs and false prophets will appear and perform signs and miracles to deceive the elect – if that were possible. ²³So be on your guard; I have told you everything ahead of time.

²⁴'But in those days, following that distress,

> *' "the sun will be darkened,*
> *and the moon will not give its light;*
> *²⁵the stars will fall from the sky,*
> *and the heavenly bodies will be shaken."*

²⁶'At that time men will see the Son of Man coming in clouds with great power and glory. ²⁷And he will send his angels and gather his elect from the four winds, from the ends of the earth to the ends of the heavens.

²⁸'Now learn this lesson from the fig-tree: As soon as its twigs get tender and its leaves come out, you know that summer is near. ²⁹Even so, when you see these things happening, you know that it is near, right at the door. ³⁰I tell you the truth, this generation will certainly not pass away until all these things have happened. ³¹Heaven and earth will pass away, but my words will never pass away.

³²'No-one knows about that day or hour, not even the angels in heaven, nor the Son, but only the Father. ³³Be on guard! Be alert! You do not know when that time will come. ³⁴It's like a man going away: He leaves his house and puts his servants in charge, each with his assigned task, and tells the one at the door to keep watch.

³⁵'Therefore keep watch because you do not know when the owner of the house will come back – whether in the evening, or at midnight, or when the cock crows, or at dawn. ³⁶If he comes suddenly, do not let him find you sleeping. ³⁷What I say to you, I say to everyone: "Watch!" '

This whole passage is often referred to as the 'little Apocalypse' (because of its sustained use of a different style of expression from that in the rest of the gospel – see below), or the 'synoptic Apocalypse' (because of similar passages in Mt. 24 and Lk. 21, but not in John's gospel).

Apocalyptic, as a recognizable genre of literary expression, has significant characteristics.[6] There is a keen sense of the battle between good and evil, pessimism about that process working out

---

[6] For a full discussion of this complex subject, see Stephen H. Travis, *Christian Hope and the Future of Man* (Inter-Varsity Press, 1980).

well in natural terms, a conviction that things will end in crisis, and the need for God to put everything right in and through the crisis. The language is often vivid and full of imagery, the content ascribed to the visions of the writer. A typical Old Testament example is the book of Daniel, significantly quoted three times in Mark 13 (14, 19, 26).

Yet, over against claims that this may be simply a piece of Jewish-Christian apocalyptic, and not from Jesus himself, one has to note that it is not typical apocalyptic. There is no visionary claim. It is not couched in the familiar first person singular, with the visionary being addressed by God and telling of this experience. The language is symbolic, but restrained in its imagery. It also contains considerable exhortation, not typical of apocalyptic material. Moreover although much of it deals with calamity and suffering, there is a rich vein of purposefulness running throughout, enabling clear warnings to be given about how to react effectively in each situation (5, 7, 11, 13, 14–16, 21). It is not markedly pessimistic about history, a characteristic of apocalyptic material, but purposeful even about its worst developments. It may not represent a long single sustained speech by Jesus (unusually long for Mark's gospel), but a collection of such sayings. Yet the fittedness of it at this point in the story, when the storm clouds of unbelief and opposition in relation to his ministry have gathered over the temple, the symbol of Jewish religion and history, makes it natural that we hear the words of Jesus in this vein. After this the story will be dominated by his passion. What more natural than that he should at this point offer the perspective of a longer view.

There is a naturalness, too, about the move from this chapter into the account of his passion. The 'necessary' sufferings of the disciples match the 'necessary' passion of their Master (8:31, 9:31, 10:33–34). This understanding of Christ's death and resurrection not only as the basis of the disciples' salvation but also as the pattern for their lives as disciples will emerge more and more clearly from now on. Even the repeated emphasis on the need to 'watch' in chapter 13,[7] and the direct reference to the watches in verse 35, is perhaps picked up by Mark's deliberate reference in timing to the official watches – evening, 14:17; cock-crow, 14:68; morning, 15:1, with midnight as the likely but unspecified time in Gethsemane 14:32–42 where, ironically, his closest circle of disciples did not watch but slept (Hooker).[8] The prediction of 13:2 about the

[7] See verses 5, 9, 23, 33 where the word means 'be on your guard', and 35 and 37 where it means 'keep watch' or 'watch'.

[8] The verb used by Jesus to exhort them to do so is that of 13:35 and 37 (Hooker, p. 116).

destruction of the temple will be quoted against him in 14:58, and in taunts at Calvary in 15:29. The Son of Man reference (13:26) will also recur in 14:62.

Chapter 13 is a distinctive chapter in Mark's gospel, but it fits well in relation to the rest. It sets out starkly what has increasingly been hinted at by Jesus about his own ministry (8:31, 9:31, 10:33–34 are all about the necessity of his death and resurrection – 'the Son of Man must . . .'). He was certainly 'leading the way' (10:32) there! What they may have missed, however, was the corollary of that insistence on death, namely that this was the way for the disciple also (8:34). The question set by this gospel is why people do not come to faith, either because they are family, friends, religious leaders, or because they have heard teaching with authority, and seen miracles. The answer that becomes increasingly clear is that none of those is the basis for our salvation. That still lies ahead in his death and resurrection. But a second reason is now emerging. None of those things would prepare a person for true discipleship, which is itself the way of the cross and the resurrection. What is right for the Master is right for the disciple, though for different reasons. This may be the main reason why this gospel was written, to help people to see that true faith does not save one from hard times and difficult experiences, as many may have hoped. True faith often leads one into hard times and difficult experiences. The glory of faith in Christ is that we are not saved *from* them but *in* them. Chapter 13 certainly makes that clear.

One other issue must be faced in relationship to this exegetical minefield of a chapter. To which time is Jesus referring in his warnings of catastrophe, hardship, persecution and betrayal? Some commentators see it all in terms of the destruction of Jerusalem in AD 70. This brings with it the additional question of whether Mark's gospel was written before or after that date. If earlier, as this exposition has suggested (p. 20), then Jesus prophesied the fall of Jerusalem. Others see it as a reference to the end of everything, some concluding that Jesus (wrongly) expected it to happen almost at once, hence the confusion between AD 70 and the Parousia. But supposing, as R. P. Martin[9] and many others have suggested, that there are at least two focal points of vision, the ultimate coming of the Son of Man (13:26), *and* the earlier destruction of Jerusalem as a harbinger of the eventual end? This double perspective offers the best outline, though this chapter is not straightforward on any interpretation, not least because in part at least it speaks of things we do not understand, and with which we have nothing to compare.

[9] Martin, *Action*, pp. 111–112.

The establishing of the destruction of Jerusalem as one mountain peak, and the Parousia as the ultimate one may be making demands on us. (Looking at two physical mountain peaks raises problems of focus, as any photographer knows.) But it may likewise help us to get the most realistic view.

On this construction the chapter can be divided as follows:

13:1–4   Warning about the temple.
13:5–13   The continuing experience of hardship by disciples.
13:14–23   The destruction of Jerusalem.
13:24–27   The end of all things.
13:28–37   Watchfulness during the entire end time – *i.e.* from now onward.

This whole chapter can be seen in terms of Jesus' instruction to his disciples to 'be on their guard'. He is specific about what they should guard against. In the first section (13:1–4) it is trust in buildings and the accoutrements of religion. The disciples (1) had every right to be proud of this third temple on this site, well rebuilt by Herod. Jesus' reply must have shattered them. *'Not one stone here will be left on another'* (2).

Their question about this comment is placed on the Mount of Olives, supremely an apocalyptic setting (Zc. 14). They ask two questions, both predictable, 'When?' and 'What sign?' Equally typically, he answers neither, because their priorities are yet again wrong. He does not encourage 'almanac discipleship'. The question should have been, 'How are we to live in the light of such a prophecy?' It is knowledge which feeds spiritual and moral well-being and the lifestyle that they need.

If they ought not to trust the buildings and the religious ceremonies, neither should they trust everyone who claims to be Messiah (13:5–13). There will be wars, international strife, physical disaster (7–8). They will be accused, condemned, punished, called to answer. Even families will split and become betrayers of one another. The advice is that, whatever the consequence, they are to hold to the truth (including the true leaders) and speak it (even in places of threat). All need to hear the good news (10); it is intended for all peoples. (There is a hidden time bomb there, the word 'nations' really means 'Gentiles'.) With a rare reference to the Holy Spirit in Mark's gospel the promise in verse 11 is not intended to encourage lazy preachers who don't prepare properly. It is the unexpected moment, in a hostile setting, where they are not to fear. We may reflect that even in such situations the more one knows already, the more material is available for the Holy Spirit to use. (See Acts 2:22 ff. and 4:18–22 as good examples.) Nineham's comment here is timely: 'When we remember that most of the early Christians were simple and unlearned people, for whom a speech in court would have been a terrible ordeal, we realise how much such a promise will have meant to them.'[10]

Not only will people not rush with open arms to receive the disciples of Jesus: rather they will largely reject them. The word 'hate' is from the same verb as that in Luke 14:25 ff., where people were called to 'hate . . . father and mother, . . . wife and children'. It must be sharper than Matthew's 'love me more than' (see Mt. 10:37), yet it cannot mean 'hatred' in its literal sense. Neither is Jesus encouraging his disciples to make themselves unpopular. He is saying that to be true disciples is their task. The rest will follow! The main thing is not to be deterred by it, any more than by the disappearance of the temple, the claims of false messiahs, political and natural catastrophes, and persecution. It is all par for the course.

The next section (13:14–23) seems to be clearly about an historical event. Luke's version (Lk. 21:20) quite specifically mentions armies surrounding Jerusalem. The reference to *the abomination that causes desolation* (Mk. 13:14) also suggests a quite specific reference. In Daniel 12:11 the same expression is used, often linked to the act of Antiochus Epiphanes in setting up a heathen altar on the altar of burnt offerings in the temple in 168 BC. If that is so then Jesus sees that as a mountain peak in the past, but now turns his gaze forward to the next desecration, and this of a building in which his own disciples showed such pride (13:1).

The rest of this section is a story of utter chaos, everyone running for their lives, in the midst of which charlatans will again appear with easy solutions and impressive actions, attempting to distract the believers from their main task, which is to endure (21–22). They should be on their guard (23), forearmed with foreknowledge.

Particular verses here require comment.

The shortening of the days (20) is a point at which what little optimism there is in this account breaks through. However terrible the times, we must not imagine they represent divine neglect. We never know the whole story. Jesus is recorded here as saying that (perhaps when his own people will be complaining about his absence) God actually shortens such times for the good of his people. We are unwise to pass judgment as though we had the full story. Living by faith does often mean simply trusting where one cannot see.

A significant difference between the false messiahs and the true

[10] Nineham, p. 349.

Messiah in this gospel is the way the others show off their signs and miracles (21, 22). They need people to be impressed by that because they have nothing else to offer. By contrast Jesus is restrained, not from performing signs and wonders as the need of people reaches him, but from using these to impose or compel faith. It isn't fundamentally what his good news is about, though these signs and wonders are signposts to the good news. He embodies the good news, and his death and resurrection are to be the heart of it. That is the gold in the bank, giving meaning to the notes and coins of signs and wonders. The false messiahs have only counterfeit money, impressive but with nothing to back it up.

The section on the end of all things (24–27) appears to lift the gaze from the immediate mountain peak of the destruction of Jerusalem to the ultimate peak of the second coming. The picture now is of a shaking of the universe, described by quotation of Isaiah 13:10. It, too, had an earlier, 'midst-of-history' fulfilment, but one which pointed on, evidently, to the end of time.

The image of the Son of Man requires careful study. Old Testament passages like Psalm 97:1–5, Isaiah 19:1, Zechariah 9:14 and Psalm 18:5–16 have all probably contributed to the ideas which build up the picture of disturbances in the heavens signifying powerful divine activity. But Daniel 7:13 must be the basis of verse 26. In Daniel 7 the vision of four kingdoms represented by four beasts is replaced by the vision of 'one like a son of man'. He comes (in Daniel's vision) 'with the clouds of heaven', and is 'led into' the 'presence' of 'the Ancient of Days'. He, says Daniel, 'was given authority, glory and sovereign power; all peoples, nations and men of every language worshipped him. His dominion is an everlasting dominion that will not pass away, and his kingdom is one that will never be destroyed' (Dn. 7:13–14). We may contrast that picture, in its depth, majesty and authority, with that of the false messiahs who needed endlessly to be performing religious tricks to gain support. By contrast, this Son of Man will send his angels to gather the chosen *from the ends of the earth to the ends of the heavens* (Mk. 13:27). This is another signal to those with eyes to see, a whisper to those with ears to hear, that wherever they are scattered and however they are being treated, or however they perceive themselves, God will gather them all in at the end. The pathway through history is only partly perceived by observation. The story will be completed at the end both by its fulfilment *and* by our total picture of it from that vantage point.

We note that Jesus does not here say that he is this Son of Man. At this point the messianic reticence operates once more. We are left to decide on the basis of Mark's account, so far in the story, but even more by the end.

The call to watchfulness (28–37) in view of the ultimate scenario recently described now takes a number of forms. As they read the signs of nature (28–29) so they must learn to read the spiritual signs of the times also. They will be more reliable, because nature (included in heaven and earth) will pass away; the words of Jesus will not.

The meaning of verse 30, about *this generation* not passing away, has caused vast reflection and disagreement. Those who see this entire chapter as referring only to the destruction of Jerusalem have least problem over this verse. But much in the chapter seems to preclude so limited a view. Those who concentrate on the Parousia in this chapter have difficulty if Jesus' words are taken at their face value. *This generation*, in the Greek, could mean humankind, or the Jewish people, or disciples of Jesus in each generation. But its most natural meaning is the generation alive at the time when Jesus spoke the words. The best solution to hold together all the diverse considerations in this chapter seems to be that which joins the destruction of Jerusalem and the ultimate Parousia as two parts of God's one activity, the former prefiguring the latter. The 'signs of the end' begin when Jesus' ministry is complete, and Jerusalem's destruction was terrible evidence of the end times. Jesus' generation would see that, and proleptically would be recipients of the promise of the rest. Such an interpretation does not settle every issue, and our separation from the first century does not help our struggle to understand, but this makes most sense of all the elements involved.

In verses 32–34 another homely image warns again about getting caught up with times and dates. They are not what matters. Even the Son (surely here a much clearer indication of Jesus' filial self-consciousness to God the Father, 32) does not know the day nor the hour (see Acts 1:7). All the greater need to be ready! (35–37).

a. Realism and hope

This chapter does not hold out great encouragement for 'triumphalistic' or 'prosperity' versions of Christianity. The descriptions chill the spine. We do well to remember that something of this account of Jesus has actually been happening to some Christians in every age. We do not await much of this. Persecution, false teachers, natural disasters are not elements of a future age, they happen now. Any true account of discipleship, and any call to believe, must include these factors as possible parts of the experience. In recent decades these things have been the daily reality for Christians in South Africa, South America and Eastern Europe.

Yet the situation described is not hopeless – quite the opposite. The Christian's calling is to watch and to endure. We are not part of the world of 'quick spiritual fixes' or 'flashy impressive messiahs'. To be on guard and to last out are more impressive testimony to the gospel of Jesus Christ, and more realistic too. There is no escapism here.

b. Like master like disciple

The clue to surviving the difficult days, which will increasingly in Mark's gospel be seen to be the secret of all the life of the disciple, is to follow in the steps of Jesus himself. The way he took for our salvation was death and resurrection. He went the way of the cross. God raised him from the dead. So we are called to take up our cross and follow day by day, in faith that day by day God will raise us to new life in Christ (Rom. 8:9–11). As we die to all to which he died, we shall live to all to which he rose.

c. The present and the eventual

Written into the challenge to watch is the exhortation to perceive the meaning of things. (See 28–29 especially.) Ordinary (and extraordinary) everyday events have an eternal significance, if only we can see it. The relationship of the destruction of Jerusalem in AD 70 to the Parousia is a case in point. Jesus is hinting that everything that happens to us is projected on to the screen of eternity. We are becoming what eternally we shall be. Everything has a double point of reference – now and then. We are called to live the now in the light of the then. To live by this perspective is to be truly 'broad-minded'.

Mark 14:1 – 16:20
7. Passion and resurrection

Mark now concentrates attention wholly on the death of Jesus. Having given a middle distance and long distance perspective in what we know as chapter 13, he now turns to the immediate present for Jesus. As usual the story is told starkly and with no attempt to soften the blow or ease the pain of those who read.

1. Encouragement, and plotting (14:1–11)

Now the Passover and the Feast of Unleavened Bread were only two days away, and the chief priests and the teachers of the law were looking for some sly way to arrest Jesus and kill him. ²'But not during the Feast,' they said, 'or the people may riot.'

³While he was in Bethany, reclining at the table in the home of a man known as Simon the Leper, a woman came with an alabaster jar of very expensive perfume, made of pure nard. She broke the jar and poured the perfume on his head.

⁴Some of those present were saying indignantly to one another, 'Why this waste of perfume? ⁵It could have been sold for more than a year's wages and the money given to the poor.' And they rebuked her harshly.

⁶'Leave her alone,' said Jesus. 'Why are you bothering her? She has done a beautiful thing to me. ⁷The poor you will always have with you, and you can help them any time you want. But you will not always have me. ⁸She did what she could. She poured perfume on my body beforehand to prepare for my burial. ⁹I tell you the truth, wherever the gospel is preached throughout the world, what she has done will also be told, in memory of her.'

¹⁰Then Judas Iscariot, one of the Twelve, went to the chief priests to betray Jesus to them. ¹¹They were delighted to hear this and promised to give him money. So he watched for an opportunity to hand him over.

A plot for Jesus' arrest and death (1, 2) gives deeper meaning to the warnings at the end of the previous chapter to be watchful. He had entered Jerusalem to the 'Hosanna' cries associated with the Feast of Tabernacles, a confident celebration of Israel's future. Now, however, it is near to Passover, also a feast of liberation, but with awful cost as the angel of the Lord brought death to the Egyptian first-born, and only the blood of sacrificial lambs on the door frames protected the Israelites (Ex. 12).

The Festival of Unleavened Bread was closely associated with the Passover, the Passover Meal being held on the evening of the final day of Unleavened Bread. Leaven, causing the loaves to rise, was usually taken from a piece left over from the day before, joining one baking to the next. As the Festival of Unleavened Bread (see Ex. 23:15; 34:18) was celebrated for a week, the use of unleavened bread stood for a break with the past and the commitment to a new start. How significant that these two meaningful feasts, virtually one,[1] should mark the beginning of the story of the passion of Jesus. Matthew records it in Matthew 26:1–2, referring only to the Passover. Luke (Lk. 22:1) also refers to this celebration, identifying the Feast of Unleavened Bread as the Passover. For all the synoptists it was a significant point of departure, as it was also for John, using it in his own particular way (Jn. 11:55; 12:1).

Sadly, the chief priests and teachers of the law are not trying to get rid of 'leaven', but of a troublesome young rabbi who has now gone well beyond 'too far'. The crowds were in the city, gathering and preparing for the Feast, so the time was not right, since the crowds (a regular point of Mark's) were still, in their own way, for Jesus.

The anointing of Jesus with expensive perfume by a woman, (3–9) takes place in the house of Simon the Leper, another reminder of Jesus' identifying with outcasts or former outcasts. The story of this woman's actions stands in stark contrast both with the plotting of verses 1–2 and the criticism of her action by some of the onlookers. There are four gospel accounts of such an event, in Luke 7:36–50, Matthew 26:6–13 and John 12:1–8 as well as here. In general it seems most likely that Matthew, John and Mark describe one incident, though the accounts are far from identical, while Luke describes another. Or we may have descriptions of three separate incidents. The problem is not easily soluble.

The woman used expensive perfume. The breaking of the jar meant that all the perfume was to be, extravagantly, used for this occasion. The anointing of the head was not in itself restricted to

[1] Dt. 16:1–8.

royal or priestly anointing. It may simply have been the woman's dramatic and expensive way of expressing devotion and gratitude. At this point in the story as Mark tells it, however, the significance for the Christ, the Messiah ('anointed one of God') of being so treated, must not be missed. Whether she knew it or not, this woman was encouraging him at the outset of the final phase of his ministry. Nor should we miss the fact that it was a woman, and that as this gospel proceeds it will be the women who are increasingly the most faithful and reliable of Jesus' followers.

The imprecise *some* of verse 4 probably means some of the disciples. If so, they have tried to keep children away and have been corrected for it (10:13–16); now they criticize a woman for her form of devotion, and are rebuked for it (6–9). Their plea for the poor was well grounded (5), but in so arguing they had shown their lack of awareness of this epoch-making time in their lives and in the history of their people (7). Wittingly or unwittingly, her actions were instinctively in harmony with Jesus' repeated prediction of the immediate future (8:31; 9:31; 10:33–34). She has prepared him for his burial (8). Nor will it be left here. Her action will be recounted wherever the good news is told (9). This last saying has significance beyond the event. It suggests that Jesus did not, as some commentators have suggested, expect the final consummation of everything to occur shortly after his death (13:10 bears this out strongly). There is to be a telling of the good news, and *wherever the gospel is preached throughout the world* (14:9) she will be part of the story.

Verses 10 and 11, telling of Judas Iscariot's first step towards betraying Jesus seems to provide another example of Mark folding one story into another to make a point, since 1–2 and 10–11 could have run naturally into one another. Mark's point is probably a double one. Religious leaders and a disciple of Jesus who are all trusted men, conspire to kill God's anointed while a woman who is not supposed to know anything performs the anointing of God's anointed. No doubt the second, sharper, point is that while Judas will get money for betraying Jesus, the woman extravagantly lavishes her money on supporting him.

a. Caring for the poor

What has been called God's 'bias to the poor'[2] is plain in the gospels. We need to note, therefore, that it is not the supreme

---

[2] A popular phrase, used by David Sheppard and others (see David Sheppard, *Bias to the Poor*, Hodder & Stoughton, 1983).

concern of Jesus. More important is being in harmony with God's will and God's timing (which will include caring for the poor but never allowing it to become the dominant factor). The gospel is good news to the poor (Is. 61:1; Lk. 4:16, 21); but the poor are not the heart of the good news. Jesus in his self-giving love to save humankind is at the heart of the good news. Moreover the salvation offered to humankind is more than caring for the poor.

b. Women in the gospels

The story of the alabaster jar of perfume lavished upon Jesus by a woman, in face of harsh criticism, is a reminder that contrary to much that has been written about certain biblical verses being oppressive of women, there is in the gospels a strong vein of teaching about the vital role of women, and about the superior contribution they make in their own way at absolutely crucial points in the story. This becomes clearer, significantly, as the gospels move to their highest point in death and resurrection.

2. The Lord's Supper (14:12–26)

On the first day of the Feast of Unleavened Bread, when it was customary to sacrifice the Passover lamb, Jesus' disciples asked him, 'Where do you want us to go and make preparations for you to eat the Passover?'

[13]So he sent two of his disciples, telling them, 'Go into the city, and a man carrying a jar of water will meet you. Follow him. [14]Say to the owner of the house he enters, "The Teacher asks: Where is my guest room, where I may eat the Passover with my disciples?" [15]He will show you a large upper room, furnished and ready. Make preparations for us there.'

[16]The disciples left, went into the city and found things just as Jesus had told them. So they prepared the Passover.

[17]When evening came, Jesus arrived with the Twelve. [18]While they were reclining at the table eating, he said, 'I tell you the truth, one of you will betray me – one who is eating with me.'

[19]They were saddened, and one by one they said to him, 'Surely not I?'

[20]'It is one of the Twelve,' he replied, 'one who dips bread into the bowl with me. [21]The Son of Man will go just as it is written about him. But woe to that man who betrays the Son of Man! It would be better for him if he had not been born.'

[22]While they were eating, Jesus took bread, gave thanks and broke it, and gave it to his disciples, saying, 'Take it; this is my body.'

²³Then he took the cup, gave thanks and offered it to them, and they all drank from it.

²⁴'This is my blood of the covenant, which is poured out for many,' he said to them. ²⁵'I tell you the truth, I will not drink again of the fruit of the vine until that day when I drink it anew in the kingdom of God.'

²⁶When they had sung a hymn, they went out to the Mount of Olives.

The last supper is now described, after due preparations have been made for it. Mark's narrative raises two problems of timing. Passover Day itself was celebrated on 14 Nisan: on it the lambs were killed during the late afternoon or early evening, literally 'between the two evenings' (Ex. 12:6; Lv. 23:5). Then after sunset, when according to Jewish reckoning a new day had begun (*i.e.* 15 Nisan), the Passover meal was eaten. This was 'the first day of Unleavened Bread'.

The first problem is raised by Mark's statement that *it was customary to sacrifice the Passover lamb* on *the first day of the Feast of Unleavened Bread* (12), since the custom was actually to *eat* the lambs that day, having *sacrificed* them the previous day. A possible solution is that, although (strictly speaking) the first day of Unleavened Bread *followed* Passover Day, yet in loose, popular speech (as used by Mark here), it was thought of as including and indeed *beginning* the Passover.

The second problem is that Mark, followed by Matthew and Luke, sees the last supper as the Passover meal (*cf.* verses 14 and 16), enjoyed on the day after the lambs were killed; whereas John depicts Jesus as dying a day earlier, at the very time when the sacrificial lambs were being slaughtered (*e.g.* Jn. 18:28; *cf.* 1 Cor. 5:7). Several theories have been propounded to resolve this discrepancy. One is that two different calendars were in operation at that time, one used by the Pharisees and the other by the Sadducees, with a gap of one day between them – in which case the synoptic and Johannine chronologies are both correct. Another explanation is that Jesus was indeed on the cross while the lambs were being killed, but that he deliberately brought his own Passover meal forward a day because, as he said, he 'eagerly desired' to eat it with his apostles before he died (Lk. 22:15–16).

There is no easy solution to either of these problems, and no scholarly consensus about them. What is clear, however, is that for both the synoptic writers and John, Jesus sees the Passover as a basis for understanding the meaning of his forthcoming death.

The disciples ask where they may prepare a place because as

visitors they have to find one within the prescribed boundaries (12). The answer and its fulfilment has been accounted for in terms of Jesus having made a prior arrangement, but Mark seems to intend something more impressive than this, more on the lines of 1 Samuel 10:1–8 (13–15). The Master is fully in control of even what is to them the unknown. The two disciples find it so and prepare (16).

The meal, apart from Jesus' blessing of the bread and the cup, has only one piece of recorded conversation, and it concerns Jesus' prophecy that he would be betrayed (18–21). Mark does not, like Matthew (Mt. 26:25), identify Judas as the one of whom Jesus deliberately speaks. John also has Jesus identifying Judas, and even locates the significant turning point for Judas when he accepted the piece of bread from Jesus (Jn. 13:26). Mark has already, of course, let his readers know who the betrayer is (14:10–11). The point made here is that even the betrayal is not outside God's plan (*as it is written*, 21), perhaps referring to Old Testament passages like Psalm 41:9 or, less likely, Obadiah. Even the person who so betrays does so by his own choice and will be held responsible (21).

The other main contribution of this story relates to the meaning given by Jesus to the bread and wine. There is no mention of the sacrificial lambs eaten, though Mark's account does not preclude it. But it is the meaning of the bread and wine that is central, both because Jesus said these things and because the early church broke bread and drank wine to represent his dying for them. Much else must have been done and said that evening which is nowhere recorded.

As to the things said by Jesus about the bread and wine, the words of Nineham are apt:[3]

> For St. Mark and his readers it went without saying that Jesus was here instituting a sacramental rite (cf. 1 Cor. 11:24, 25 which makes this explicit); he made the loaf his body in the sense that those who partake of the loaf (originally the disciples, but later all who participate in the Eucharist) participate in his body, i.e. through communion with him, and hence with one another, they share all the various benefits which the early Church associated with being 'in Christ', 'members of his body'. By his words over the cup Jesus defines the meaning of his forthcoming death as a sacrificial shedding of blood, the means of inaugurating a new covenant between God and man (v. 24); and the drinking of the wine (whether by the original disciples (v. 23) or by the later participants in the Eucharist) is the means of participating in the

---

[3] Nineham, pp. 381–382.

atoning effects of his death and in the blessings of the new covenant it inaugurates.

Words like *This is my body* (22) about bread must have electrified the atmosphere. So must his reference to the wine as *my blood of the covenant* (24). The old covenant, inaugurated through Moses, included sprinkling of sacrificial blood (Ex. 24:6–8). In it God committed himself to his people and called for their commitment to him. The repeated failure on their part led to a yearning for a better way, designated in the 'new covenant' promised by God through Jeremiah (Je. 31:31). The new covenant will involve an inner writing of God's law on their hearts and minds. He will be their God and they his people, and all of his people will truly know him. What is more, their sins and wickedness will be forgiven and forgotten (Je. 31:33–34). No wonder, before *covenant*, some manuscripts have added *the new*, as Paul has it in 1 Corinthians 11:25. God's new, inner covenant is being symbolized in the upper room, and will shortly be realized by the death of Jesus, represented here by the bread and wine. They are invited to enter all of that as they participate by eating and drinking.

That it is imminent is signalled by Jesus' words, like the Nazirite vow of Numbers 6:2 ff.,[4] that he will not again drink *of the fruit of the vine until that day when I drink it anew in the kingdom of God* (25).

If this was a Passover meal, then the hymn referred to in verse 26 would be the second part of the Hallel (Pss. 114–118 or 115–118) normally sung at that point in the Passover meal.

The Mount of Olives was outside Jerusalem, whereas Deuteronomy 16:7 was understood to require all visitors to be in for the night of Nisan 15th, but in practice at the time a larger district was allowed, including Bethphage. The last supper link with the Passover meal is not threatened by this information, therefore.

3. Jesus predicts Peter's denial (14:27–31)

'You will all fall away,' Jesus told them, *'for it is written:*

> *' "I will strike the shepherd,*
> *and the sheep will be scattered."*

[28]*But after I have risen, I will go ahead of you into Galilee.'*
[29]*Peter declared, 'Even if all fall away, I will not.'*
[30]*'I tell you the truth,'* Jesus answered, *'today – yes, tonight – before the cock crows twice you yourself will disown me three times.'*

---

[4] Moule, p. 115.

217

[31]*But Peter insisted emphatically, 'Even if I have to die with you, I will never disown you.' And all the others said the same.*

We now, in predictions of Peter's denial, return to the familiar theme of how hard a way is discipleship of the kingdom of God. Of all people, impetuous, well-intentioned Peter becomes the focal point, and by his own hapless choice. Jesus begins with a general prediction that all the Twelve will fall away from him, using part of Zechariah 13:7 as the basis for his words (27). They should not be too desolate, however, because after rising he will *go ahead* of them into Galilee, back home (28).

This is all too much for Peter! He protests that even if all the others deserted Jesus (is there just a hint that Peter would not be surprised if they did?), he would not (29). (And does this relate to Jn. 21:15, 'Do you love me more than these?')

Jesus' reply is stunning in its precision. He says, *'today – yes, tonight – before the cock crows twice you yourself will disown me three times'* (30). Peter's rebuttal of this now goes further. Should he have to die with Jesus (how near to the truth we can stumble without knowing it), he will not disown his Master. This, evidently, is too much for the others! They also protest their loyalty. Neither their desire to stand with him, nor their sincerity, are in doubt. The question is whether the quality of their commitment will see them through what was to come.

a. Privilege and responsibility

If the Twelve did from time to time see their position as one of enormous privilege, they were now beginning to see the other side of the coin. 'To whom much is given, from them much will be expected.' How wonderful to be in the upper room witnessing and sharing the last supper! How equally heinous to have so witnessed and shared and then betrayed the central character. This is not simply a lesson for Christian leaders. It is a universal principle of life. Whether at national or local government level, or in societies, work or family, our major concern should not be the attitudes of voters, or employees, or loved ones. Behind it all stands a greater answerability, to the God who gave it all and sees all.

b. The heart of discipleship

Repeatedly Mark's story has shown the sad failure of group after group to grasp the meaning of, or enter into, the experience of true discipleship of Jesus. In one sense we have been better placed to see what it does not involve than what it does. The last supper puts the balance straight. Eating and drinking was understood in the first century as a deep and intimate form of acceptance and sharing. Jesus has encouraged his disciples to eat his body and drink his blood. There could be no deeper symbol of total dependence on him and commitment to him. Even more significant still are the background themes of Passover and covenant. At the first Passover God defeated the enemies of his people and set his people free, protected as they were by the blood of the sacrificial lambs. Christ now offers his life sacrificially to defeat the enemies of God's kingdom and to set free those who will be joined by faith (symbolized here by their eating and drinking) to him.

And it means covenant. God in Christ brings about the new covenant prophesied in the Scriptures. The shedding of blood confirms the covenant at the most total and serious level of all. The covenant people will henceforth not be one natural race, like the Jews, entered into by physical birth. People who respond to the invitation by faith will be the people of the new covenant of the kingdom of God.

c. Human frailty and discipleship

The story of Peter's protestation of loyalty to Jesus makes sad reading for us, knowing as we do what will eventually take place. That Peter and the others meant what they said is not in doubt. The mistake they made was to be too confident in their ability to stand faithfully on their own when the battle became fiercest. Yet, despite their coming failure, they will not be given up. The message from the risen Christ will be for 'his disciples and Peter' (16:7).

4. Gethsemane (14:32–42)

They went to a place called Gethsemane, and Jesus said to his disciples, 'Sit here while I pray.' [33]*He took Peter, James and John along with him, and he began to be deeply distressed and troubled.* [34]*'My soul is overwhelmed with sorrow to the point of death,'* he said to them. *'Stay here and keep watch.'*

[35]*Going a little farther, he fell to the ground and prayed that if possible the hour might pass from him.* [36]*'Abba, Father,'* he said, *'everything is possible for you. Take this cup from me. Yet not what I will, but what you will.'*

[37]*Then he returned to his disciples and found them sleeping. 'Simon,'* he said to Peter, *'are you asleep? Could you not keep watch for one hour?* [38]*Watch and pray so that you will not fall into*

219

temptation. The spirit is willing, but the body is weak.'

³⁹*Once more he went away and prayed the same thing.* ⁴⁰*When he came back, he again found them sleeping, because their eyes were heavy. They did not know what to say to him.*

⁴¹*Returning the third time, he said to them, 'Are you still sleeping and resting? Enough! The hour has come. Look, the Son of Man is betrayed into the hands of sinners.* ⁴²*Rise! Let us go! Here comes my betrayer!'*

The experience at Gethsemane showed how weak that ability was. Jesus again took the inner group with him, Peter, James and John (33). To them he showed the depth of his distress and sorrow at what lay ahead (33–34). They were asked to *stay here and keep watch* (34).

'Gethsemane' probably means 'oil-press' or 'olive-press'. The area, identified by Mark only as *a place called Gethsemane* (32) is located by John as a garden beyond the Kidron ravine (Jn. 18:1–2). It is therefore taken to be on the lower slopes of the Mount of Olives, some half a mile from the wall of the city.

The powerful verbs used of Jesus' condition – *deeply distressed . . . troubled . . . overwhelmed with sorrow* (33–34) underline the fact that for Jesus, too, being faithful to the end was costly. The battle begun with baptism and temptations (1:9–12) is now reaching its climax. Only he knew the full implications of his words at the last supper about his body and blood – in the context of Passover and covenant. In this situation we can understand that he genuinely needed his closest friends to watch with him in Gethsemane.

His prayer, in so far as we are allowed to listen in on it, constitutes one of the most poignant events in the gospel. He addresses God as *Abba*, a word in the Aramaic language Jesus would speak. We are probably to understand that this word was used when elsewhere in the gospels the Greek word for 'Father' is recorded from the lips of Jesus. *Abba* is intensely personal and intimate. On the rare occasions of its use in addressing God, 'which art in heaven' was added.[5] Jesus uses it without such 'screening' protection. Here, of all places, the intimacy of his Father's love was needed, and his reciprocal response. (The Christian church daringly came to use this address for God, too, in describing the believer's deep, inner sense of belonging to God's family – Rom. 8:15; Gal. 4:6.)

Whichever way we interpret the prayer of Jesus in Gethsemane the seriousness of the occasion must be underlined. It is not a drama acted out for the benefit of the faithful. It represents a

---

[5] Cranfield, p. 433.

real struggle by Jesus who alone on earth knew what was involved. *'Take this cup from me'* (36). For the cup see on 10:38. R. P. Martin suggests that the cup here may refer to the fierce struggle of temptation to go another way than his Father's way. It is usually, however, understood to represent a request by Jesus that if there is any other way possible for his work to be done than the awful sin-bearing death set out, as we have seen, in relation to the suffering servant of Isaiah 53 and the ransom of Mark 10:45, then that way should be followed. It is not an opposition to his Father's will, but a facing of the horror of the death he faces. Yet even with this horror ahead he reaffirms his Father's will (36). This brief insight into the intimate prayer life of Jesus shines a light not only on the cost of our redemption but also on the nature of Jesus as God and man. The two are seen as one in this crucial moment for the redemption that will be offered to all.

By contrast (37–41), the disciples cannot even remain awake. Three times he returned to find them sleeping – perhaps heavy with fear as well as tiredness. On the third occasion the word *'enough'* can have the meaning 'the bill is paid', as though there in the garden of Gethsemane everything was finally established. What had been settled in prayer would be carried out in life – and death (41).

The reference to the Son of Man in this context shows clearly that this is his self-designation. The betrayal of the Son of Man means the betrayal of Jesus. Are the disciples beginning to see it more clearly now? Some things must have fallen into place with the appearance of *my betrayer* (42).

Praying and doing

Much is quite properly made these days in books on spirituality about the importance of 'praying as you go', of the interrelation of prayer and action at every point of life. The aim is to emphasize prayer's great value and no Christian would wish to disagree with that. On its own, however, such an emphasis can lead to a devaluing of prayer by a trivializing of its purposes. Prayer in the Bible and in Christian tradition is much more than spiritual injections into the interstices of life. It is also about wrestling with big issues, about prolonged time in God's presence precisely away from all the pressures of life's busy round of activities. It is for gaining a perspective on those activities from the vantage point of being alone with God. The use of the mountain as the place for such encounters in the Bible contains rich symbolism (see on 9:2–8).

5. Jesus arrested (14:43–52)

Just as he was speaking, Judas, one of the Twelve, appeared. With him was a crowd armed with swords and clubs, sent from the chief priests, the teachers of the law, and the elders.

⁴⁴*Now the betrayer had arranged a signal with them: 'The one I kiss is the man: arrest him and lead him away under guard.'* ⁴⁵*Going at once to Jesus, Judas said, 'Rabbi!' and kissed him.* ⁴⁶*The men seized Jesus and arrested him.* ⁴⁷*Then one of those standing near drew his sword and struck the servant of the high priest, cutting off his ear.*

⁴⁸*'Am I leading a rebellion,' said Jesus, 'that you have come out with swords and clubs to capture me?* ⁴⁹*Every day I was with you, teaching in the temple courts, and you did not arrest me. But the Scriptures must be fulfilled.'* ⁵⁰*Then everyone deserted him and fled.*

⁵¹*A young man, wearing nothing but a linen garment, was following Jesus. When they seized him,* ⁵²*he fled naked, leaving his garment behind.*

The arrest of Jesus is the next stage of his abandonment. His inner disciples could not stay awake with him. Now they could not even be with him. They chose that way for themselves, in any case (50). Worst of all was Judas, who by pre-arrangement identified Jesus with a kiss, a typical greeting of a rabbi by a pupil (44–45). This enables a small group to take Jesus quietly, away from the crowds (14:1–2). Yet violence still erupts with a disciple (John says it was Peter, Jn. 18:10) cutting off the ear of one of the assailants (47). Jesus complains about such force and secrecy, since he had been so readily available (48–49). He accounts for their actions in terms of the fulfilment of Scripture, no doubt those already alluded to earlier in connection with 14:18 and 27 (namely, Ps. 41:9 and Zc. 13:7). At this, all his disciples, despite their recent protestations (29, 31) run away for safety. Jesus' application of the Scripture to his own situation was correct (27).

Verses 51–52 are wonderfully inexplicable except as one more piece of evidence from someone who was there. Wearing nothing but a linen garment (to judge by the word, a high quality piece of clothing), was he wearing only one garment because he had jumped out of bed on hearing the crowd make their way? Was he hoping to get on ahead to warn people? And who was he? There is a not surprising tradition that it was Mark himself. The last supper might have taken place in his home, and Acts 12:12 has the early Christians meeting there. Someone might have warned the residents of that house about the crowd making its way to capture Jesus. A young man who had run at speed could easily have got too far into the centre of things and been apprehended. We do not know, and many fascinating guesses have been made. We need not have the answer to every question, but one thing is clear – Jesus is now deserted by everyone allegedly on his side.

The betrayal by Judas

Various reasons have been adduced for Judas' treachery. His name might suggest he was from the south while all the others were from the north. John's gospel suggests he was greedy for gain (Jn. 12:6), an idea with some grounding in Matthew 26:14–16. But that could hardly be the main reason. Some have suggested that he was frustrated at what seemed to him to be Jesus' failure to take opportunities available to take over the kingdom from the Romans. Others even, most kindly, guess that the act of betrayal was an attempt to force Jesus' hand, and make things develop. Mark shows no interest in any of this. He realistically says that it happens, that it is a terrible thing to do, and that nevertheless God will work it into the pattern for the Messiah.

For us these things are equally true. We all may, and we all do, betray our Lord, though not as dramatically as Judas. It remains a heinous thing to do, and we are answerable. What Judas did not discover, though Peter did, and we now know, is that there is forgiveness even for such betrayals. (Judas took his own life, Mt. 27:3–5; Acts 1:16–20; while Peter was restored, Jn. 21:15–22.) And God can still take the broken and spoiled strands of life and weave them into the total tapestry (Rom. 8:28). We should never be complacent about sin, since all sin betrays Jesus: but nor should we be destroyed by remorse or guilt when sin overtakes us – there is forgiveness and restoration (1 Jn. 1:8–10).

6. The trial before the Sanhedrin (14:53–65)

They took Jesus to the high priest, and all the chief priests, elders and teachers of the law came together. [54]*Peter followed him at a distance, right into the courtyard of the high priest. There he sat with the guards and warmed himself at the fire.*

[55]*The chief priests and the whole Sanhedrin were looking for evidence against Jesus so that they could put him to death, but they did not find any.* [56]*Many testified falsely against him, but their statements did not agree.*

[57]*Then some stood up and gave this false testimony against him:* [58]*'We heard him say, "I will destroy this man-made temple and in*

three days will build another, not made by man."' [59]Yet even then their testimony did not agree.

[60]Then the high priest stood up before them and asked Jesus, 'Are you not going to answer? What is this testimony that these men are bringing against you?' [61]But Jesus remained silent and gave no answer.

Again the high priest asked him, 'Are you the Christ, the Son of the Blessed One?'

[62]'I am,' said Jesus. 'And you will see the Son of Man sitting at the right hand of the Mighty One and coming on the clouds of heaven.'

[63]The high priest tore his clothes. 'Why do we need any more witnesses?' he asked. [64]'You have heard the blasphemy. What do you think?'

They all condemned him as worthy of death. [65]Then some began to spit at him; they blindfolded him, struck him with their fists, and said, 'Prophesy!' And the guards took him and beat him.

The trial of Jesus is now described, as economically as ever, by Mark. The different gospels emphasize different parts of the story, giving rise to much discussion about what happened and when. Mark suggests an informal, preliminary hearing, late at night, in view of a more formal gathering in the morning, followed by an appearance before Pilate.

Of the hearing at night, R. P. Martin writes, 'What is given in these verses is best called a preliminary hearing. It was informal and not too careful about strict legal procedures. So it was held at night, contrary to legal requirements for an official trial. But it wasn't such a trial, so this may explain the irregularities.'[6] This also fits well with John 18:13 ff.; 24; 28 ff.

The purpose, as Mark sets out this preliminary hearing, seems to be to convince themselves that Jesus deserved death for blasphemy, then to hand him over to the Roman authorities for execution on the charge of being a threat to Roman authority. It is not certain whether or not at that time the Sanhedrin would have had authority to have Jesus stoned to death for blasphemy, but in any case consideration of the response of the people certainly made it politically wiser to use the Roman power if possible.

As Jesus is being taken for his hearing, Mark once again neatly folds in the first part of the story of Peter at this point, following at a distance, then sitting at the guards' fire, warming himself (14:53–54). The contrast between the experiences of Jesus and Peter seems to be the point.

[6] Martin, *Action*, p. 132.

Mark says that the authorities had difficulty in getting an accusation to stick (55). The various false testimonies conflicted with one another (56). More serious was the misuse of his words, possibly those in 13:2, or more likely in John 2:19 (57–58). Even those attempts failed, however (59). In desperation the high priest turns to Jesus himself with a question about the evidence (60). Jesus puts himself in contempt of the court by retaining a regal silence (61). Then, however, the high priest touches on the crucial point, that of the identity of Jesus (61). The title he uses – *the Christ, the Son of the Blessed One* may well have been built up on the strength of things Jesus was reported to have said and done, and on conclusions based upon them. (For 'the Christ' see on 8:29.) 'The Blessed One' is a periphrasis (way of speaking about God without using his name) for God. In such a setting Jesus makes one last attempt to enable the leaders of his nation to see the truth about him (*I am*). But he immediately, and typically, reinterprets his status and role in terms of the Son of Man picture (62).[7] This statement actually provides what his accusers need. It is adjudged to be blasphemous. The high priest acts appropriately for such an occasion, puts the question to the Sanhedrin, and gets the response he seeks (63–64). The blasphemy was not claiming to be Messiah, but claiming that he was the Son of Man *sitting at the right hand of the Mighty One* (62, another periphrasis for God). The genuine anger this aroused is reflected in their behaviour towards Jesus (65). His claim is to them at once offensive and literally incredible, but ironically, as they taunt him with the challenge to prophesy, they are actually fulfilling a prophecy he has made again and again (8:31; 9:31; 10:33–34). The most likely source of all this information would be Joseph of Arimathea and Nicodemus, members of the Sanhedrin who became Christians (Jn. 19:38–42).

7. Peter disowns Jesus (14:66–72)

While Peter was below in the courtyard, one of the servant girls of the high priest came by. [67]*When she saw Peter warming himself, she looked closely at him.*

'You also were with that Nazarene, Jesus,' she said.

[68]*But he denied it. 'I don't know or understand what you're talking about,' he said, and went out into the entrance.*

[69]*When the servant girl saw him there, she said again to those standing around, 'This fellow is one of them.'* [70]*Again he denied it.*

---

[7] For this title used in this way, see commentary on 8:31; 9.31; 10:33–34 and 13:26.

After a little while, those standing near said to Peter, 'Surely you are one of them, for you are a Galilean.'

[71]He began to call down curses on himself, and he swore to them, 'I don't know this man you're talking about.'

[72]Immediately the cock crowed the second time. Then Peter remembered the word Jesus had spoken to him: 'Before the cock crows twice you will disown me three times.' And he broke down and wept.

Peter denying his Lord while the preliminary trial takes place is Mark's way of once more returning to his theme of true (and false) discipleship.

Peter's story is simply told. Under pressure, twice from a serving girl and once from bystanders, he first pleads ignorance, then denies he belongs to the group of disciples, then disclaims any link with Jesus (68, 70, 71). The kindest thing said about him is that he at least called curses down on himself, not on anyone else. But he need not have bothered, *the cock crowed a second time. Then Peter remembered . . .* (71). He had grace to break down and weep. There might yet be a chance for him.

Truth and falsehood

Mark's double story provides alarming evidence of how easily institutions and corporate pressure can totally misrepresent the truth. In the Sanhedrin the only totally innocent person is declared guilty by the religious leaders of the day! Outside a good, full-hearted disciple finds himself denying the Lord whom he is follow-ing, at some risk to himself even if at a distance. There is a mystery about corporate evil which carries people along to do things which in their better judgment, and on their own they would never do. Our own century has provided several instances of the operation of what the New Testament calls 'principalities and powers' at that corporate level. Corporate evil flourishes when we believe that we are not responsible, that there is little we can do, that others make the policies, we only carry them out. It enables nations to exploit nations, corporations to exploit workers, workers to exploit cor-porations. Alongside any individual interpretation of evil there must be the corporate perspective too, and the question of corpor-ate salvation also.

8. Jesus is turned over to Pilate (15:1–15)

Very early in the morning, the chief priests, with the elders, the

teachers of the law and the whole Sanhedrin, reached a decision.
They bound Jesus, led him away and turned him over to Pilate.
²*'Are you the king of the Jews?' asked Pilate.*

'Yes, it is as you say,' Jesus replied.

³*The chief priests accused him of many things.* ⁴*So again Pilate*
asked him, 'Aren't you going to answer? See how many things they
are accusing you of.'

⁵*But Jesus still made no reply, and Pilate was amazed.*

⁶*Now it was the custom at the Feast to release a prisoner whom*
the people requested. ⁷*A man called Barabbas was in prison with*
the insurrectionists who had committed murder in the uprising. ⁸*The*
crowd came up and asked Pilate to do for them what he usually
did.

⁹*'Do you want me to release to you the king of the Jews?' asked*
Pilate, ¹⁰*knowing it was out of envy that the chief priests had handed*
Jesus over to him. ¹¹*But the chief priests stirred up the crowd to*
have Pilate release Barabbas instead.

¹²*'What shall I do, then, with the one you call the king of the*
Jews?' Pilate asked them.

¹³*'Crucify him!' they shouted.*

¹⁴*'Why? What crime has he committed?' asked Pilate.*

But they shouted all the louder, 'Crucify him!'

¹⁵*Wanting to satisfy the crowd, Pilate released Barabbas to them.*
He had Jesus flogged, and handed him over to be crucified.

Jesus before Pilate is an encounter which has captured the imagination of people in every century since then.

In 15:1 the Sanhedrin met formally and *reached a decision.* Then, either to avoid the anger of the people, or because they were not allowed to carry out the death sentence themselves (see Jn. 18:31), they decided to hand him over to Pilate. Interestingly, the word used for *turned him over to* occurs frequently in Mark's gospel, usually in connection with Jesus' journey to Jerusalem and death (9:31; 10:33; 14:10, 11, 18, 21, 41, 42, 44; 15:1, 10, 15). It is used in the Greek version of the Old Testament to translate 1 Samuel 24:4, meaning 'delivered over to death', based on a Hebraic passive form. The idea seems to be that although we are reading accounts of what men are doing to Jesus, behind it all we must also be aware of the guiding hand of God. The same verb is used of John the Baptist's arrest in Mark 1:14. This is significant when we recall that in Mark's gospel John the Baptist is not only forerunner of Jesus but also prototype.

For this they needed something more substantial than blasphemy to motivate Pilate to do what they wanted. Pilate's question in verse 2 *'Are you the king of the Jews?'*, suggests the line they took. Luke fills in some of the detail perhaps implied by Mark 15:3, *accused him of many things*. In Luke 23:2 they make the most of their religious complaints against him 'subverting our nation . . . opposes payment of taxes to Caesar . . . claims to be Christ, a king'. Pilate's question about his being the king of the Jews therefore brings together Jewish religious issues and Roman secular scruples. To this question Jesus gives an affirmative answer, but putting the responsibility for the description on to Pilate himself, *'Yes, it is as you say'* (2). The meaning of Jesus' answer is not abundantly clear. It could, for example, be translated, 'You do well to ask.' Even here, however, the balance is towards accepting the description, not rejecting it. Having answered the crucial question, however, he declines to deal with the direct accusations of the Sanhedrin, as he had in their preliminary hearing (4). Jesus' silence, on an issue of life and death, amazes Pilate (5). Moule's comment sums up the situation well:

> The irony of the situation is overpowering: Jesus, who is, indeed, king of the Jews in a deeply spiritual sense, has refused to lead a spiritual uprising. Yet now, condemned for blasphemy by the Jews because of his spiritual claims, he is accused by them also before Pilate for being precisely what he had disappointed the crowds by failing to be – a political insurgent. Jesus refused either to plead guilty or to defend himself.[8]

The silence of the suffering servant in Isaiah 53:7 again comes to mind. Pilate's attitude of 'amazement' picks up a characteristic theme of Mark's gospel, a sense which people have that more is going on than meets the eye.

The nature of the custom mentioned in verse 6 is not known outside the New Testament. Nor do we know about the insurrection mentioned in verse 7. The reference in verse 8 to *what he usually did* suggests an idiosyncratic custom of Pilate himself. *The crowd* referred to may well have been a group of Barabbas' supporters.

The introduction of Barabbas into the story is itself interesting. The words translated *a man called Barabbas* (7), are literally 'the one called Barabbas', giving rise to the question 'Which one?' It is usually employed as a device to distinguish two people with the same name but, perhaps, a different extra name or title (see Mt. 27:22, 'Jesus who is called Christ'; Mt. 26:3, 'the high priest, whose name was Caiaphas'; and Jn. 9:11, 'the man they call Jesus', in this

---

[8] Moule, p. 124.

case a known teacher/healer is the point). But there is no such equivalent for Barabbas, except that a good number of reliable manuscripts of Matthew 27:16 ff. actually have 'Jesus, called Barabbas'. The tendency to drop the name Jesus, for any ordinary person, was strong among Christians for reasons of devotion to their Lord, and among Jews because of the unpleasantness caused by memory of Jesus Christ. But if it was originally present, then it explains the language used here, heightens the contrast between Barabbas and Jesus, and adds further irony to the choice made by the pro-Barabbas crowd.

Pilate's question to the crowd in verse 9 suggests that Jesus had made a positive response to his enquiry in verse 2. Mark concentrates now on the various motives of the different participants. Pilate perceives the envy of the chief priests where Jesus is concerned (10). The desire to please the crowd guides Pilate himself (15). The crowd want an insurrectionist set free by the Roman authorities (8, 11) urged on now by the chief priests. The one motive not clear is that of the crowd in calling for Jesus to be crucified. If all they wanted was Barabbas' freedom they did not have to oppose Jesus so vehemently. We might guess that because Jesus had resisted the way of insurrection they saw him as an enemy of all that Barabbas represented. But that would be only a guess. Mark simply leaves it as a mystery, not that they should choose Barabbas but that they should so strongly condemn Jesus. Are we meant to perceive the power of evil (which all disciples of Jesus will also meet) gathering strength as the battle lines are more firmly drawn up? Pilate's action confirms such a view, with a flogging for Jesus before he was passed on for crucifixion. Yet the word used for that passing on is that referred to in 15:1. A greater mystery than that of evil in the world is God's capacity to be at work even when men and women choose to do evil things for which they are answerable, and yet which God will weave into his pattern for his world.

The opposition to Jesus

The operation of evil in this story had a particular focal point. Each group was threatened by the largely silent figure at the centre. For the religious authorities his interpretation of messiahship in terms of the Son of Man, with strong overtones from the suffering servant of Isaiah 53, yet given with such divine authority, was too much for them to accept. For Pilate the prospect of a king of any kind put his position in jeopardy, both his location in Jerusalem and his reputation with Rome. The crowd, especially if it was a pro-

Barabbas protest, had no time for this 'lowly service of love' approach. They wanted the Romans away. The story continues to have strange relevance, since the teaching, dying, rising and ascending of Jesus are a constant rebuke to our human values and systems. 'Giving to gain', 'dying to live', 'measuring time by eternity', 'estimating greatness by the degree of lowly service', 'first being last and last first', and 'the meek inheriting the earth' do not simply cause derision, they produce great anger. Mark's story not only tells how it happened to Jesus. Perhaps, with a sad shake of the head, he is preparing Jesus' followers for much of the same.

9. The mocking of Jesus (15:16–20)

The soldiers led Jesus away into the palace (that is, the Praetorium) and called together the whole company of soldiers. [17]They put a purple robe on him, then twisted together a crown of thorns and set it on him. [18]And they began to call out to him, 'Hail, king of the Jews!' [19]Again and again they struck him on the head with a staff and spat on him. Falling on their knees, they paid homage to him. [20]And when they had mocked him, they took off the purple robe and put his own clothes on him. Then they led him out to crucify him.

The mocking of Jesus serves to drive the point about suffering home more sharply. *Praetorium* is a Latin word describing the governor's residence (16). Matthew identifies the *purple robe* more precisely as a 'scarlet military cloak', the nearest they could get to the purple usually worn by kings and emperors. The *crown of thorns* was a painful imitation of a diadem, worn by the emperor as a sign of divinity, oddly enough. Their greeting was a transposition of a traditional welcome for Caesar (17–18). A 'king' who goes so meekly and without abuse or resistance was an obvious target for mockery from the world's tough men – precisely Mark's point.

Their fun over, the soldiers put Jesus into his own clothes again, and took him to his death.

10. The crucifixion of Jesus (15:21–41)

A certain man from Cyrene, Simon, the father of Alexander and Rufus, was passing by on his way in from the country, and they forced him to carry the cross. [22]They brought Jesus to the place called Golgotha (which means The Place of the Skull). [23]Then they offered him wine mixed with myrrh, but he did not take it. [24]And they crucified him. Dividing up his clothes, they cast lots to see what each would get.

²⁵*It was the third hour when they crucified him.* ²⁶*The written notice of the charge against him read:* THE KING OF THE JEWS. ²⁷*They crucified two robbers with him, one on his right and one on his left.* ²⁹*Those who passed by hurled insults at him, shaking their heads and saying, 'So! You who are going to destroy the temple and build it in three days,* ³⁰*come down from the cross and save yourself!'*

³¹*In the same way the chief priests and the teachers of the law mocked him among themselves. 'He saved others,' they said, 'but he can't save himself!* ³²*Let this Christ, this King of Israel, come down now from the cross, that we may see and believe.' Those crucified with him also heaped insults on him.*

³³*At the sixth hour darkness came over the whole land until the ninth hour.* ³⁴*And at the ninth hour Jesus cried out in a loud voice, 'Eloi, Eloi, lama sabachthani?' – which means, 'My God, my God, why have you forsaken me?'*

³⁵*When some of those standing near heard this, they said, 'Listen, he's calling Elijah.'*

³⁶*One man ran, filled a sponge with wine vinegar, put it on a stick, and offered it to Jesus to drink. 'Now leave him alone. Let's see if Elijah comes to take him down,' he said.*

³⁷*With a loud cry, Jesus breathed his last.*

³⁸*The curtain of the temple was torn in two from top to bottom.* ³⁹*And when the centurion, who stood there in front of Jesus, heard his cry and saw how he died, he said, 'Surely this man was the Son of God!'*

⁴⁰*Some women were watching from a distance. Among then were Mary Magdalene, Mary the mother of James the younger and of Joses, and Salome.* ⁴¹*In Galilee these women had followed him and cared for his needs. Many other women who had come up with him to Jerusalem were also there.*

Once more, Mark tells his story, even this most important part, almost without comment or interpretation. Jesus makes only one statement from the cross. Yet we are not left totally without help to understand what it all means.

There is, for example, a strong reliance on Old Testament prophecies and allusions. This does not mean that the account is constructed as an imaginary collage of Old Testament texts. If God was preparing over the centuries for the coming of the Messiah, it is hardly surprising that the clues to the experiences of that Messiah will be found in the passages that spoke of his coming.

Such references include the particular influence of Psalm 22, on

Jesus' cry of dereliction (34; Ps. 22:1); the dividing of the garments and casting lots (24; Ps. 22:18); the shaking of heads and mockery (29–32; Ps. 22:7–8); the offer of wine mixed with myrrh (23; Ps. 31:6) and of vinegar (36; Ps. 69:21). And of course throughout is the suffering servant of Isaiah 52:13; 53:12. Yet each of these events fits naturally into the story, too. The cry of dereliction reflects the enormity of what Jesus was enduring. Since the victims were crucified naked their clothing was taken as the possession of the soldiers, to apportion as they chose. The head-wagging and mockery reflect the surprise of his enemies that at last they had him trapped, and the general inability of all present to perceive what was actually happening. The offer of *wine mixed with myrrh* (23), and later of *wine vinegar* (36), were in the first place probably a regular form of help to the crucified, and in the second an attempt to prolong the drama in a misunderstanding of the cry of dereliction (34–35). Mark did not create these elements to pick up Old Testament themes. They happened, and were fulfilments.

Another source of understanding is the way the crucifixion draws together some of the main features of Mark's gospel itself. The battle against evil was foreshadowed in the temptations (1:12). The opposition from religious authorities began in Capernaum (2:6). The inability of his disciples to be what he needed was signalled in their slowness about the parable of the sower (4:10–13). The unwillingness of people to accept the grace of God given in Jesus was embodied in the action of the local residents after Legion was cured; they asked Jesus to leave (5:17). The opposition of Herod became clear in the matter of John the Baptist (6:14–29). The necessity of the cross and its implications were regularly repeated (8:21; 9:31; 10:33–34). The transfiguration established its continuity with God's purposes in the past (9:2–8). The unbelief which constantly threatened his work kept breaking out (10:19). The price of following God's will through to its conclusion, and the difficulty people faced, was illustrated by the rich young man (10:17–26). The future for Jesus, in terms of cup, baptism, ransom, blood of the Covenant, was sketched in different sayings and occasions (10:38, 45; 12:22–24). The enormous spiritual struggle involved in the meaning of his death was most closely revealed by his prayers in Gethsemane (14:32–42).

Running through it all was the calm control of Jesus on all occasions, the bumbling support of his disciples, the way in which the women perceived and could be relied on more than the men, the growing storm clouds of opposition, and the regular response of awe and amazement at the sense of God's hidden hand at work in it all. He who has ears to hear, and she who has eyes to see, can perceive that in the story of the crucifixion the gospel has almost reached its conclusion. Mark's plain account of the death of Jesus is meant to enable those who can to draw insight from the Old Testament and from his gospel. But in the end each reader has to decide.

As to the detail, verse 21 introduces Simon of Cyrene as the father of Alexander and Rufus in a way which suggests that the sons at least were known to the readers of the gospel. Is this the Rufus of Romans 16:13? Simon could hardly have been travelling from Cyrene in North Africa. This must have been his place of origin. Roman soldiers had the right to enforce tasks upon citizens (see Mt. 5:41). To Jew and Gentile alike the picture of a so-called Messiah needing someone else to carry the *patibulum* or cross-piece (the upright section would already be at the site and in the ground) must have been at once shocking and incomprehensible. Those who had learned the words of Jesus with care from this gospel would more likely be thinking of 8:34, 'If anyone would come after me, he must deny himself and take up his cross and follow me'. Not exactly to the letter of that verse, but certainly in its spirit, Simon unwittingly became the first to carry a cross and follow Jesus. If, at the time of reading, the Christians at Rome were suffering persecution, or about to do so, the story of Simon, and the possible link with Rufus and Alexander, would have meant much to them.

Golgotha (22) means 'a skull'. Presumably there was a skull-shaped hill, or it could just have been 'bad-land', and thus used for executions. Jesus refused the offer of wine mixed with myrrh, the purpose of which was to dull the senses. The Talmud records that women from Jerusalem provided a narcotic for condemned criminals, as a charitable act. Was he keeping his vow of 14:25, or not wishing anything to dull what he now did in obedience to the Father's will? (23). While this ministry was being offered, the soldiers were dealing with one of the few perks of their thankless work (24).

The inscription, not over his head but on a notice, shows clearly that the charge was treason, despite Pilate's protestation of Jesus' innocence. The irony of his being executed on the basis of a wrong interpretation of what he truly was, is all the clearer because of Mark's unadorned account (26).

He tells nothing of the robbers (compare Lk. 23:39–43 and Mt. 27:44 where two different moods are described). The insults hurled at Jesus again pick up reports of what he was alleged to have said. Once more the irony of the salvation language (31) is very strong. What they taunt him for not doing, saving himself, is precisely so because he is doing what they ridicule, saving others. He could not do both. Mark sees both robbers crucified with him as at this point reviling Jesus (32).

For once Mark is quite precise about the details of time. It was the third hour (9 a.m.) when they crucified Jesus (25). There was darkness over the whole land from the sixth hour (noon) until the ninth hour (3 p.m.) when Jesus cried out and died (33–34, 37).

The 'cry of dereliction', Jesus' only words from the cross in Mark's account, has been variously interpreted. Some see it, quite properly, as the beginning of Psalm 22, and argue that we are meant to see it as an affirmation of the whole of that Psalm as the mood of the cry, since the Psalm ends with victory and assurance. But this is much too subtle, and fails to meet the exact circumstances of the story. Neither do they match the mood of Mark's gospel throughout. These are the only words of Jesus from the cross in Mark because Mark wishes to underline the enormous cost, to Jesus, of obedience to the Father's will. This cry is wholly in harmony with the prayers in Gethsemane, where he was 'deeply distressed', 'troubled', and 'overwhelmed with sorrow' (14:32–34). 'This cup', about which he then prayed, is now being drunk to the dregs (36). The ransom price is being paid to set 'many' free (10:45). The bread and wine on which the new covenant is based are being offered and poured out (14:22–24). The cry of dereliction reflects the awfulness of fulfilling that task, described elsewhere in Scripture so graphically (Rom. 3:21–26; 2 Cor. 5:18–19, 21; 1 Pet. 1:18–20). He was bearing on himself all the awful consequences of human sinfulness before God, so that any who come by faith in him might be set free of those consequences, and follow his way of obedience to the heavenly Father. From the deepest point of darkness emerged the cry of desolation. How else could it be expressed?

The words Jesus used, presented here by Mark as a Greek transliteration of an Aramaic form of Psalm 22:1, were probably said originally in the Hebrew, since the first word, repeated, would in Hebrew be most likely misunderstood as a call for Elijah (35), which led to the renewed offer of liquid sustenance, this time the drink with which the soldiers were issued (36). But there was nothing more to happen now (37), for Jesus died. (Death by crucifixion could linger for days. Mark wishes us to know that when Jesus had completed his work, he died. Even here he was in control.)

The tearing of the temple curtain *from top to bottom* (38) obviously has great symbolic meaning. There were two curtains in the temple to which he might be referring. One was over the entrance to the Holy Place (Ex. 26:37). The other was between the Holy

Place and the Most Holy Place (Ex. 26:31–35), where God's immediate presence was felt to be. The high priest would enter through that curtain once a year on behalf of all the people on the Day of Atonement (Lv. 16). The penetrating of this second curtain is used symbolically elsewhere in the New Testament to describe the immediate access of Christians to God, particularly in the Letter to the Hebrews (6:19; 9:3; 10:20). This makes most sense for Mark's account, too. As Jesus dies, bearing in mind all that his death signifies for the saving of sinners (see on verse 34 above), the way is truly opened directly to God for all who come by faith. This is the glorious meaning of the tearing of the curtain, and particularly from top to bottom, signifying God's action in Christ (2 Cor. 5:19), a point to be constantly remembered in all our reflections on the meaning of Christ's death.

The question is raised as to whether the curtain in the temple was literally torn. Since we cannot prove it we come back once again to the degree of historicity we ascribe to Mark's account, and to the accuracy we attach to what he records. There is no specific reference outside the New Testament to the tearing of the curtain. Josephus does describe certain unusual events but does not mention that event on that occasion. On the other hand, if such a thing did happen it could well have been reported by priests who became Christian (Acts 6:7), since the ordinary public need not have known. The question is not whether this could have happened but whether God would do such a thing. Since mostly in the biblical records the understanding of concepts and meanings is related to a prior divine activity, the balance points towards an actual event, though it is the meaning which matters more.

Ironically, once more, when the curtain masking the immediate presence of God from Israel in the temple is torn open, it is a Gentile who first enters into the newly offered spiritual access through Christ (39). He stood in front of Jesus, heard his cry and saw his death. He made a statement of his own faith, 'Surely this man was the Son of God' (39). The Greek requires only the translation 'a son of God', but the definite article is not needed in such a construction for its presence in the translation. Again we have to discuss what Mark means. The point seems to be that an unbiased observer, religiously speaking, can see what the religiously trained cannot (39).

The women now feature strongly once more (40–41). Another trait displayed by Mark is the using by God of the least plausible witnesses, from the eccentricity of John the Baptist, through the unreliability of his chosen apostles, and the commission of the man Legion as proclaimer of the good news, to the setting up of a child as the example of the man of faith. Now, and increasingly, the reporting of vital events will depend on the word of women, not highly regarded in Jesus' day, but relied upon by him.

Mary of Magdala (a town on the west of Lake Gennesaret) had been healed by Jesus (Lk. 7:36–50). In Luke also (8:1–2) she belongs to a group of women supporting Jesus with their resources (see verse 41 here on this point). In John 19:25 she is with a group of women near the cross, and in John 20:1–18 there is the memorable account of her meeting with Jesus after his resurrection. In Luke 24:10 she is one of the women who, finding the tomb empty, went to tell the disciples. James the younger and Joses, whose mother Mary was there, were presumably known to the Christians for whom Mark was writing. Of Salome, Matthew says that she was the mother of Zebedee's sons, presumably meaning James and John (Mk. 3:17). For all the strong protestations of loyalty by the men (14:31), at the end it was the women who saw it through.

11. Jesus is buried (15:42–47)

It was Preparation Day (that is, the day before the Sabbath). So as evening approached, ⁴³Joseph of Arimathea, a prominent member of the Council, who was himself waiting for the kingdom of God, went boldly to Pilate and asked for Jesus' body. ⁴⁴Pilate was surprised to hear that he was already dead. Summoning the centurion, he asked him if Jesus had already died. ⁴⁵When he learned from the centurion that it was so, he gave the body to Joseph. ⁴⁶So Joseph bought some linen cloth, took down the body, wrapped it in the linen, and placed it in a tomb cut out of rock. Then he rolled a stone against the entrance of the tomb. ⁴⁷Mary Magdalene and Mary the mother of Joses saw where he was laid.

The burial of Jesus is described in six verses in all. Yet some very important points are made here by Mark.

Crucifixion was such a shameful way to die that the corpses were normally treated with scant respect. But in Jesus' case a prominent member of the Council who had tried Jesus, Joseph from Arimathea, went to Pilate to ask for the body, and having obtained it, wrapped it appropriately, put it into a rock tomb, and sealed the place with a stone.

The other synoptic writers add further information. Luke says he was 'a good and upright man, who had not consented to their (the other Council members') decision and action' (Lk. 23:50–51). Matthew goes further and adds that Joseph 'had himself become a disciple of Jesus' (Mt. 27:57). This is probably what Mark and Luke mean by saying that Joseph was *waiting for the kingdom of God* (Mk. 15:43; Lk. 23:51). Mark simply says that Joseph put the body into a rock tomb (46). Luke says it was a wholly unused tomb (Lk. 23:53). Matthew says it was Joseph's 'own new tomb' (Mt. 27:60). (John's gospel points out why Joseph has not been heard of till now. He 'was a disciple of Jesus, but secretly because he feared the Jews', Jn. 19:38.) This was evidently the moment that he made his open testimony. John also includes Nicodemus, another member of the Council, whom he has featured in John 3. He too apparently openly acknowledged his commitment by this action.

When Mark includes something not in the other gospels we do well to note it carefully. He simply adds that Joseph went *boldly* (43). A better translation might be 'took courage'. He does not come out of the accounts as a naturally brave man, though Luke says he was 'a good and upright man' (Lk. 23:50). He did what was necessary.

Another significant detail occurring only in Mark is the observation, *Pilate was surprised to hear that he was already dead*. He also called the centurion to check even the time of his death (44). Criminals sometimes lingered for days. Jesus lasted a surprisingly short time. Is this also part of the irony of Mark's account? He who was not strong enough to resist death's onslaught for very long is nevertheless the one who by his death is setting the many free (10:45). But this is only for those who see with the eye of faith.

The other point emerging from Mark's story of Pilate's intervention is that it provides evidence, and not from a supporter, that Jesus did actually die. This was significant in rebutting a heresy suggesting that he only 'appeared' to die.

Mark now hints at another important factor. Pilate gave the body to Joseph (45). Since the bodies of the crucified normally went into a common grave, unmarked, uncelebrated and unrecorded, is Pilate's consent for Joseph's special burial of Jesus his way of acknowledging that Jesus was not a common criminal, or worthy of crucifixion? We hear again echoes of Mark's word 'delivered', carrying overtones of God doing the delivering for purposes not perceived by most of those caught up in the events. Yet they are not thereby stripped of responsibility for what they did.

The wrapping of the body with a linen shroud was customary. So was the rolling of a large stone down a slope to block the entrance to a tomb (46).

This all took place on the Preparation Day, the Friday before the Sabbath, Saturday (42). Some of the women who will come on the third day, including the Friday, now see where the tomb was (47).

237

Light in darkness

This is the darkest moment of the gospel story. Mark's simple account highlights this. Yet the darkness is not total. Although the apostles are still in a state of shocked absence, an unexpected disciple emerges (two in John's gospel) to do what was reverently appropriate. Bravery was not Joseph's normal characteristic. Maybe it took the crisis of Jesus' death, as a result of the decision of his fellow Council members, to bring out the spark of courage to face Pilate, ask for the body, and be known by the act as a disciple. If it was his own tomb he gave then the witness is even more moving and complete. We may be grateful that the gospel story includes men like Joseph (and Nicodemus) – not easily persuaded, not naturally given to public demonstration of their loyalties, but in the crisis ready to rise to the occasion as disciples.

12. The resurrection of Jesus (16:1–8 [9–20])

When the Sabbath was over, Mary Magdalene, Mary the mother of James, and Salome bought spices so that they might go to anoint Jesus' body. ²Very early on the first day of the week, just after sunrise, they were on their way to the tomb ³and they asked each other, 'Who will roll the stone away from the entrance of the tomb?'

⁴But when they looked up, they saw that the stone, which was very large, had been rolled away. ⁵As they entered the tomb, they saw a young man dressed in a white robe sitting on the right side, and they were alarmed.

⁶'Don't be alarmed,' he said. 'You are looking for Jesus the Nazarene, who was crucified. He has risen! He is not here. See the place where they laid him. ⁷But go, tell his disciples and Peter, "He is going ahead of you into Galilee. There you will see him, just as he told you." '

⁸Trembling and bewildered, the women went out and fled from the tomb. They said nothing to anyone, because they were afraid.

[⁹When Jesus rose early on the first day of the week, he appeared first to Mary Magdalene, out of whom he had driven seven demons. ¹⁰She went and told those who had been with him and who were mourning and weeping. ¹¹When they heard that Jesus was alive and that she had seen him, they did not believe it.

¹²Afterwards Jesus appeared in a different form to two of them while they were walking in the country. ¹³These returned and reported it to the rest; but they did not believe them either.

[14]Later Jesus appeared to the Eleven as they were eating; he rebuked them for their lack of faith and their stubborn refusal to believe those who had seen him after he had risen.

[15]He said to them, 'Go into all the world and preach the good news to all creation. [16]Whoever believes and is baptised will be saved, but whoever does not believe will be condemned. [17]And these signs will accompany those who believe: In my name they will drive out demons; they will speak in new tongues; [18]they will pick up snakes with their hands; and when they drink deadly poison, it will not hurt them at all; they will place their hands on sick people, and they will get well.'

[19]After the Lord Jesus had spoken to them, he was taken up into heaven and he sat at the right hand of God. [20]Then the disciples went out and preached everywhere, and the Lord worked with them and confirmed his word by the signs that accompanied it.]

The text of the resurrection narrative above has been divided into two parts, verses 1–8 and verses 9–20, in order to draw attention to a difficulty. As the NIV note puts it, 'the most reliable early manuscripts and other ancient witnesses do not have Mark 16:9–20'. They conclude the gospel with verse 8.

Is it possible that Mark intended his gospel to end with a statement of the women's fear and silence, and without any stories of Jesus' resurrection appearances? A growing number of scholars think so. In spite of the abruptness of such a conclusion, it would be in harmony with Mark's emphasis on the necessity of faith, faith now in the women's testimony, even without resurrection appearances.

Other scholars have speculated that the autograph of Mark's gospel was somehow damaged and that its original ending was lost. It certainly seems very odd that Mark's good news about Jesus should end with the blunt information that the women *said nothing to anyone, because they were afraid*. Since the *young man* in the tomb told the women both that Jesus had risen and that he was going before them to Galilee, where they would see him (5–7), one would naturally expect Mark to go on to describe this promised encounter with the risen Lord.

It was this sense of anomaly about verse 8 being Mark's intended conclusion that evidently led early scribes to try to fill the gap. Two attempts have survived. The so-called 'shorter ending', which occurs in some later manuscripts, is translated by RSV in these words: 'But they reported briefly to Peter and those with him all that they had been told. And after this, Jesus himself sent out by means of them, from east to west, the sacred and imperishable proclamation of eternal salvation.' This is clearly not a genuine piece of writing by Mark. Not only is its attestation late, but its vocabulary and style are very different from Mark's.

The other and so-called 'longer ending' is printed in several English versions as verses 9–20. As in the 'shorter ending', their language and style are quite different from the rest of the gospel; their connection with verse 8 is extremely awkward; and they read like a summary of the details of post-resurrection appearances taken from the other gospels. In consequence, a number of early church fathers declared them unauthentic, and suggested that they had been added by a later scribe in order to give Mark's gospel what seemed to him a proper ending, expressing what he believed Mark had written or intended.

None of the proposed solutions to the problem of the ending of Mark is without objections or difficulties. Whether Mark meant to finish with verse 8, or his original ending got lost, verses 9–20 cannot with any confidence be accepted as an authentic part of his gospel. On the one hand, the scribe who added this conclusion did well by taking up Mark's theme of belief and unbelief, as we shall see, but on the other hand he credited Jesus with making promises of spectacular signs which do not harmonize with the main body of Mark's gospel.

We turn now to the text of chapter 16.

The women who were faithful at the cross, and two of whom were there for his burial, now come on the day after the Sabbath to anoint Jesus' body (1). Mark has all through his account been blunt about the failings of the apostles. This story is wholly in harmony with that. It is the story of the women's pilgrimage and the women's discovery which he chooses to highlight.

There is a second point here. Part of Mark's gospel is the mystery of unbelief. One reason for unbelief by people who should know better is that they are looking for all the wrong evidence. Jesus refuses to beguile them with a display of earthly power, or oratory about messiahship or fitting into their patterns. They will find the truth only as they look through the evident circumstances and by faith perceive the hidden realities. This story, ending at Mark 16:8, underlines this fact. It is on the testimony of women that the gospel miracle of resurrection has to be believed in. The testimony of women did not count in the judicial hearings of the day. It was not the status of the witnesses, but the truth to which they testified which was the ground for believing.

The evidence for the women was clear – and alarming (3–5). They wondered how they would get the stone away from the tomb (where *were* the men?). But the stone was rolled away, and a young man in a white robe (Mark probably means an angelic messenger) gave the necessary message to them (5). It is contained in two contrasts.

Jesus the Nazarene (6) reminds them of the origin of all this, and roots these events in the real humanity of Jesus. *Was crucified . . . has risen* (6) is the first contrast, and it draws the gospel towards its climax. We now begin to see why Jesus in Mark's story would not try to persuade people to commit themselves by impressing them about messiahship, or encouraging them to spread stories of his identity or of his miracles. Only now are the grounds for faith properly in place. He interpreted messiahship in terms of the suffering servant reflected in his use of Son of Man because death and resurrection, as the redeeming work for the many, was what he was really here to achieve. They could not truly know till they understood that. This is why seeing they did not perceive, and hearing they did not understand (4:12). Now they would be in a better position to do so. If there is a 'messianic secret' in Mark, this is it, and the secret is now out.

We may also understand now why Mark introduced so early the little parable of the bridegroom being taken away after the bridal feast (2:19–20), and why the second half of the gospel is punctuated with an insistence on what will happen to him in Jerusalem (8:31, 9:31, 10:33–34). This is the destiny to which Jesus, and so Mark's gospel, was drawn from the outset. Nothing else could take its place earlier in the story and nothing else could be the basis for the adequate faith that Mark seeks from his readers.

Here, too, lies the key to Mark's understanding of discipleship. The breath-taking procession of miracles in the first half of the gospel, with the insistence of 'immediately' joining one to another in the story, has given way to a different model for discipleship. It is not the endlessly triumphal power display for which perhaps many longed – but the lowly path of obedient service on which Jesus' miracles were actually based. But that lowly obedient service would bring him eventually to death and resurrection, its ultimate expressions. Only so could the major miracle be achieved, the redemption of sinful men and women. The discipleship significance is underlined by Jesus' command to those who would follow to take up their cross too (8:34–38). This is the true path of discipleship, not the permanently clear, bright and shining way but the lowly path of service, or rejection, or persecution, discovering daily the joy that is found not necessarily in happy circumstances but in faithful service and daily rising with him.

There is, however, one final point. The second contrast from the

241

angelic messenger is, *'He is not here . . . He is going ahead of you into Galilee. There you will see him . . .'* (7). The evidence they needed, of his life and death and resurrection was there as the adequate basis for their faith and the abiding model for their discipleship. But the very entering into it must be a faith act. They must travel to Galilee (back home) as though he were there in order to discover that he was there. Faith is to be a daily exercise of walking to where the Lord has gone, believing him to be there and finding him to be so. It is not a procession of cast-iron certainties, but an experience of trust in him who lived, and died, and rose to be with them forever. And they will find him at home. This is the faith and the discipleship to which the gospel has drawn us from the outset.

There is one further point in this section (16:8). Here Mark's realism is at its height. The sheer frailty and humanity of those first disciples are not to be forgotten. The men are not even there. The women (at least at first) are *trembling . . . bewildered . . . afraid.* They *fled* and *said nothing.* Our first-century forebears in the faith were not naturally superior (or inferior) to us. Neither did faith and discipleship come any easier for them. Yet despite all, they went on believing and laid the foundation for us.

The more traditional gospel ending (9–20) has clear links with the other gospels in its contents. The resurrection appearance to Mary Magdalene (9) is linked to John 20:14–18, the encounter with the disciples in the country offers a parallel to the Emmaus road story of Luke 24:13–35, while the appearance to the Eleven (14) at table has in common with Luke 24:36–38 the rebuke to those present. The commission to preach the good news throughout the world ties in with that of Matthew 28:19.

Yet as they are gathered together here, one theme predominates which is very much in harmony with the rest of Mark. The reference to 'believing', or 'not believing' constantly recurs. The disciples did not believe Mary's report of seeing the risen Christ (11). Nor did they believe the two who returned from the country (13). Jesus berates the Eleven for their lack of faith and *their stubborn refusal to believe those who had seen him after he had risen* (14). When they preach, those who believe (and are baptized) will be saved; those who do not believe will be condemned (16). The various signs, in the form of gifts and abilities, will be experienced by *'those who believe'* (17–18). Clearly 'signs and wonders' are being promised to those who faithfully engage in mission. The prevalence of unbelief, and the contrasting blessings of believing, described again and again within this gospel, are here at the end. But not at the very end. In verses 19 and 20 Jesus is taken up into heaven. The ascension completes the story, and the disciples do now believe, do go out to preach, and do receive the confirmation they had been promised.

The final choice is clear, whether we follow the shorter or the longer ending. In face of a remarkable unwillingness to believe, in the disciples as well as those to whom they went, the commission is to take the good news of what God has done in Jesus – of all that God has done in Jesus. If we take the shorter ending, then the centre of the commission is the going in faith, back home to where life's harsh realities awaited them, and there they would find him in his risen power.

If we take the longer ending, then unbelief is rebuked, and evidence of the risen Christ is provided to various groups and individuals. Yet still they have to risk themselves in the mission.

If Mark's story is the completed one of the longer ending, then the invitation is to learn the lesson which the disciples finally grasped. If Mark's gospel is truly 'open-ended', it is that we may complete the story in our lives.

Study guide

Mark's twentieth-century Christian readers face a problem. We know the story (at least in outline), and how it ends. We are so familiar with the individual parables and miracles that we are no longer able to sense their full impact. Yet many of us have a nagging feeling that our knowledge of Mark's gospel is, after all, fairly superficial. Indeed, we are not always sure what Mark, or Jesus as recorded by Mark, was getting at. Their world seems so alien to us. How can we break through this strange combination of over-familiarity and bewilderment?

Two complementary activities may help us.

First, set aside a quiet period of time to read the whole gospel through at one sitting. Don't pause to unravel puzzling passages at this stage. Read it as an unfolding narrative, using your imagination to think yourself back into the events Mark relates. Put yourself in the shoes of the disciples, the religious leaders, the ordinary people who saw and heard Jesus. Sense the mounting tension as opposition to him swells. Feel the catastrophe of his death, and then the awesomeness of the revelation that 'He is risen'.

Then dig more deeply into the meaning of Mark's narrative with the aid of this study guide. Whether you work as an individual or as a group, it should help you not only to grasp the meaning of each passage, but also to trace Mark's main themes, and to see what he was intending to communicate by putting his gospel together in the way he did. The guide follows the seven main sections of Donald English's exposition, and each question, or group of questions, relates to a sub-section. If you work as a group, with limited time, you will get the most from each session if you do some 'homework' and come prepared to share your answers.

When you read the gospel straight through and when you study it in depth, allow the character, actions and teaching of Jesus to make a fresh impact on you. Mark constantly notes the reactions of those who saw and heard him. How will *you* respond?

SESSION ONE

Introduction *(pages 14–24)*
and **The beginning** *(Mark 1:1–13; pages 25–47)*

1 What clues does Mark give us about his purpose in writing his gospel (see pp. 14–17)?

2 What does Mark tell us about who Jesus was, through (a) the way he has structured his gospel, (b) the titles he uses for Jesus, and (c) his emphasis on the kingdom of God (see pp. 17–20)?

3 How do people respond to Jesus in Mark's gospel? What does this tell us about the nature and demands of discipleship? (See pp. 20–22.)

4 How does Mark target his readership? Given that his readers' culture is alien to us, what point is there in our studying Mark's gospel? (See pp. 22–24.)

5 **Read 1:1**
On a casual reading, Mark's opening phrase may seem rather prosaic. How does a closer look reveal that this is very far from the case (see pp. 25–28)?

6 **Read 1:2–3**
These Old Testament quotations remind us that generations of God's people had waited for the momentous events that Mark is about to describe. What does this have to teach us (see pp. 29–30)?

7 **Read 1:4–5**
How does Mark characterize John the Baptist's ministry? Why was the desert such an appropriate location for it? (See pp. 30–33.)

8 **Read 1:6–8**
How do you understand John's message about his own role and that of Jesus, and the two 'baptisms' (see pp. 33–38)?

9 **Read 1:9–11**
Try to imagine the scene, with the man from Nazareth and the voice from heaven. What is this startling event all about (see pp. 38–43)?

10 **Read 1:12–13**
   a Although Jesus had no human companionship, he was not alone. What does the reference to 'animals' and 'angels' tell us (see pp. 43–44 and 46–47)?
   b No sooner had the Spirit come upon Jesus than he drove him out into the desert. What can we learn from this for our own discipleship (see pp. 45–46)?

SESSION TWO

The ministry opens up
(Mark 1:14 – 3:6; pages 48–80)

1 **Read 1:14–15**
   What did Jesus mean when he proclaimed the message recorded here? What implications can we draw from it? (See pp. 48–52.)

2 **Read 1:16–20**
   How did Jesus summon these fishermen to follow him? What lessons are there here for the way we call people to follow him? (See pp. 52–53.)

3 **Read 1:21–31**
   a This passage twice mentions Jesus' authority. How is it manifested in the incidents recorded here (see pp. 53–55)?
   b The encounter between Jesus and the demons here speaks of the larger conflict between the kingdom of God and the powers of darkness. How do we see it being worked out today (see pp. 55–58)?

4 **Read 1:32–39**
   What was Jesus' priority? How did his healings and exorcisms, and his time of prayer relate to this? What can his disciples today learn from his example (see pp. 59–62)?

5 **Read 1:40–45**
   What is remarkable about Jesus' response to the plea of the man with leprosy? How does this challenge us (see pp. 62–64)?

6 **Read 2:1–12**
   What significance do you see in Jesus' words in verses 9–11 (see pp. 64–68)?

7 **Read 2:13–17**
   Why does Donald English say that 'Mark touches Christians on a sensitive spot with this story of Jesus going into table fellowship with Levi and his friends' (p. 70; see pp. 68–70)?

8 **Read 2:18–22**
   What does Jesus' metaphorical language teach us about the nature of the kingdom of God (see pp. 70–73)?

9 **Read 2:23–27**
   Jesus' Sabbath activities provoke murderous hostility on the part of the Pharisees (3:6). What elements in this passage might well have enraged them? How do we Christians sometimes fall into the same trap as the Pharisees? (See pp. 73–77.)

10 **Read 3:1–6**
   Jesus' opponents are now actively seeking a reason to accuse

him. How does his question confound them? How does it challenge us when our zeal to obey God tips over into legalism? (See pp. 77–80.)

SESSION THREE

Words and deeds in Galilee
(Mark 3:7 – 6:13; pages 81–126)

1 **Read 3:7–12**
  a What grounds are there for seeing Jesus' withdrawal as a positive move rather than as an escape from opposition (see pp. 81–82)?
  b What can we learn from this passage that is relevant to the debate between those who emphasize preaching and those who emphasize 'power' in evangelism (see pp. 82–83)?

2 **Read 3:13–19**
  What was the threefold task of the twelve (14)? How does this apply to us as disciples? How can we maintain a balance between the three aspects? (See pp. 83–86.)

3 **Read 3:20–35**
  a How does Jesus explain what God was doing through him (23–30)? (See pp. 86–88.)
  b Some Christians, on reading verse 29, fear that they may at some time have committed the 'unforgivable sin'. What in fact do Jesus' words mean, and what do they *not* mean (see pp. 88–89)?
  c Read 3:31–35 (and look back at 3:21). Put yourself in Mary's position. What do you think was going on in her mind in this interaction with her son? What point did Jesus make? (See pp. 89–91.)

4 **Read 4:1–20**
  a What is a parable, and why did Jesus use this teaching method (see pp. 92–93 and 98–101)?
  b What was Jesus communicating in the parable of the sower (or, as some prefer to call it, of the soils)? How does this guide us as we share the faith? (See pp. 93–97.)

5 **Read 4:21–25**
  What is Jesus' point here (see pp. 97–98)?

6 **Read 4:26–34**
  How does Jesus encourage his disciples (and us) through these further 'seed' parables (see pp. 101–104)?

7 **Read 4:35–41**
  Why did Jesus perform this 'nature miracle'? (Think about

both the overt reason and the deeper reason.) (See pp. 104–107.)

8 **Read 5:1–20**
   a What is the significance of the geographical reference in verse 1 (see pp. 107–109)?
   b Describe what was going on in the exchange between Jesus and the man/the demons (see pp. 109–110).
   c How do you think we should view a story such as this, which seems so strange to scientific Western ears (see p. 110)?
   d The episode concludes with two rather surprising facts. What are they, and what do they teach us (see pp. 110–112)?

9 **Read 5:21–45**
   a Jairus and the woman could hardly be more different. What was the one thing they had in common, and why does Mark interweave their stories (see pp. 112–115)?
   b When the news arrived of the little girl's death, what ambivalent thoughts must Jairus have had regarding the woman (see pp. 115–116)? What did 'having faith' mean for him?
   c What did Mark intend to convey through his record of these two miracles (see pp. 117–118)?

10 **Read 6:1–6a**
   Describe the dynamics of the relationship between Jesus and those of his home town (see pp. 118–120). How can we find a way through similar unbelief in ourselves (see pp. 120–123)?

11 **Read 6:6b–13**
   Discuss the significance of the resources that the twelve had, and that they did not have. Do we want to be 'safe' or 'sent' (see pp. 123–126)?

SESSION FOUR

Missionary outreach beyond Galilee in spite of the disciples' limitations
(Mark 6:14 – 8:26; pages 127–157)

1 **Read 6:14–29**
   What kind of people were Herod and his family? Even though it is most unlikely that we shall ever meet with persecution and death at the hands of such people, what does John's experience teach us? (See pp. 127–131.)

2 **Read 6:30–44**
   a Why does Mark focus on the apostles' return rather than on what they had done on their mission? (See pp. 131–133,

and look back to 3:14 and Session Three, question 2.)

   b How convincing do you find the 'explanations' of the feeding of the 5,000? How does Mark intend us to view this miracle? (See pp. 133–137.)

3 **Read 6:45–52**
What do you think was going on in this interaction between Jesus and his disciples? Can you identify with the disciples' reactions? (See pp. 137–140.)

4 **Read 6:53–56**
What is the difference between the crowds who pursued Jesus and the disciples who followed him? Is it still possible to run after Jesus for 'what you can get', without a true commitment to discipleship? (See pp. 140–141.)

5 **Read 7:1–23**
Where did those who over-emphasized tradition go wrong? Was Jesus condemning *all* tradition here? How can we evaluate our Christian traditions? (See pp. 141–147.)

6 **Read 7:24–30**
How does this incident illustrate (a) the passage that goes before it (7:1–23), and (b) the ultimate mission of Jesus and his church (see pp. 147–150)? How ready are we to break with our 'Christian' taboos in order to carry on that mission?

7 **Read 7:31–37**
What light does this miracle shed on who Jesus is? What meaning do you see in his words and actions? (See pp. 150–152.)

8 **Read 8:1–21**
   a Is the account of the feeding of the 4,000 just a duplication of the story of the feeding of the 5,000 (6:30–44)? Can you explain convincingly why it isn't? (See pp. 152–154.)

   b In what way do we tend to follow the Pharisees in asking for a sign (verse 11), and the disciples in being slow to understand what the Lord is trying to teach us (verses 14–21) (see pp. 154–156)?

9 **Read 8:22–26**
Why does Mark incorporate this story at this point? (See pp. 156–157.)

SESSION FIVE

Going to Jerusalem
(Mark 8:27 – 10:52; pages 158–183)

1 Read 8:27–33
What is remarkable about this incident at Caesarea Philippi? What makes it a 'turning point in Jesus' ministry'? (See pp. 158–161.)

2 Read 8:34 – 9:1
What did Jesus mean when he spoke of taking up a cross? What are its implications for those considering Christian discipleship and their counsellors? (See pp. 161–162.)

3 Read 9:2–13
a What are some ways of understanding what happened at the transfiguration? Which is the most satisfactory way of thinking about it? (See pp. 163–164.)
b What did the transfiguration mean (see pp. 164–165)?
c Read 9:9–13. What is the meaning of Jesus' instruction and his answer to the disciples' question (see pp. 165–166)?

4 Read 9:14–29
Jesus' words, 'Everything is possible for him who believes,' sometimes have a triumphalistic interpretation placed upon them. What did Jesus mean, and how does this encourage those who identify with the plea of the boy's father: 'I do believe; help me overcome my unbelief'? (See pp. 166–168.)

5 Read 9:30–50
a Although the disciples were eager to ask Jesus about their own ranking (34) and to safeguard what they saw as their own group exclusivity (38), they were reluctant to ask for help when they did not understand his teaching (32). How is our attitude sometimes like theirs? Why would it have been better for the disciples, and why is it better for us, to persevere till we understand Jesus' words? (See pp. 168–169.)
b What revolutionary fact did Jesus help the disciples understand in verses 33–36 (see pp. 169–170)?
c Why need they not have been concerned about the man performing exorcisms in Jesus' name? What *should* they have been concerned about? (See pp. 170–172.)

6 Read 10:1–12
What was the Pharisees' motive in asking Jesus about divorce? How does Jesus take them behind Moses' words in Deuteronomy 24:1–4 to God's ideal for marriage? In the context of today's rising divorce rates, in what practical way can we

uphold both Jesus' emphasis on God's ideal for marriage and his recognition of human sin? (See pp. 172–175.)

7 **Read 10:13–31**
   a Read verses 13–16. Why did Jesus welcome children, and adults with the attitude of a child (see pp. 175–176)?
   b Read verses 17–22. How can wealth destroy this attitude of trust in God? How does Jesus set out to teach the rich young ruler about faith in God? (See pp. 176–177.)
   c Read verses 23–31. Why were the disciples amazed at Jesus' words? In reply to Peter's exclamation, how does Jesus assure the disciples of the rewards of leaving everything to follow him (see pp. 177–178)?
   d What do you think Jesus' words about wealth and entering the kingdom mean for us today (see pp. 178–179)?

8 **Read 10:32–45**
   Donald English writes of 'the contrasting perceptions of the future' of Jesus on the one hand and James and John on the other. What does he mean? What light do Jesus' words here shed on his own imminent death? (See pp. 180–183.)

9 **Read 10:46–52**
   Verses such as verse 52 are sometimes quoted to suggest that if only we had more faith, we would be healed. What are the pitfalls in that interpretation? How do you think we should understand such passages? (See p. 183.)

SESSION SIX

Jesus enters Jerusalem
(Mark 11:1 – 13:37; pages 184–210)

1 **Read 11:1–11**
   What significance does Mark see in Jesus' entry into Jerusalem? How is this accentuated by the Old Testament passages he quotes as part of the crowd's responses? (See pp. 184–187.)

2 **Read 11:12–25**
   a Why is the cursing of the fig tree 'one of the most difficult stories in the gospels'? What do you think is the most satisfactory interpretation of it? What did Jesus intend to teach by it? (See pp. 187–190.)
   b What point was Jesus making by his action in the temple? Why did the reaction of the religious authorities again take on a murderous shape? (See pp. 190–191.)

3 **Read 11:27–33**
   How did Jesus' question about John's baptism answer the

Sanhedrin's question (see pp. 191–192)?

4 **Read 12:1–12, and as background, Isaiah 5:1–7**
The religious authorities knew that Jesus 'had spoken the parable against them' (verse 12). How do you think they would have understood it? (See pp. 192–194.)

5 **Read 12:13–17**
What made the question in verses 14–15 a trick question? Jesus again responded with a counter-question. Why were they 'amazed' by the conclusion he drew from their answer? (See pp. 194–196.)

6 **Read 12:18–27**
The test continues. What lay behind the Sadducees' question? 'There is enormous skill in Jesus' answer' (p. 197). How was that skill demonstrated? (See pp. 196–198.)

7 **Read 12:28–34**
What distinguishes this question from the others in this 'test' section? What is the significance of Jesus' answer and the teacher's further comment? (See pp. 198–199.)

8 **Read 12:35–40**
Why did Jesus introduce this 'theological knockabout' into the proceedings? What was the serious point he wanted to make? (See pp. 199–201.)

9 **Read 12:41–44**
In what sense were the widow's two very small coins 'more' than the large amounts given by others? How are Jesus' disciples – then and now – challenged by her action? (See pp. 201–202.)

10 **Read 13:1–37**
  a In what respects is this passage like typical apocalyptic material, and in what is it different (see pp. 202–204)?
  b How does it fit in at this point in Mark's gospel (see pp. 204–205)?
  c What answer would you give to the question, 'To which time is Jesus referring' (see pp. 205–206)?
  d Read verses 1–13. 'You must be on your guard,' Jesus tells his disciples (verse 9). Against what, specifically? How does this command tie in with Jesus' injunctions not to be alarmed or to worry (verses 7, 11)? (See pp. 206–207.)
  e Read verses 14–23. How should we understand the 'abomination that causes desolation' and the events described in this section (see pp. 207–208)?
  f Read verses 24–27 and Daniel 7:13–14. Jesus' description of a historical shaking leads on to a picture of the final cosmic shaking, in which 'the Son of Man' is central. What does the

title indicate? (See pp. 208–209.)

g Read verses 28–31. How can we best understand the difficult verse 30? What is Jesus emphasizing by his use of the two 'homely images' here? (See pp. 209–210.)

SESSION SEVEN

Passion and resurrection
(Mark 14:1 – 16:20; pages 211–243)

1 **Read 14:1–11**
   a What significance can you see in verse 1–2 (see pp. 211–212)?
   b How does the account of the woman's action fit appropriately into the 'plot' of Mark's story at this point? How does her attitude contrast with that of Jesus – and challenge us? (See pp. 212–214.)

2 **Read 14:12–26**
   a How do the events of this passage demonstrate that, even under the conspirators' threat, Jesus was entirely in control and conscious of the working out of God's plan (see pp. 214–216)?
   b What was the significance of Jesus' words and actions during the Passover meal (see pp. 216–217)?

3 **Read 14:27–31**
   We know that, despite Peter's protestations, he did betray his Lord. Assuming that he was sincere in what he said, why do you think he failed so soon afterwards? (See pp. 217–219.) Can you think of parallels in your own Christian experience?

4 **Read 14:32–42**
   What indications are there here of the depth of Jesus' struggle and suffering (see pp. 219–221)?

5 **Read 14:43–52**
   Trace the tragic irony in Jesus' betrayal and capture (see pp. 222–223).

6 **Read 14:53–65**
   While the religious authorities were struggling to pin evidence on Jesus, he 'actually provides what his accusers need' (p. 225). Why did they regard his statement as blasphemy? (See pp. 223–225.)

7 **Read 14:66–72**
   Trace the thoughts and emotions that must have torn Peter apart as these events unfolded (see pp. 225–226).

8 **Read 15:1–15**
   a How do you explain the reclassifying of the charge from

one of blasphemy to one of political insurgency (see pp. 226–228)?

b From what motives (explicit or implicit) did the various protagonists in this episode act (see pp. 228–230)?

9 **Read 15:16–20**

What point is Mark making by describing the soldiers' mockery (see p. 230)?

10 **Read 15:21–41**

a Mark continues his tragic narrative in his usual stark, factual style, yet it is rich in Old Testaments allusions and quotations. Which can you pick out? What does Mark's awareness of their 'fulfilment' tell us about the unique nature of this particular execution? (See pp. 230–232.)

b There is also a good deal of irony in Mark's account. Look particularly at the inscription of the charge against Jesus, and at the language about 'salvation' (see pp. 233–234).

c How do you understand Jesus' cry of dereliction in verse 34 (see pp. 234–235)?

d How do you understand Mark's statement that the temple curtain was torn in two (verse 38; see p. 234)?

e What is remarkable about the centurion's conclusion and the women's presence (see pp. 235–236)?

11 **Read 15:42–47**

There are several significant points here. What are they (see pp. 236–238)?

12 **Read 16:1–8, 9–20**

a Mark 16:9–20 does not appear in the most reliable early manuscripts of the gospel, yet verse 8 seems an unsatisfactory ending. Which solution to the problem seems the most satisfactory to you? (See pp. 238–240.)

b How do verses 1–8 put the themes of the preceding chapters into perspective? (See pp. 240–242.)

c How do verses 9–20 link up with the post-resurrection sections of the other gospels? What is a central theme of this ending? (See pp. 242–243.)

d 'The final choice is clear, whether we follow the shorter or the longer ending' (p. 243). What is that final choice? How will we respond?